DON BRECKON'S
COUNTRY RAILWAY PAINTINGS

DON BRECKON'S COUNTRY RAILWAY PAINTINGS

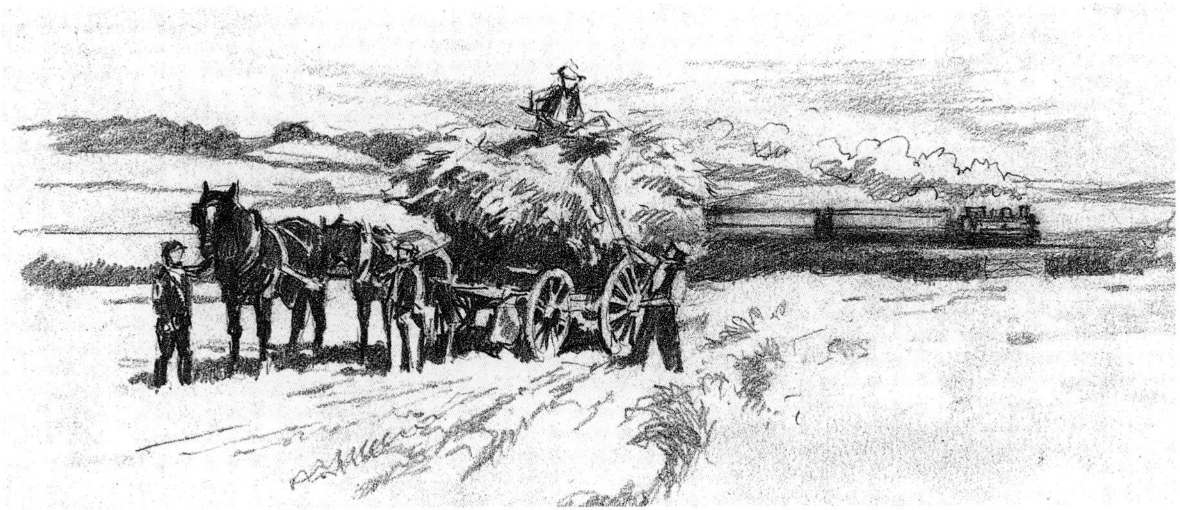

David & Charles

Special thanks to Meg for her assistance with the writing and compilation of this book

A DAVID & CHARLES BOOK

First published in the UK in 1991
First paperback edition 2003

Distributed in North America
by F&W Publications, Inc.
4700 East Galbraith Road
Cincinnati, OH 45236
1-800-289-0963

A catalogue record for this book is available from the British Library.

ISBN 0 7153 1507 2

Printed in Singapore by KHL Printing Co Pte Ltd
for David & Charles
Brunel House Newton Abbot Devon

Visit our website at www.davidandcharles.co.uk

David & Charles books are available from all good bookshops; alternatively you can contact our Orderline on (0)1626 334555 or write to us at FREEPOST EX2110, David & Charles Direct, Newton Abbot, TQ12 4ZZ (no stamp required UK mainland).

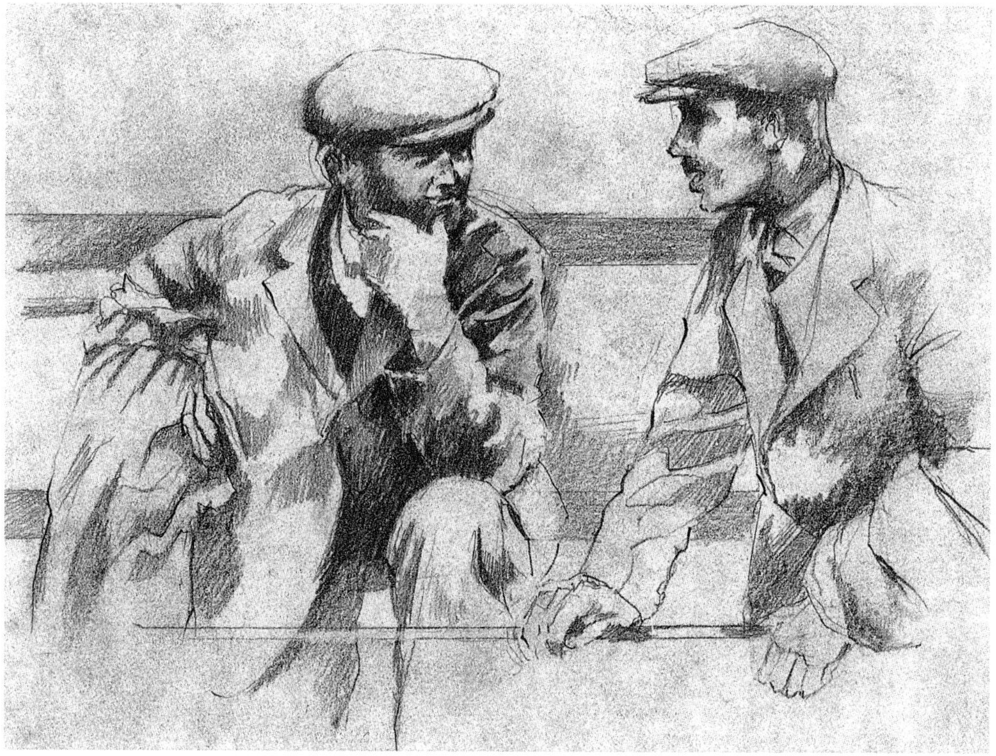

CONTENTS

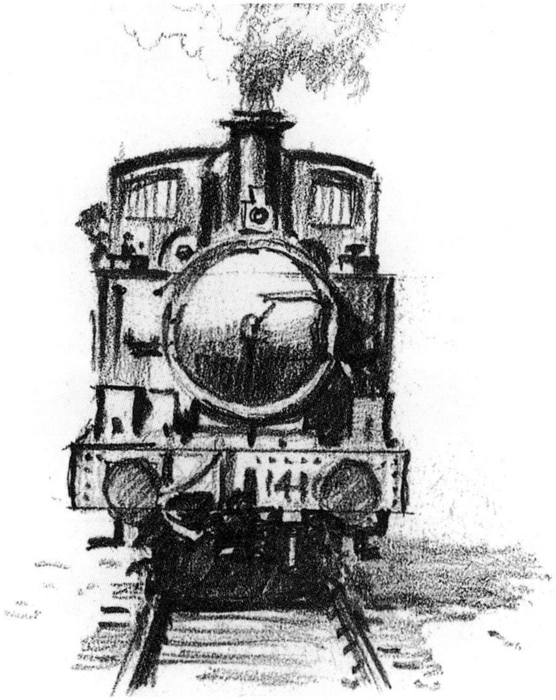

THE PLATES

ACKNOWLEDGEMENTS

Thanks are due to the following who have agreed to their paintings being reproduced in this book:

Mr P. Alderman
Mr M. Armstrong
Mrs N. Banbury
Mr T. Boddington
Mr P. Conway
Mr B. Dawson
Mr W. Doe
Miss E. Downe
Miss L. Downe
Mr S. Eagling
Mr D. Gee
Mr J. Harries
Mr J. Liardet
Mr J. Longman
Mr B. Moses
Mr B. Pillinger
Mrs T. Pillinger
Mr R. Robertson
Mrs J. Stephens
Mr D. St John Thomas
Mr N. Williams
Mrs J. Worden

Acknowledgement is also due to Solomon & Whitehead (Guild Prints) Ltd for allowing reproduction of *Dumbleton Hall* published as a signed limited edition in 1984, *Riverside Local* published as a signed limited edition in 1987, *Much Wenlock* published as a signed limited edition in 1988, and *Country Connections* and *Skye Boat Train* which are available as fine art prints.

I would also like to thank Mr J. Guyatt for historical information on Rowfant station and Mr George Brewer for his clear and lively memories of life in Lostwithiel in the pre-war years.

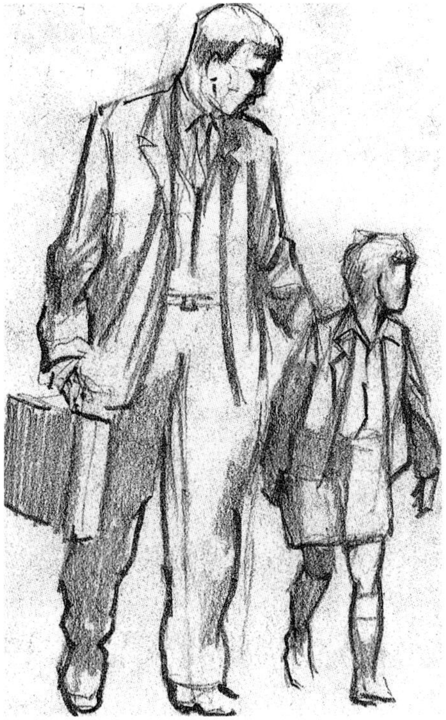

A Local Train of Thought

Siegfried Sassoon

Alone, in silence, at a certain time of night,
Listening, and looking up from what I'm trying to write,
I hear a local train along the Valley, And 'There
Goes the one-fifty', think I to myself; aware
That somehow its habitual travelling comforts me,
Making my world seem safer, homelier, sure to be
The same tomorrow; and the same, one hopes, next year.
'There's peacetime in that train.' One hears it disappear
With needless warning whistle and rail-resounding wheels.
'That train's quite like an old familiar friend', one feels.

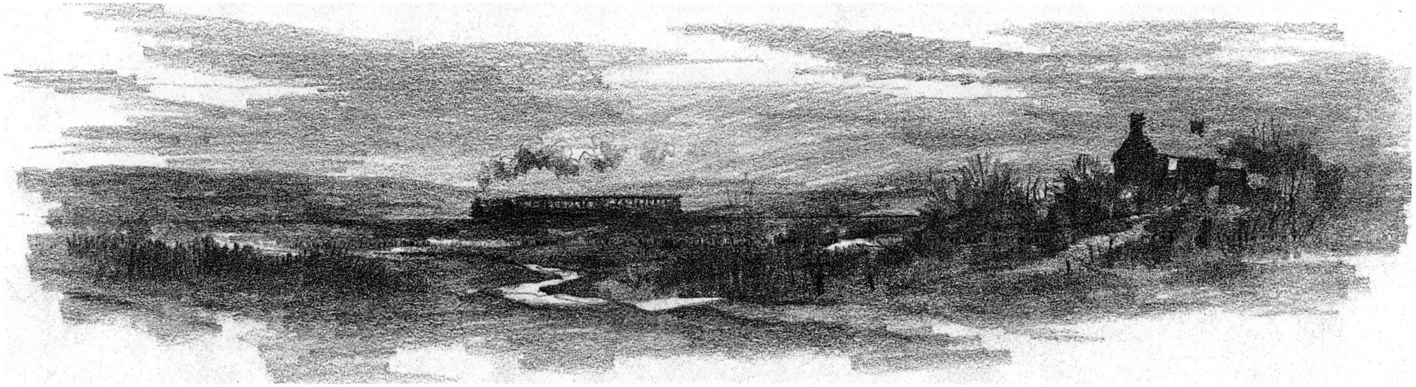

FOREWORD

Kevin Crooks (*Arts Producer for TSW*)

Considering the era of the steam railway, it's easy to welter in a nostalgia that bewilders the modern generation. The conditions that cause things to change also rapidly modify our opinions and, in its time, the steam engine was heralded as a monster that frightened the horses and blackened the weekly wash. Taking such a view is clearly unproductive. Steam has a particular place in our history; it powered the Industrial Revolution and changed our lives forever. So where might lie the evidence for its best effect on the lives of ordinary people?

Flying over the Devon and Cornish countryside reveals something of recent industrial archaeology, including the many branch railway lines that were axed during the Beeching period. Now grown over with carpets of gorse and bracken are the ingeniously engineered routes that once connected remote villages with a rapidly developing world. The removal of these branch lines seems like an act of vandalism, making a sorry nonsense of what the Victorians referred to as the Permanent Way. The main routes for Britain's railways remain intact, only modified here and there to increase the speed of the locomotive. Trunk lines have changed little in a hundred and fifty years, but the best part of the railway has gone – the mycelium of branch lines that reached out from the major body and formed a reticulated pattern across the countryside.

The branch lines and the country connections that once drew communities together offered a cheap and reliable means of transport. Travelling by train was an adventure then, offering a passage through rows of suburban back gardens, glimpses of other people's lives and a countryside as neat as an Ovaltine label. The ephemera remains: photographs of double-headers hauling up Shap Fell, and faded first-class tickets from Tavistock crop up from time to time. But where is that sense of bustle and steam on bright sunny mornings, and coal splinters in the eye – where is the atmosphere best displayed?

I think the answer is, in the work of Don Breckon. I first met Don, about whose work I have been privileged to make a BBC documentary, on the Looe to Liskeard branch line at St Keyne in Cornwall. Well, not exactly; my eye had been taken by a painting of the scene in a local art gallery. I gladly forked out twenty-five pounds to take the picture home. A small tank locomotive had pulled a carriage into the station. Through a curtain of steam, a group of waiting passengers held the driver in earnest discussion. I mused over the possible conversation. News of some event far up the line, a timetable enquiry, or was the small boy simply itching to see inside the engine cab? I felt an immediate response to the painting. It wasn't that the scene had convinced me or that its technical accuracy had moved me, it was the distinct impression that I was standing within the picture.

Artists have a certain advantage over others who record history. The play of light, the choice of colour, the composition and the brush strokes give clues to the artist's love and understanding for his subject. Some years after Don became a personal friend, he once remarked that in order to do justice to any subject, the artist must understand it intimately.

Recalling those country connections of fifty and sixty years ago provides us with a tacit pleasure. To some it is bound to be nostalgic and to others it is the pleasure of discovery. Recreating our bright images of the past takes skill and artistry. I look at these brilliantly painted pictures of an age of steam and know that no one does it better.

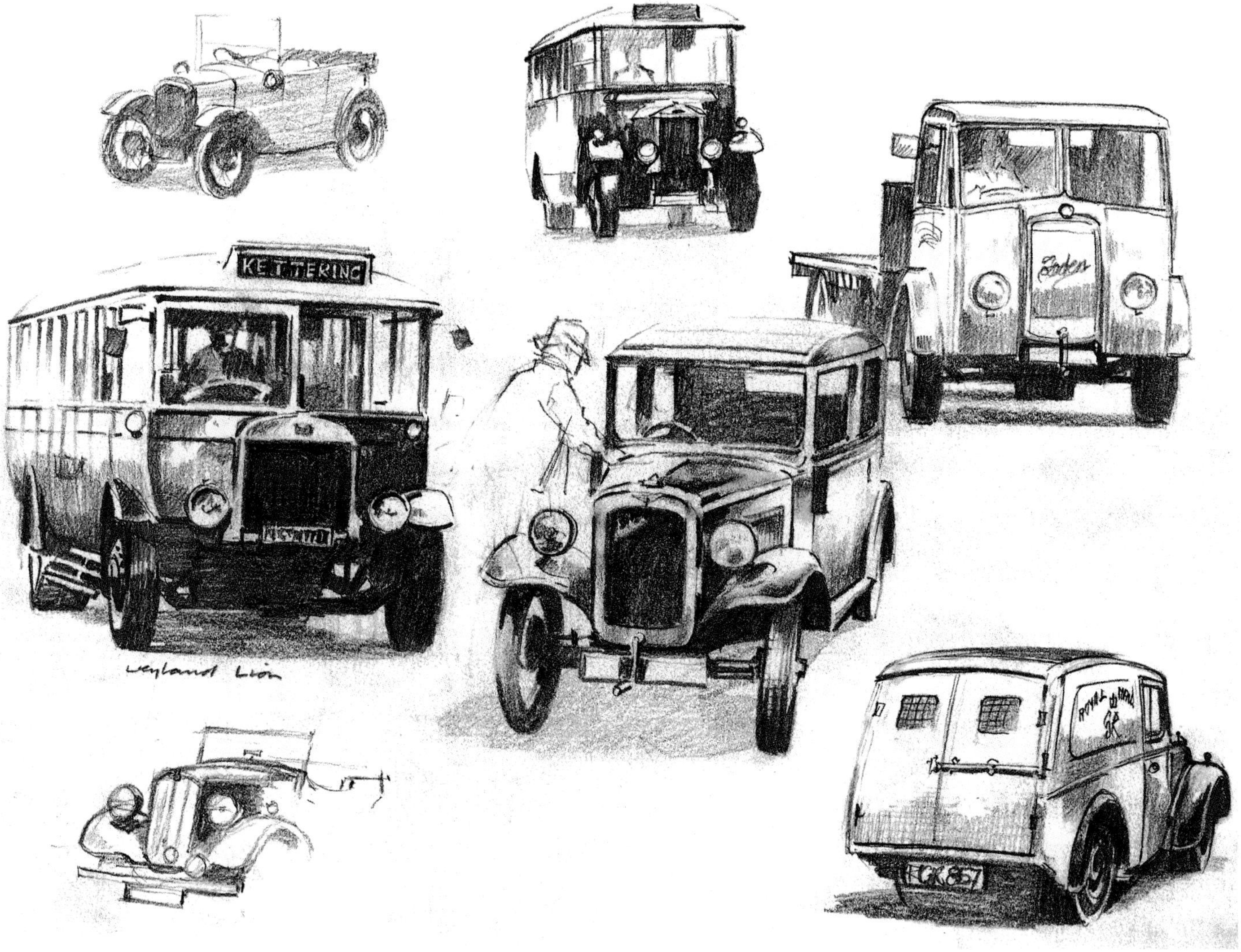
KETTERING
Leyland Lion
ROYAL MAIL
FGK 857

INTRODUCTION
Don Breckon

Sometimes in conversation we might say, 'that reminds me of the time when . . .', and some memory of long ago will be taken out, inspected, and put away again. But now and then there is the sudden realisation that the moment being recounted was an important turning point, or the awakening of an interest which helped to shape the person we are today.

I suspect that the most important little things are completely forgotten and yet they have moulded our attitudes ever since they occured. If I dig back into my childhood to discover what 'nudged' me towards the road of Art – or 'drawing' as I would have called it then – I begin to find many lost moments which must have played their part in shaping my future career.

My first drawing lesson is a very clear memory. It was from my father. Home on leave from the army during the war, he said he would show me how to draw ships. To my knowledge he had never drawn anything before, so I was most intrigued. On a scrap of paper he drew the upright bow of a ship, then off to one side made a dot with his pencil. He then joined the top and bottom of the bow to the dot. The superstructure and funnels followed, all flowing down and away to the dot. It was amazing! The ship seemed to be about five miles long but it was sailing towards us, seeming to come out of the paper. It was my introduction to perspective and, armed with this 'secret weapon', I went off to school to be the 'envy of all my friends', as the adverts say.

In those early years the only art which meant anything to us was the dramatic kind. On the way home from school we would hang around the front of the Odeon cinema, admiring the film posters and ready for the really good ones which got the accolade 'Cor – look at that!' The cinema was the main source of entertainment for adults and children alike in the 1940s, and although it was certainly not regarded by us as an 'art form', it fired our imaginations and would lead to hours of games inspired by what we had seen 'at the pictures'. Our surroundings were comparatively drab at that time and the colour and excitement on the screen compensated for this to a great extent. I can still remember the suppressed excitement when the curtains rolled back and the dramatic theme music swept through the cinema as the screen lit up in glorious technicolor. If a Western was showing that week there would be the strange sight of the local lads trotting along the pavement making clopping sounds whilst whacking themselves on the rear!

At home in the evenings, in the pre-TV era, it was time for the *Boys' Golden Wonder Book* or some such, filled with exciting line drawings illustrating the stories. Even better were the occasions when we could get hold of American comic books in full colour. Later in the 1950s, the *Eagle* comic arrived on the scene, featuring the artwork of Frank Hampson with 'Dan Dare'. The centre spread cutaway illustrations of L. Ashwell Wood were a visual treat, heralding a new approach to comic-book art in Britain.

Cartoon drawings always interested me. I can remember trying to copy Giles and Illingworth from newspapers, becoming aware that art could be funny or dramatic in cartoon or poster form respectively, in both cases conveying a clear message to everyone at a glance.

There was also the form of magazine art which merited a rather longer look. The covers of Ronald Lampitt for *John Bull* and Norman Rockwell for *Saturday Evening Post* could be appreciated for the detail which often emerged only after studying them for some time. Lampitt's views of country villages, usually from a high viewpoint, may have prompted my own drawings of country churches. Cycling around the Welland Valley near Corby and sketching churches was my first experience of drawing from life. Every Christmas a drawing book was amongst my presents and I would draw for hours, listening to the radio at the same time. My parents liked the 'country church' phase, preferring silent subjects to the drawings of trains or aerial dogfights when I could not resist making the sound effects while I worked!

At school I looked forward to the art lessons, unless they turned out to be 'object drawing' which we considered at the time to be very dull. It must have been much worse for those boys who were not interested in art in the first place! Later, in the sixth form, there was less supervision; when opportunity arose, I drew racing cyclists and cartoons – definitely not part of the syllabus.

Later, the experience of 'square bashing' at RAF Hednesford at the beginning of National Service would have been even more traumatic had it not been for the therapeutic benefit of my cartoon drawing. When writing home I would include my visual interpretation of the more startling aspects of 'basic training', trying to find the funny side of things. This made me feel more able to take the whole episode in my stride.

When I arrived at Art College after National Service it was with a rather lowbrow idea of art. On being confronted with a nude model in life drawing class, cartoon drawing seemed no longer appropriate! Gradually I was made aware of the history of painting and design, and my artistic horizons began to broaden. The saying was that when students went home after their first term they would see their home towns with new awareness – and it was certainly true.

Most of the time, however, I was slightly at odds

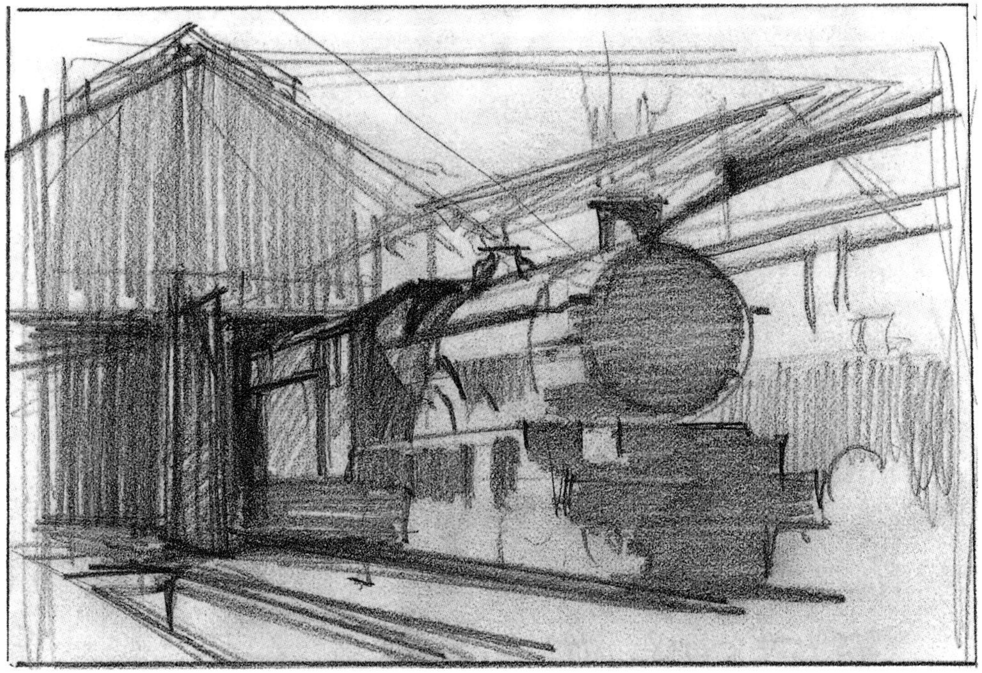

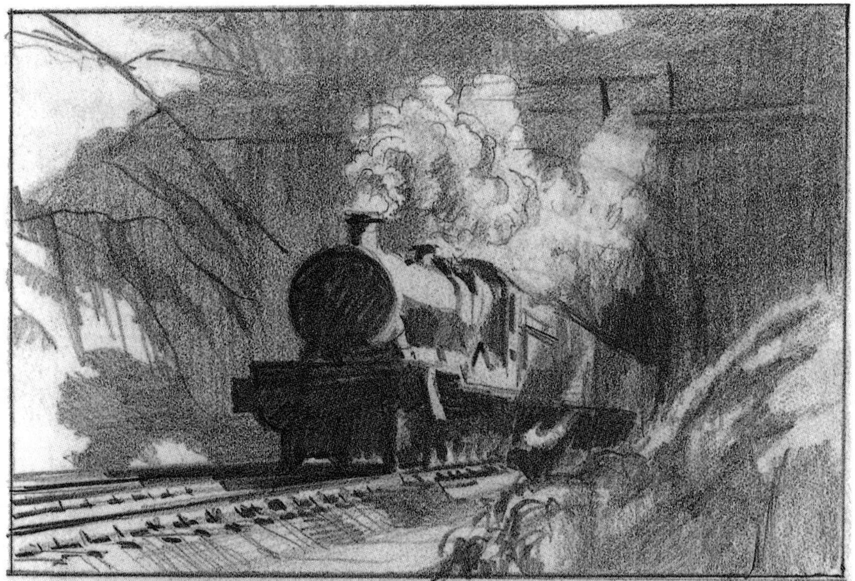

Tonal rough for Tunnel

with the college teaching, as many of my earlier ideas of art refused to go away. On a visit to the Tate Gallery, when we were supposed to be studying contemporary painting, I was alone in the Nineteenth Century rooms admiring Stanhope Forbes' *Health of the Bride*, Millais' *Order of Release* and Ward's *Gordale Scar*. The tutors struggled on manfully. In one painting class my palette had become clogged with several layers of paint – it was becoming more interesting than the painting I was working on! The exasperated tutor ordered me to go and clean it forthwith. At that time it was acceptable to put a little turps on the palette, put a match to it, and scrape off the burning paint. Hidden among the cycle racks I set fire to the turps but I must have overdone the amount because it blazed up like a beacon, singeing the leaves of the trees. I returned to the class with a charred piece of wood which had once been my palette!

Leaving college and starting work as an art teacher was a sobering experience. There were no tutors now to help out with ideas and organisation, only the rest of the school staff curious to see how the 'new art man' would shape up. All aspects of art were now used in connection with the children's work, and the college training began to mean something at last.

When I did eventually get back to my own painting I was strongly under the influence of the art college approach to subject matter and was always looking for new ways of tackling familiar ideas. On holiday once in Paris, I saw for the first time colour photographs of traffic at night taken with a time exposure technique. Car lights became long lines of light weaving through the streets. Indicators were short dashes of orange. So these photographs were pictures of movement which could be interpreted in paint as brightly coloured lines sometimes dribbled on to the dark tones of the background.

At the same time in the late fifties and early sixties, the building boom was under way and scaffolding and tower cranes were part of every city and townscape. I brought the linear scaffolding structures and the flowing traffic of the night photos together and painted abstract impressions of cities.

This linear work soon included railway tracks and signal gantries as subjects for painting, although trains were not yet part of the compositions.

The railway interest was returning with these paintings, however, and with it the realisation that the steam locomotive, which had seemed such a permanent feature, was being rapidly swept away.

Visits to the scrapyards in Kettering and South Wales underlined the sadness of the situation and led on to a series of paintings on a scrapyard theme, with the shapes of broken wheels and connecting rods treated in a semi-abstract way. But there was a more sentimental reaction to the scrapyards – the desire to put things back as they were and restore these engines in a realistic manner through the paintings.

From semi-abstract work back to representational painting seemed like a return to my beginnings, and it was a slow process. Gradually the pleasure in working to make things realistic as opposed to an 'impression' increased. There were new challenges but often greater satisfaction, and I felt that I had strayed back onto home ground.

For the first few years I was content to concentrate on the train but I became increasingly aware of the importance of the setting. As I drew back to include more of the landscape through which the train was passing, other things began to find their way into the picture. Cars and buses of the period, the activities of people, farming and buildings, all contributed to give a sense of period and to add a new dimension to the work. This is a labour of love as my imagination drifts back to scenes of a period which has mellowed with the passing of time into a warm glow.

Today, in the age of the ever-present car, it is difficult to realise how important the railway was to country life. So, having chosen the title for this new collection of paintings, the selection has not been limited to a literal interpretation of 'Country Connections' – junction stations linking branch line to main line – but includes all aspects of country life where the railway became a connection to the mainstream of activity in the nearby towns and beyond.

With the rapid expansion of the railway companies in Victorian times rural communities were changed as never before. When the line arrived and the village station was built, people and goods became mobile to an extent that would change the whole character of rural life. No wonder the Duke of Wellington was reputed to have been concerned

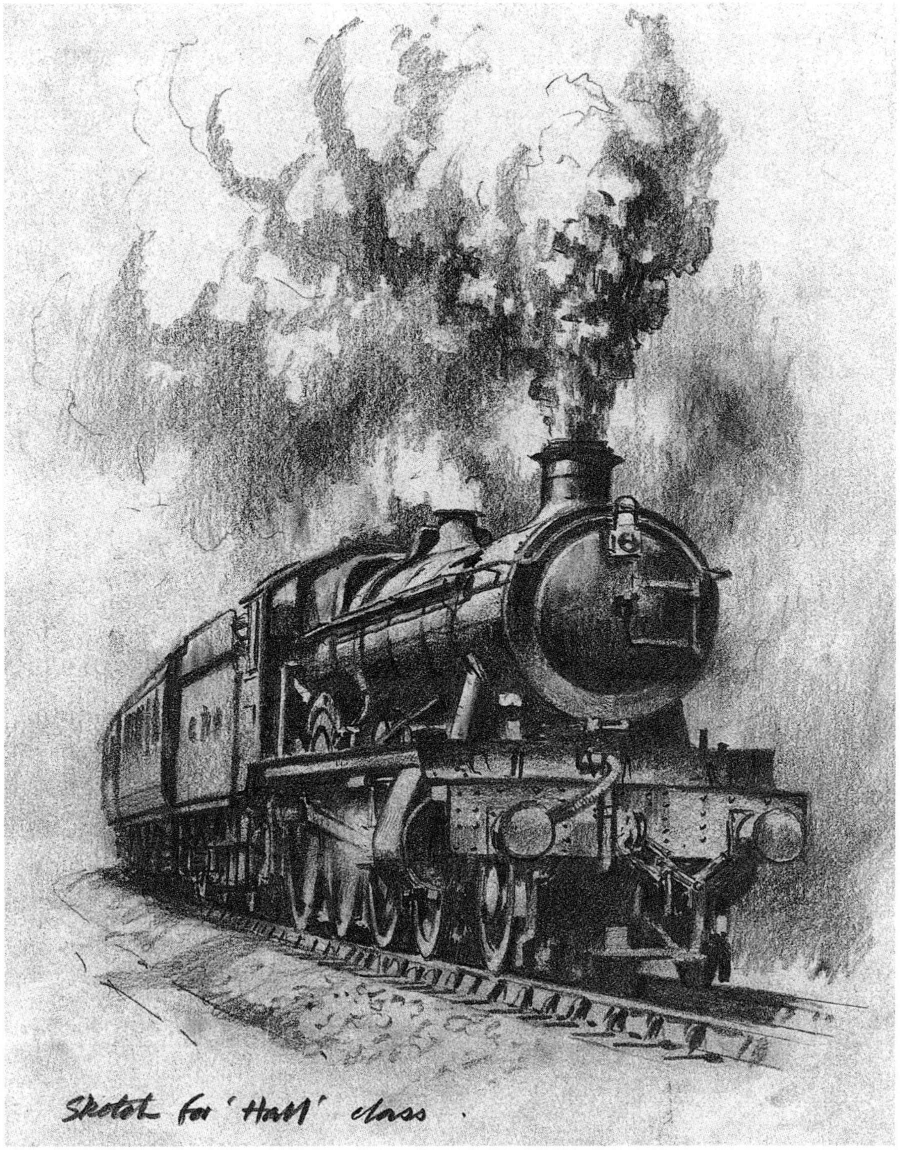

that the railways 'would encourage the working class to move about'.

The paintings in this book are my commemoration of the links which flourished with the transportation of coal, milk, and mail as well as passengers, and of the influence which the railway in all its aspects had on life in the countryside. They record the men who worked the railway, from footplate crew and signalmen to porters and track gangs. They represent the railway for the most part in its country setting – stations, viaducts and bridges, cuttings and embankments, fast trains, slow trains and goods trains.

The writing for this book has been chosen to complement the paintings by adding details of the atmosphere and day-to-day life of the rural railway. In this I have been fortunate to have the assistance of three writers, Tony Barfield, Tony Kingdom and Guy Pannell, who have contributed 'word pictures' from their research and personal experience.

This book is a reminder of a time when twin ribbons of steel fastened to thousands of wooden sleepers advanced into the countryside, establishing connections which changed the expectations and ambitions of the rural population for ever.

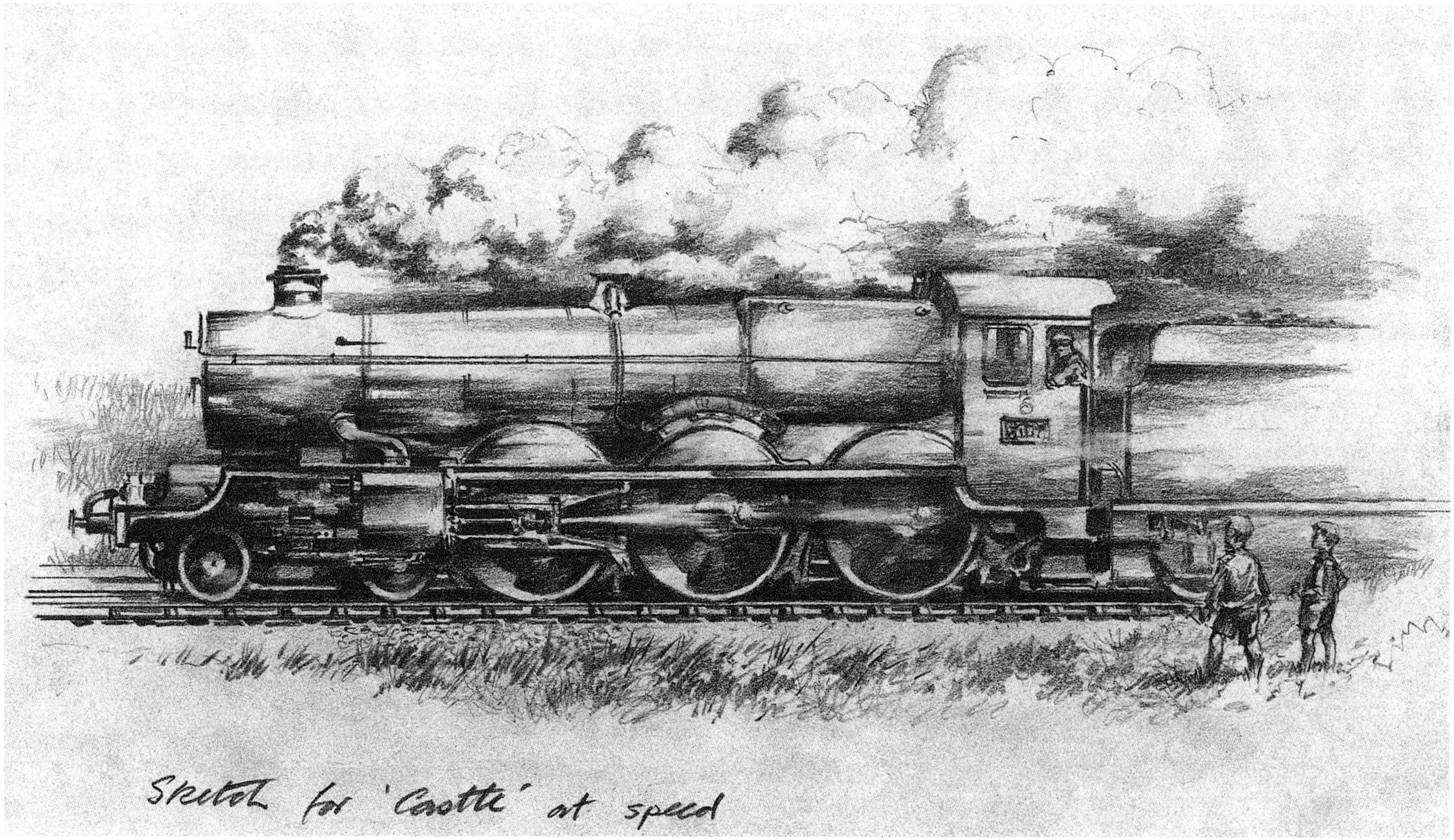

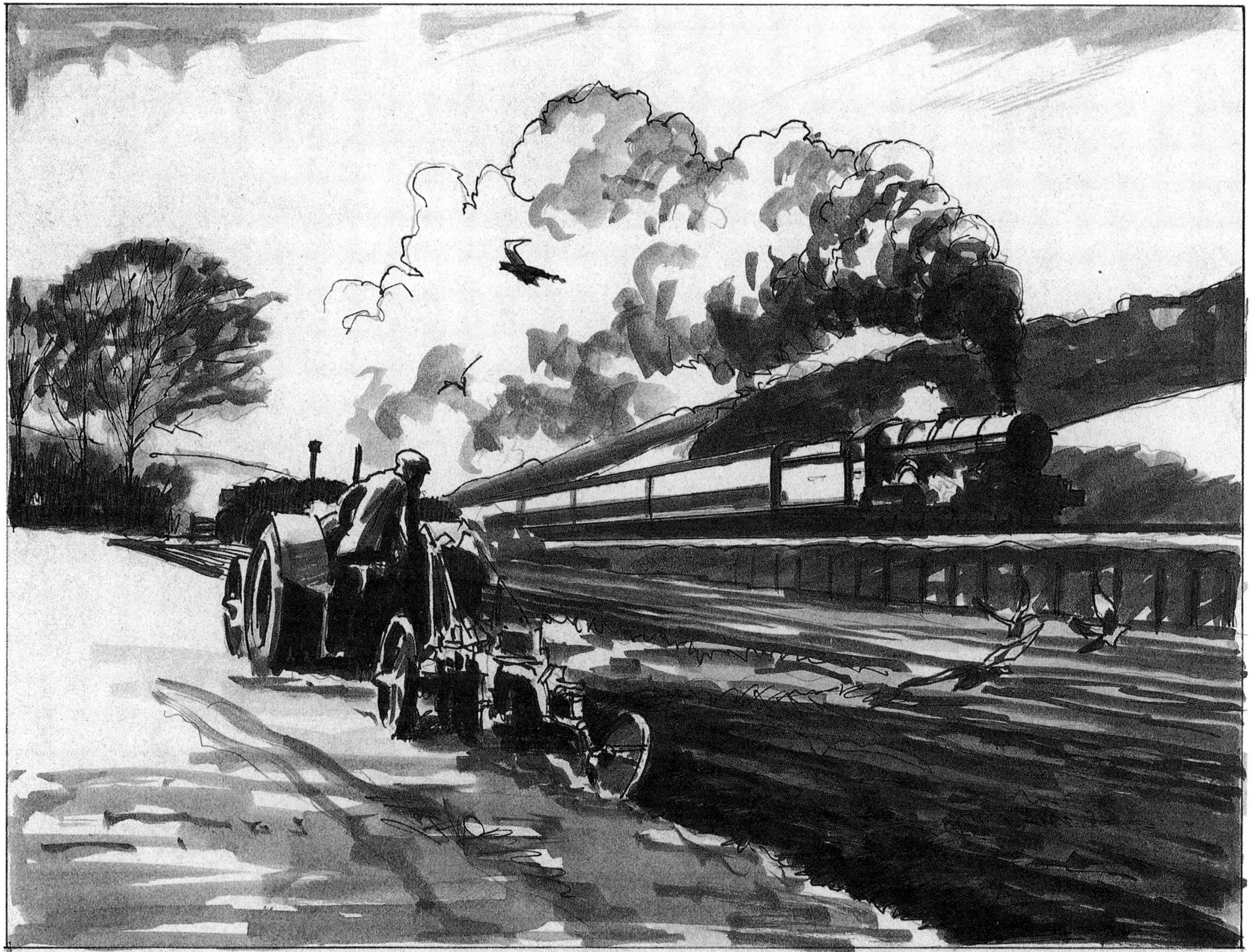

Tonal Study – "Traction"   'Castle' class loco. Fordson tractor

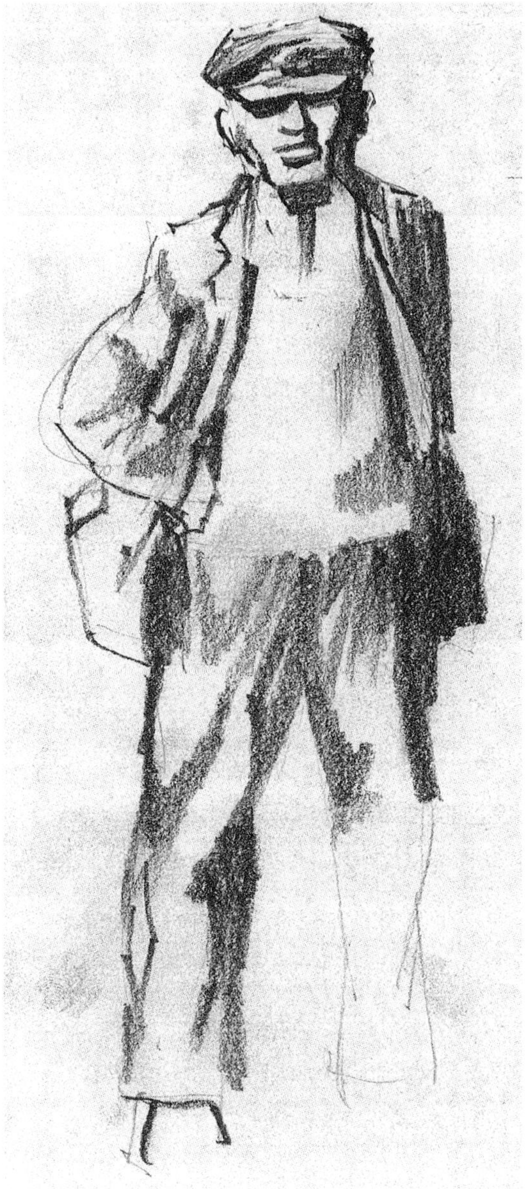

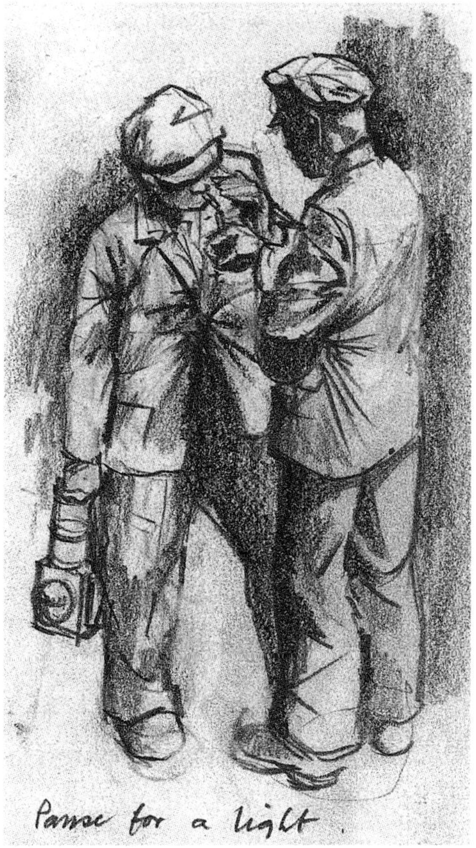
Pause for a light.

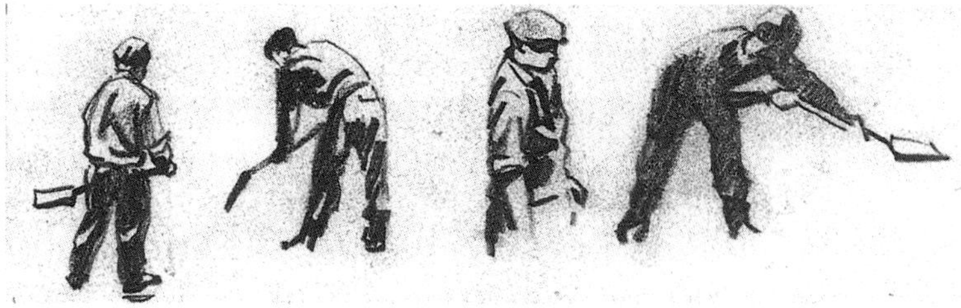

WORKING THE COUNTRY CONNECTIONS

Tony Barfield

What is a country connection? To all manner of people it was all manner of things. To city-dwellers it was the mainline station where they transferred from the express train to the branch line train, with its ancient locomotive and coaches taking them deep into the country to visit relatives or, perhaps, on the final leg of the journey to their annual seaside holiday. To the countryman or woman, the country connection was the train that took them into town every week to do their shopping and that carried their children to school. It transported the milk in large silver churns. It brought the mail that gave news of friends and relations in far-off places and, for a few minutes at various times during the day, it brought a quiet country station to life.

One such station was Wooferton, situated on the main line between Hereford and Shrewsbury. From here a branch line ran eastwards to Tenbury Wells, Cleobury Mortimer and the Wyre Forest to connect with the Severn Valley line at Bewdley. On a sunny, sleepy afternoon we were standing in the bay platform having witnessed the arrival of a train from Hereford. A few schoolchildren, a couple of countrywomen returning from market, and a solitary man transferred to our train, which consisted of two elderly coaches and an even more elderly ex-Great Western Railway (GWR) pannier tank loco 2101.

Bill, my driver, and I were sitting on a platform seat enjoying the sunshine while we finished off a cup of tea. We noticed the male passenger talking to our guard, who pulled out his pocket watch and studied it intently. The passenger climbed into the carriage and Jock, our guard, walked up the platform towards us. 'Got one in a bit of a hurry back there,' he explained as he sat alongside us. 'He's worrying about missing his connection at Bewdley. I've told him, slow we might be but we've never missed it yet. He insisted that I inform the driver of the situation, so when you two have finished your tea we'll think about making a move.'

Jock returned to his guard's van and waved his green flag with a flourish. We responded with a toot of our whistle and shuffled out of the bay platform and onto the branch line. The Tenbury Wells branch passed through beautiful countryside, but for about the first ten miles climbed steadily until it reached Cleobury Mortimer. Unfortunately, with an ageing loco, it meant that we were hard-pressed to exceed 15mph on some of the steeper gradients and, what with stopping at numerous halts and small country stations, the journey did seem to last for ever – especially to a city-dweller in a hurry. Added to this, at every stop pleasantries were exchanged between the station staff and train crew. Produce would be loaded into and unloaded from the guard's van, a basket of pigeons was released at one station and churns containing drinking water were unloaded at another. By the time we wheezed into Cleobury Mortimer 2101 was feeling a bit breathless, so while I filled up the water tanks Bill went around the loco with the oil can. This proved to be too much for the male passenger. He rushed up to the loco and accosted Bill.

'Driver, this train is getting slower and slower, and it is imperative that I connect with the Severn Valley train at Bewdley. Damn it all, man, can't you go any faster?'

Bill put his oil can down, wiped his hands on a piece of cotton waste and removed his pipe from his mouth.

'Yes, I reckon I could, but I don't reckon the loco would keep up with me!'

That remark of Bill's summed up the very essence of a country branch line. They did appear to be, and often were, slow, but invariably they ran to time. The staff who operated these lines were railwaymen and had immense pride in their job. The stations were always clean and tidy; the waiting-rooms always smelled of polish and always had a warm fire in the grate in winter, and in summer there was fierce competition for the best-kept station award.

Even the footplate crews were, in a sense, country people. Quite a few branches had their own small loco shed situated at the end of the line. These sheds usually housed one or two tank locos and the staff lived locally, visiting the parent depot on the main line perhaps three or four times a year. Some lines had their motive power provided by a depot on a through route, such as the Kidderminster yard where I worked all through the 1950s. The depot housed about twenty-four locomotives and there was a fair amount of mainline work to Worcester, Hereford, Wolverhampton and Birmingham, but the bulk of our business consisted of trains along the Severn Valley and Tenbury Wells branches. The city depot was a very vital link in the country connections of the area.

'Right Bill, shut her off!' I shouted to my driver as, standing astride the boiler of the locomotive, I saw the water bubbling up to the top of the water tanks. Bill quickly shut off the valve on the water column, and I closed the tank lids and screwed down the catches. We were replenishing the water of pannier tank number 29 before backing onto our train of three wagons and a guard's van for the run along the obscure and forgotten branch to Ditton Priors in a remote part of Shropshire. The line had closed to passenger traffic in 1938 and, although the route was forgotten by the world at large, it still carried a thrice-weekly goods train which was a necessary service for local people.

My driver had been born in the area and had

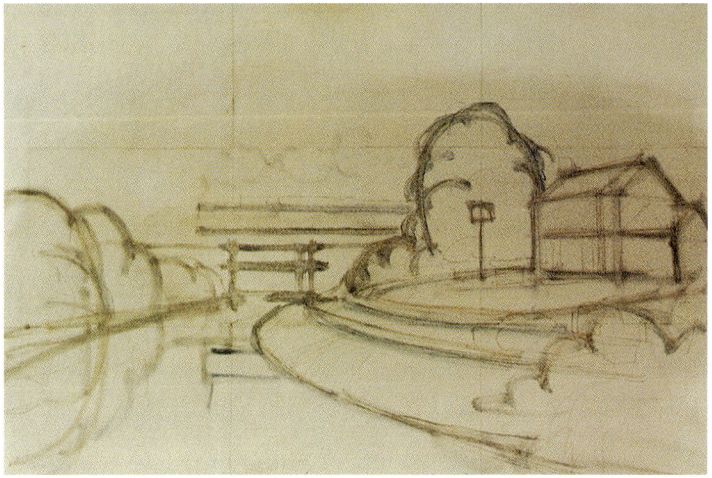

The layout for 'Riverside Local'. Outline of main shapes sketched in on the canvas use of 1/3 grid lines for inn sign & left hand edge of bridge

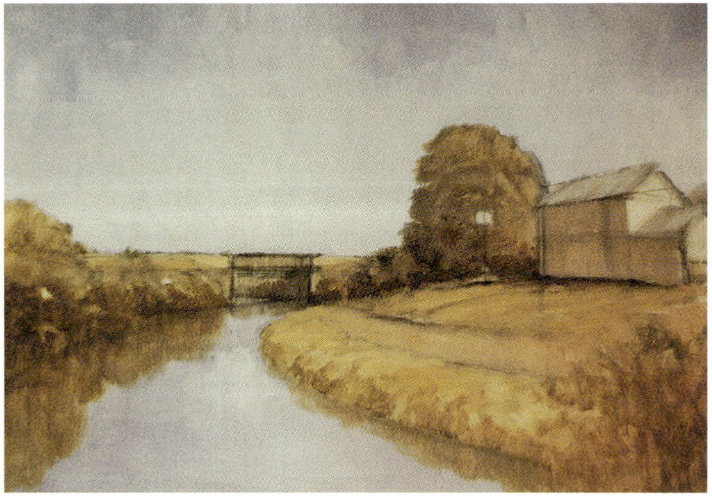

'Blocking in' of colour & tone. All to be altered later with further layers of paint though the basic idea will survive the changes!

Riverside Local

The warm summer morning brings the regulars of the Red Lion inn out onto the lawn to enjoy their drinks in the sunshine. An Austin Seven saloon and an MG sports car wait in the car park beside two children, who have been looking forward to feeding the ducks whilst their parents visit the inn. The clatter of wheels on the bridge turns most heads as a GWR 1400 class 0-4-2T locomotive crosses with a two-coach local train.

The sketches elsewhere in the book will show that this composition took different forms before it was finalised. The original idea was a branchline train crossing a river with a country pub on the river bank. After much searching through photographs of pubs and rivers in England and Wales I found nothing to fit what I had in mind, so it became an imaginary scene. The model for the pub, however, was a Herefordshire farmhouse whose image I had noted earlier and stored away for future use.

The painting started well and then came to an abrupt halt – something was not working. After various alterations, which did not seem to solve the problem, I put the painting to one side and for almost a year it was propped up in a corner of the studio in a half-finished state, an apparent failure. It attracted the attention of visitors to the studio, however, to the extent that suggestions were made as to how it could be saved. In fact everyone was taking such an interest that it was becoming something of a community project!

Seeing a photograph of a bridge on the Taunton–Barnstaple line which had a side arch for a farm track gave me new impetus. My riverside driveway curved away from the water at the railway. This new bridge could take it through to the other side and open up the foreground along the curve of the river bank. This, combined with other suggestions such as altering the line of the bank, moving the children and changing the position of the cars, gave the painting the atmosphere I had been seeking. On completion the painting was seen by Solomon and Whitehead, and in 1987 it was published as a limited edition print.

I have pleasant memories of visiting friends and going down to their 'local' on a summer Sunday morning for a pre-lunch drink, and this scene brings back those times. But most of all it is a painting of sounds – the sounds of summer. The clink of glasses mingles with conversation, children's voices echo back from the surface of the river and perhaps one can imagine the distant sound of a tractor or the Sunday sound of church bells – all added, of course, to the chuffing and hissing of the other local crossing the bridge.

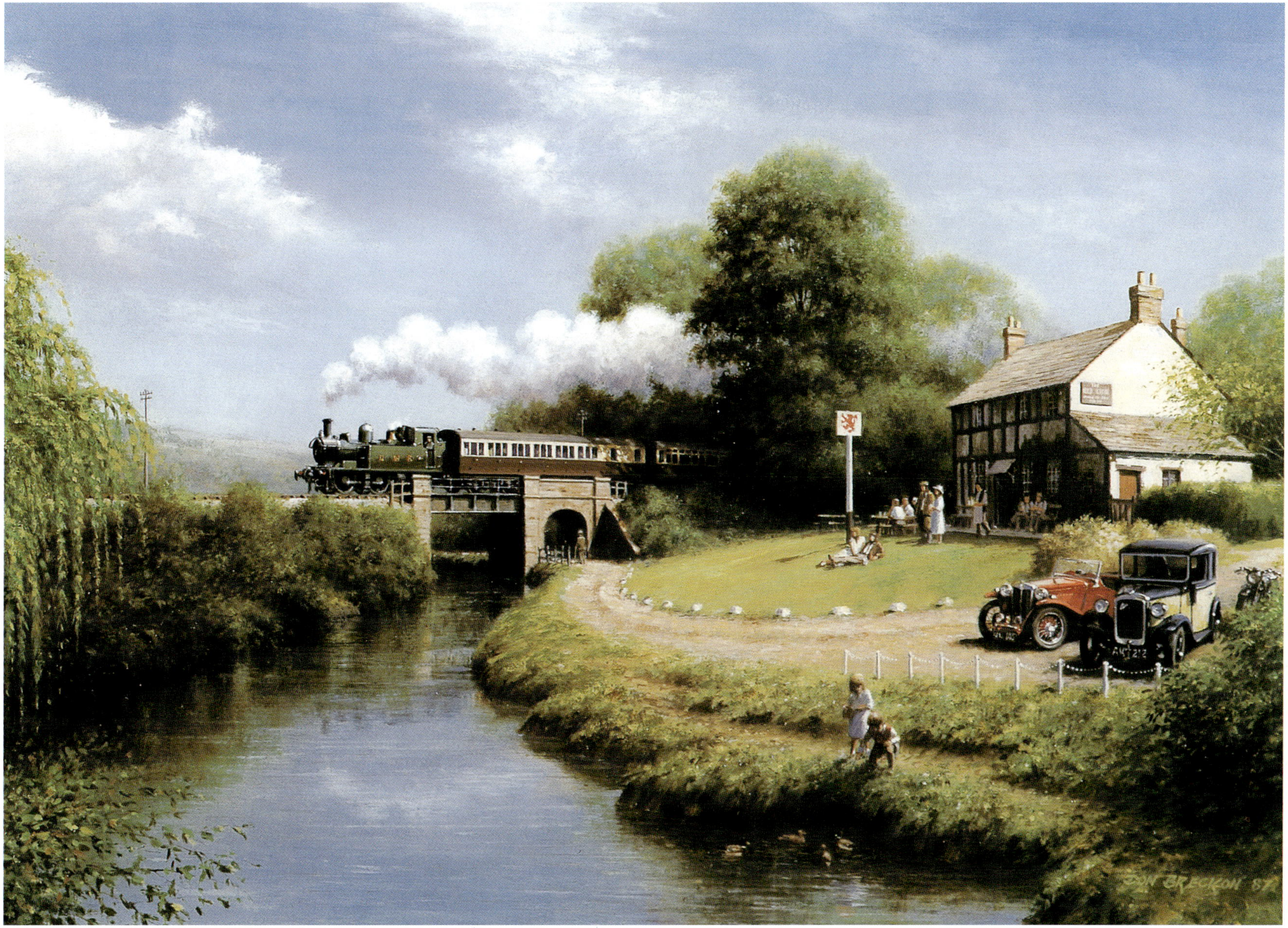

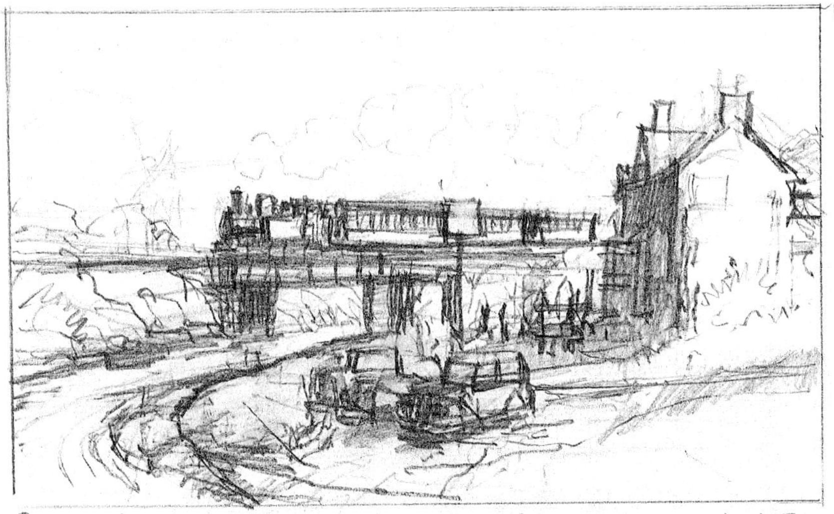

(1) 'Riverside Pub' Mid Level engine 1400 Cars - Austin 7
'Riverside Local'

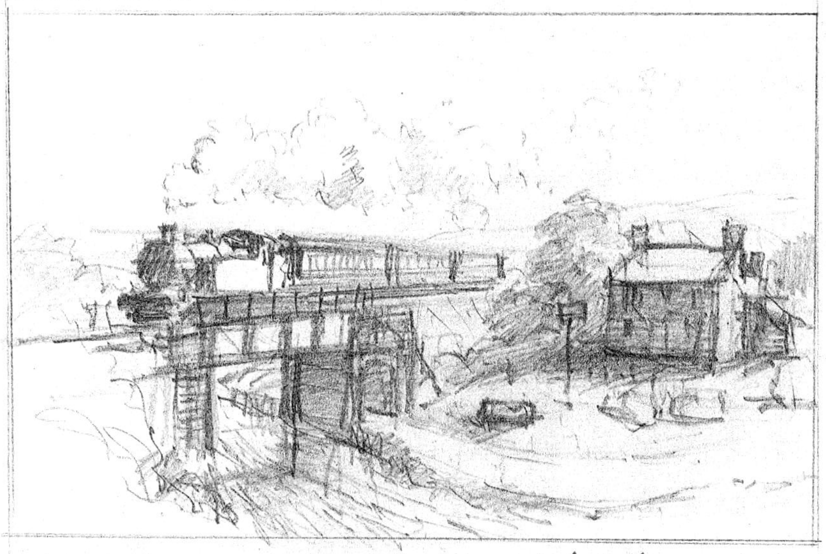

(2) High Level 'Prairie' tank - dist. hills

" No Sir, there is nothing contrived by man by which so much happiness is produced, as by a good tavern or inn " - Samuel Johnson

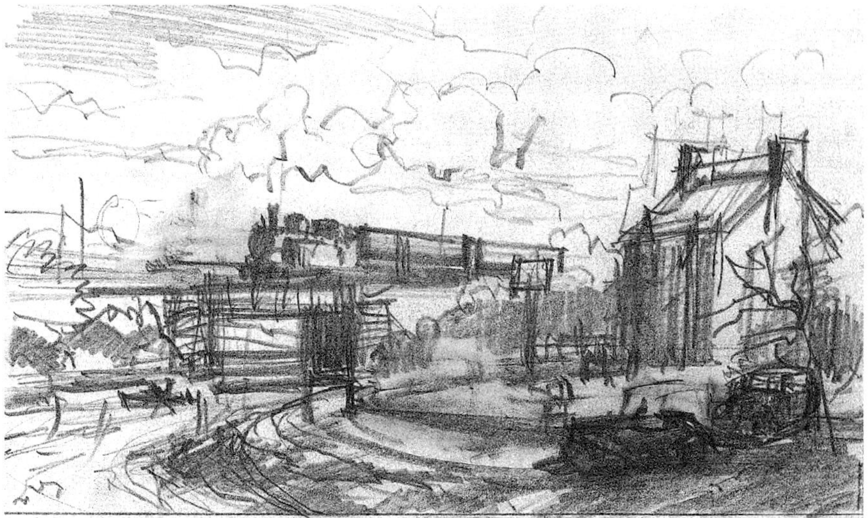

(3) Lower eye level cars to right hand corner
boat on river? engine '1400' class

started his train career when the railway had been a small independent company. So had Ted the guard, and Harold the signalman. Living 10 miles away in Kidderminster I was very much a foreigner, but accepted because Bill said I was all right!

We had left Kidderminster at mid-morning and, travelling light, the engine had taken the Severn Valley line to Bewdley and then the Tenbury Wells branch up through the heart of the beautiful Wyre Forest to Cleobury Mortimer, which was the junction for the Ditton Priors branch. Our locomotive 29 was part of the history of the line. Originally she had been built as a saddle tank for the company but, after it was taken over by the GWR, she had been converted to a pannier tank. However, she had retained her outside cylinders which gave her a rolling gait and a character of her own. Strangely enough, this feeling of 'character' seemed to apply to all country railways. Sometimes it was the old decrepit locomotives or rolling stock, sometimes the peculiar signalling arrangements, the materials used in the buildings, or the dress or accents of the staff. They all had something special or different, but whatever it was you always felt comfortable with it.

The outstanding character of the Ditton Priors branch, or 'The Gadget' as it was known locally, was without a doubt Old Ted the guard. Ted had a voice like the prophet of doom, with a slow ambling gait, rounded shoulders, and a drooping head which, when lifted, revealed a lugubrious face somewhat similar to a bloodhound. He never smiled or laughed, was miserable about everything, and when spoken to his reply was always sour and sharp. But underneath it all he was a shy and kindly man who, at the end of the day, would suddenly thrust a lettuce or a cauliflower at you, muttering to the floor, 'Here boy, take this, I've got one left over.'

No one had ever seen as much as a flicker of a smile on Ted's face, but then none of us knew what today was going to bring. Ted had climbed up into his van, Harold the signalman handed us the single-line token, and with a toot of our whistle 29 set off, waddling along like a duck. Apart from the initial 1 in 60 gradient the line was fairly level, which was just as well because I had worked out that the combined ages of loco, driver and guard came to about a hundred and eighty years!

The line followed the Rea Valley, which is a quiet and unspoilt tract of countryside in rural Shropshire, and the railway, in common with most branch lines, seemed to go through the most beautiful part of it. There were quiet deserted stations named Detton Ford, Aston Botteral, Burwarton and Stottesdon, but Bill applied the brakes and, with a sigh and a slight shudder, 29 came to a halt in the middle of nowhere. I crossed to the driver's side of the footplate, climbed down to the track and made my way to the boundary fence, where a buxom middle-aged lady was standing with a wicker basket in her arms.

'Arthur's working just past the river bridge, tell him not to be late home for tea because I'm off to the WI meeting tonight,' she told me, as she handed over the basket. 'Oh by the way, there's a little something in there for you and Bill.'

I climbed back onto the footplate, Bill opened the regulator, and 29 waddled off at her customary 15mph. The basket was put safely out of the way in a corner until, about a mile along the track, we passed over the river bridge where we found Arthur, the woman's husband, trimming back the lineside vegetation. The basket containing his lunch

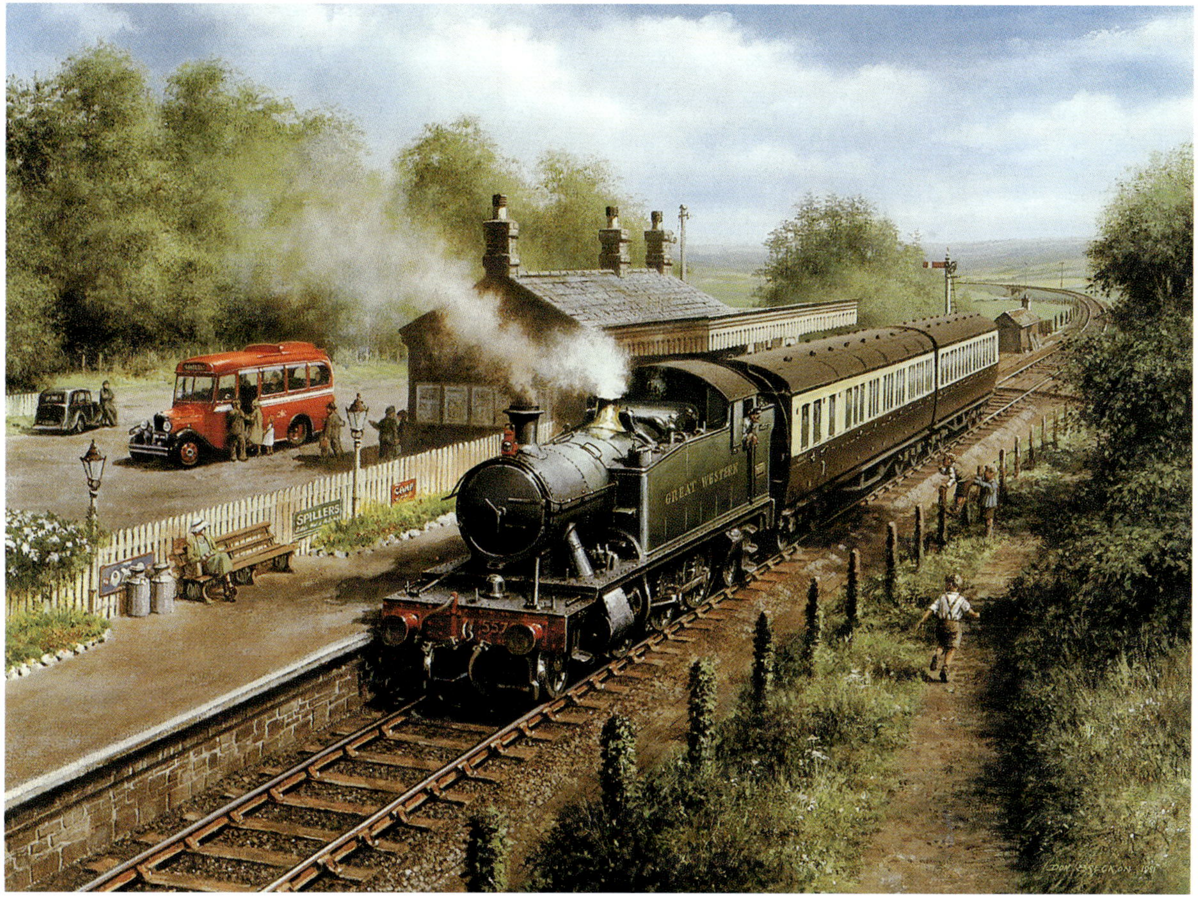

Country Connection (1981)
GWR 2-6-2T No 5572 pauses at a country station while passengers transfer to a Bedford WLB local bus in the 1930s.

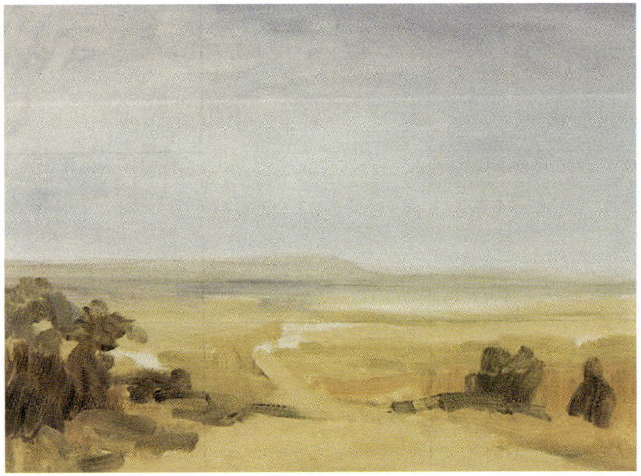

'BLOCKING IN' STAGE. SOMEONE SAYS IT LOOKS LIKE AUSTRALIA! DARK AND LIGHT MASSES JUST SUGGESTED

Four stages in the working of "Country Road"

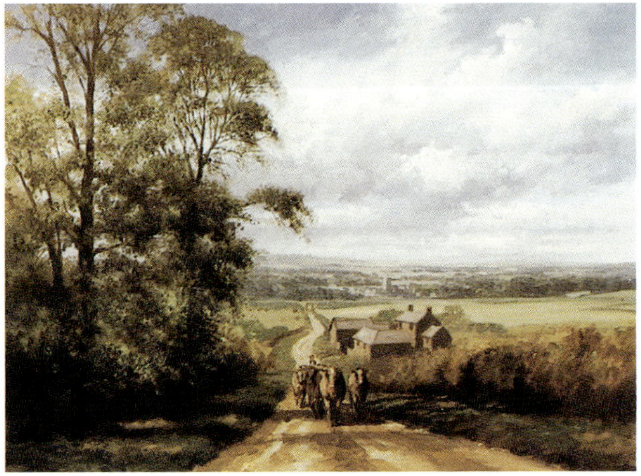

FOLIAGE ADDED TO TREES. CATTLE 'ROUGHED IN' AND FARMHOUSE BLOCKED IN. DISTANT HILLS DEFINED WITH VILLAGE CHURCH AND BUILDINGS. DECIDE ON TRAIN TO BE CROSSING SCENE ON EMBANKMENT WITH BRIDGE OVER ROAD. WORK ON CLOUDS.

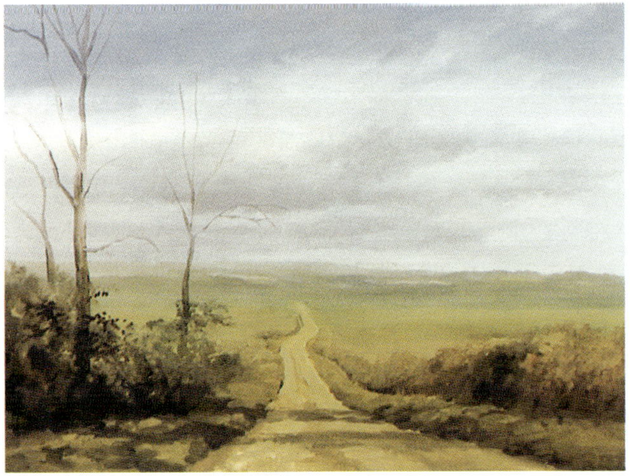

ROAD AND SHADOWS MORE DEFINED. TREE TRUNKS AND SHAPE OF CLOUDS ADDED. DISTANT HILLS ALTERED, BUT NOT YET WORKED OUT.

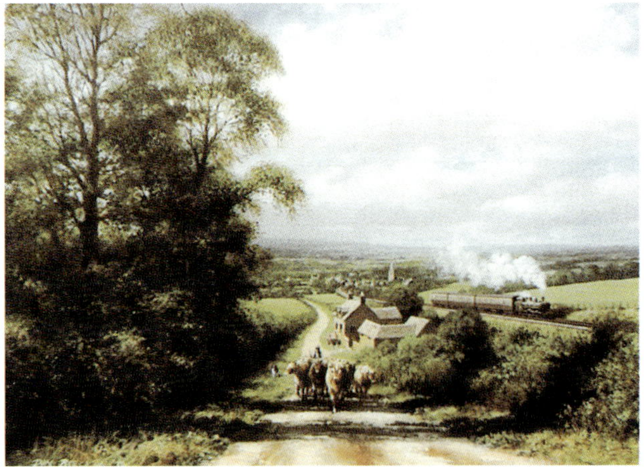

ALTERATIONS. FARM BUILDING CHANGED AND TRAIN INTRODUCED TO THE RIGHT, WITH LINE RUNNING BACK TO VILLAGE. SOFTEN CLOUDS. ADJUSTMENTS TO DISTANCE AND DETAIL WORK.

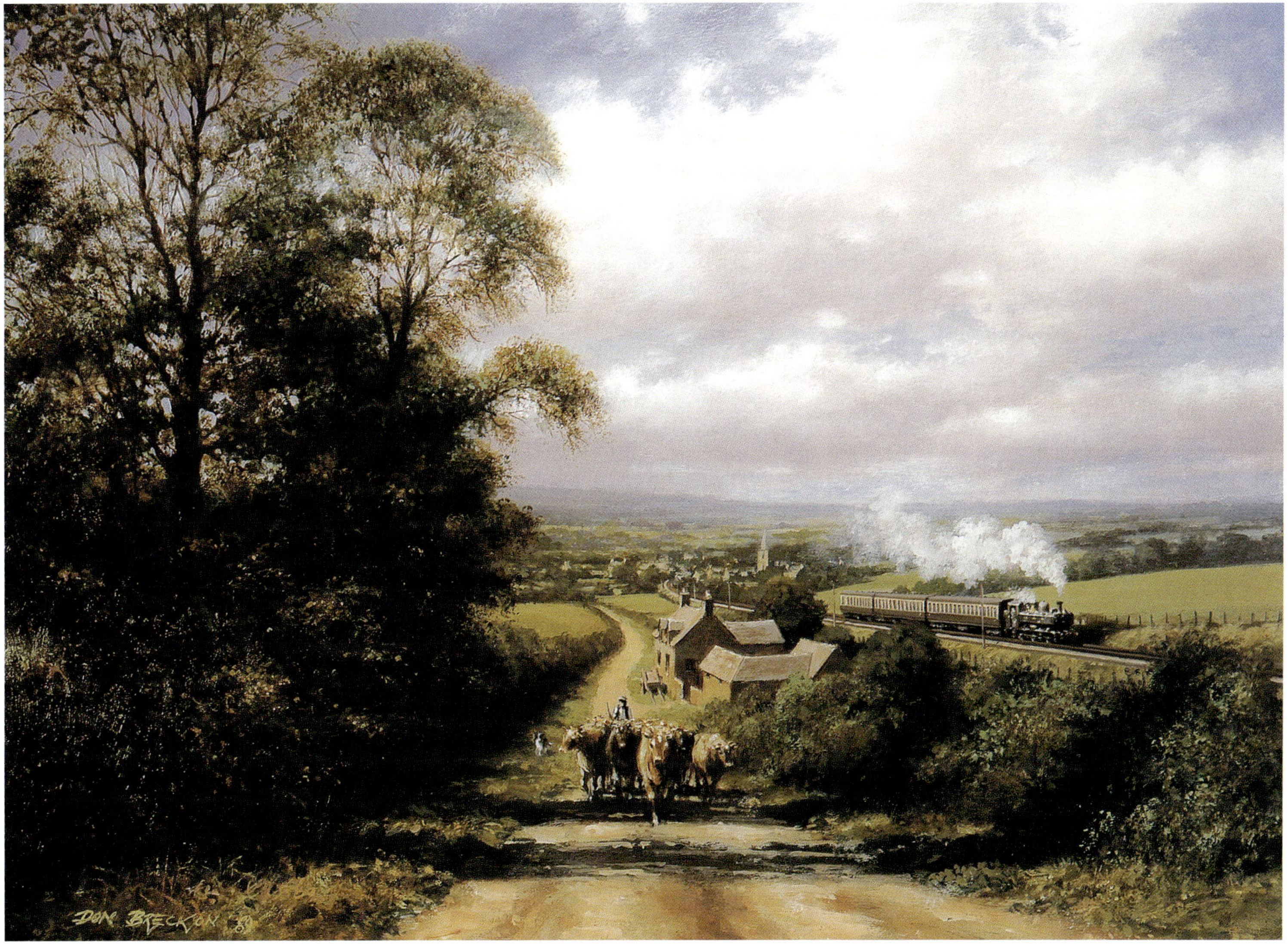

Country Road (1989)
A GWR 0-6-0 pannier tank locomotive brings a local train away from a village in the valley as a small herd of cows plod slowly along the road in the shadow of the elms.

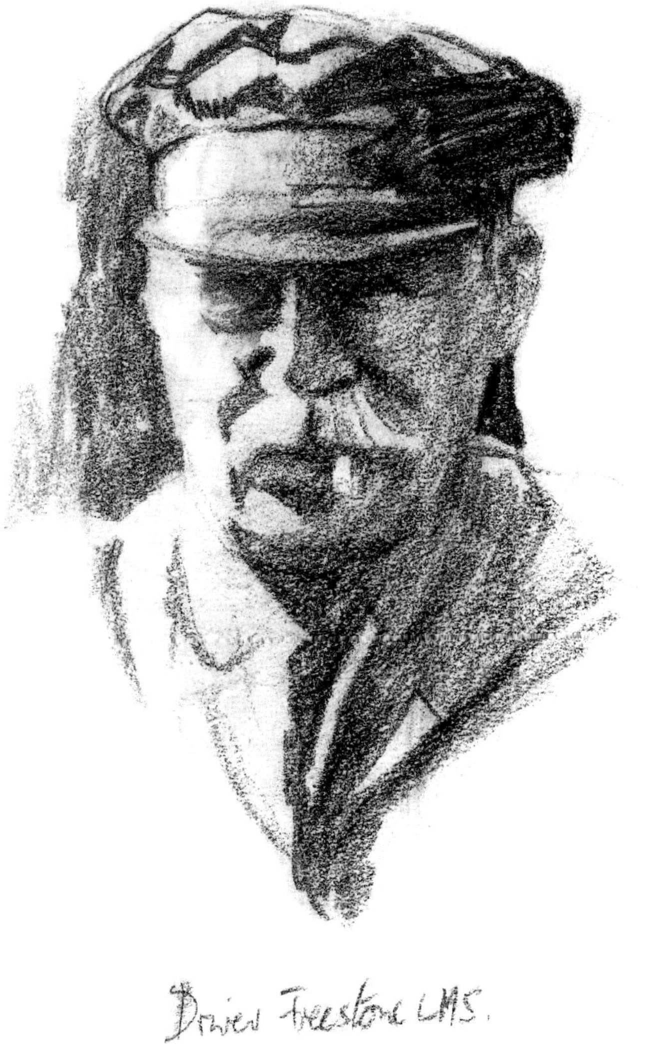

was handed over, but not before we had removed our little something. Sometimes it was fresh vegetables or a jar of home-made jam, but today it was a dozen fresh eggs. Fried on the shovel they were a meal fit for a king!

Officially, the only traffic along the Ditton Priors branch was goods travelling to and from the navy armament depot at the end of the line, but unofficially all the locals used it as their own private railway. Anyone visiting someone else would be given a lift in the guard's van, a farm gate or some fencing posts would be transferred from one farm to another, even the odd pig or sheep would be carried if we had an open wagon included in the train. Money never changed hands for any of this, but we never went short of fresh rabbits or chickens, vegetables, fruit and, at Christmas, a tree or a holly bush. It was all very much part of the country way of doing things.

The rest of the journey was uneventful until we reached Cleobury North, where there was a level crossing. It was my job to climb down from the locomotive and open the gates so that we could cross the road. As is happened, a large herd of cows was making its way along the road so I leaned on the gate enjoying the sunshine until they had all passed. 29 had gently come to a halt with her buffers nearly touching the gates, and Bill and Ted were discussing the finer points of Hereford cattle. The last cow cleared the crossing and I opened the gate I had been leaning on and then started to open the other.

Suddenly my foot slipped on one of the numerous cow-pats, and I came down heavily on my backside on top of it. Rather dazed I raised myself up into a kneeling position, but with my back towards the gate I had been pushing open. Unknown to me this was now gathering momentum as it swung back towards me. I soon found out, however, because it hit me square in the back and thrust me forward face-first into another cow-pat! As I staggered to my feet I became aware of a strange noise. It sounded like a squeaky bicycle, but looking around I realised that it was coming from Ted our guard. He was actually laughing! He was doubled up, with tears of mirth running down his cheeks, and could barely speak to ask, 'Did you see it, Bill? Arse over tip he went, lordy me I haven't seen anything so funny for years.'

That incident certainly went down in the folklore of that particular branch line.

However, not all journeys were as pleasant as the trips to Ditton Priors. Most branches were a delight in spring and summer, but it was a very different story in winter. The Severn Valley line, running alongside the River Severn, was a good example because in winter thick cold mists would rise up from the river, blotting out all the familiar landmarks, and tears would well up in our eyes as we leaned out of the side of the cab and peered ahead to see the signals. One particular job, working a coal train from Alveley Colliery, meant booking on at 4.30am and a 10 mile journey travelling tender-first. Due to the spartan, Victorian-style cabs that the Great Western 63XX class locomotives had, this left us totally exposed to all the elements. If it rained or snowed then the end result would be two very cold and miserable footplatemen. But even days like that could sometimes have their lighter moments.

With a strong, healthy exhaust note 6382 climbed out of Bewdley and headed towards Arley. Here the line follows the course of the river, a beautiful place in summer, but now, in the depths of winter, desolate and cold. The dark swirling waters gave off an icy chill and the wind blew down the valley, driving before it thickly falling snow which swept over the tender and was forced into every corner of the cab. It settled on our clothes, clogged our eyes, collected in our ears and trickled down inside our collars. It melted in the heat from the fire and soaked into our topcoats, dripped onto our overall trousers, and puddled the wooden floorboards of the footplate. Bill and myself silently took turns to drive and fire to try and keep warm, each of us wrapped up in our own personal misery. As the miles passed beneath our wheels the dawn slowly broke to reveal a white world and a grey sky, from which fell the ever-thickening snow.

I looked across at Bill, his face blue with cold, and he saw me looking and mustered up a grin. 'I bet I know what Old Fred's first words will be', said Bill as we pounded on towards Arley, where we were due to change the single-line token.

Old Fred was the stationmaster/signalman/porter/shunter/gardener and fount of all knowledge at the station, and summer or winter would always be dressed in laceless plimsolls, no socks, railway trousers, a wide leather belt, and an open-neck

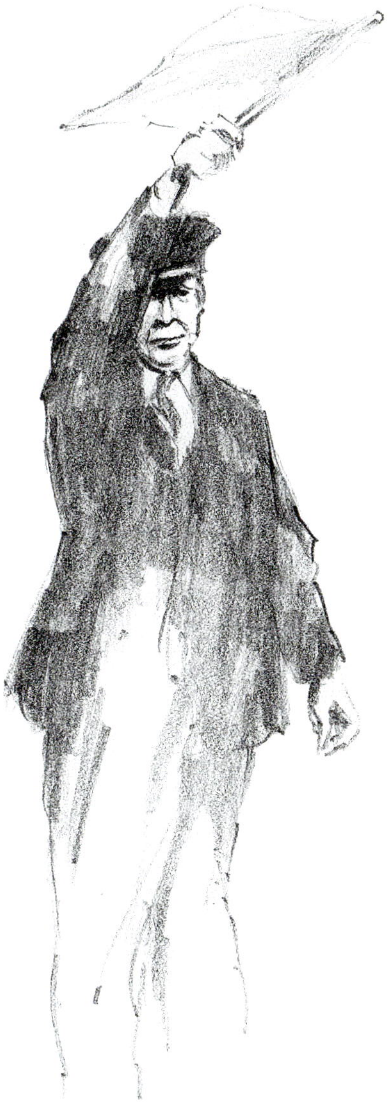

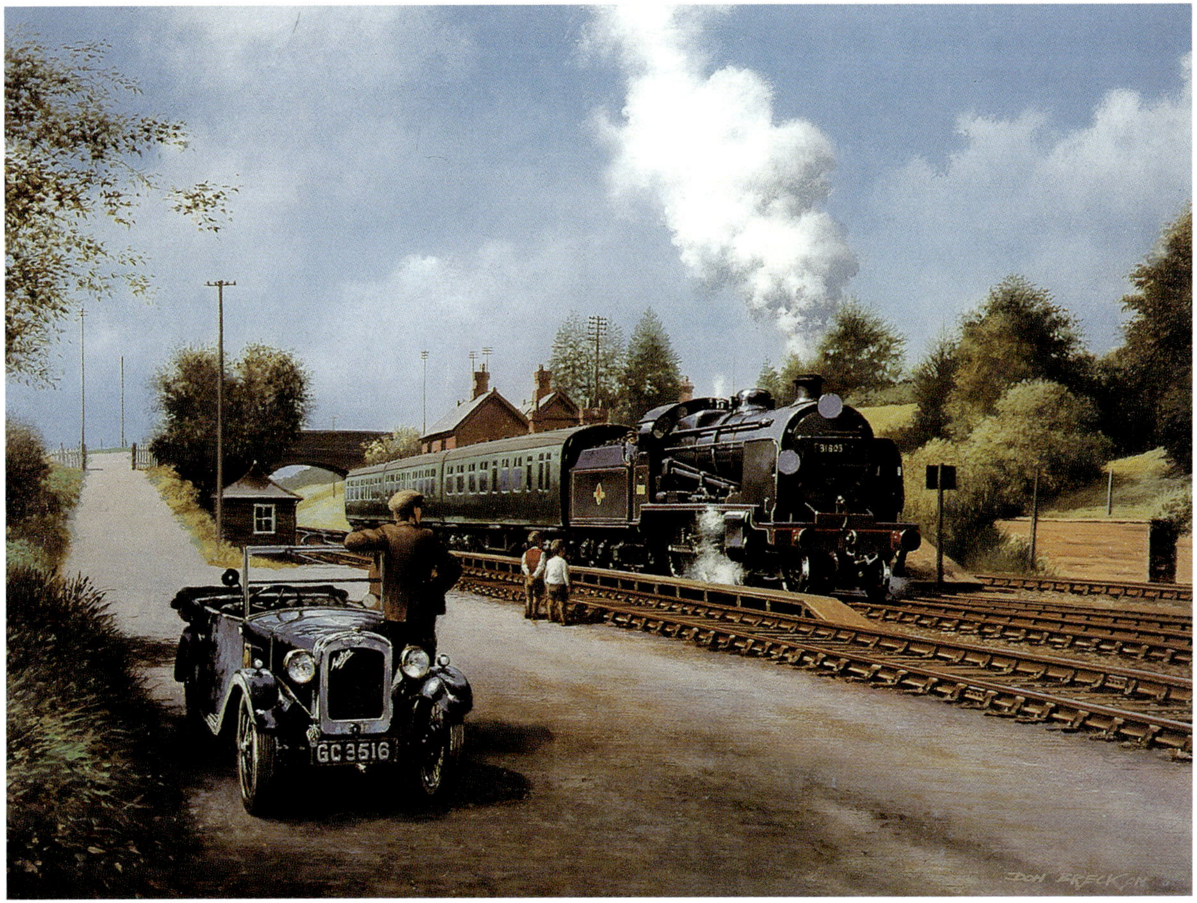

Leaving Daggons Road (1984)
The driver of a restored Austin Seven tourer waits while his sons watch the departure of a Southern Region U class 2-6-0 from Daggons Road station in the 1950s.

khaki army shirt with the sleeves rolled up, although if he was meeting a passenger train he grudgingly wore a cap! He had two speeds, dead slow and stop, and was the bane of every fireman's life because he never seemed to be waiting ready to change the single-line token, but just when it seemed that the train would have to stop, Fred would appear with the token held aloft.

Bill gave a prolonged blast of the whistle to let Fred know that we were on the way, but, peering ahead, I could not see any sign of him. Another shriek of the whistle, but still no Fred. I braced myself to hang over the side of the cab to exchange the token. Sometimes this operation could be carried out quite smoothly, but catch the token at the wrong angle and you could end up with a badly bruised hand. With the wind and snow making my eyes water it was not going to be an easy task.

Another blast of our whistle, and Fred appeared out of the station buildings. Slowly he ambled along the platform, stopped, looked up at the sky and the falling snow, and then resumed his slow course down the slope towards the wooden-sleepered crossing between the tracks. As usual he had no socks or jacket on, and already he wore a coating of snow. 'He's left it too late this time,' I thought, as I leaned over the side of the swaying cab. The wind tore at my clothes and my eyes watered with the cold as I watched Fred's slowly moving figure. The slush and the wet beneath my feet made me feel very insecure, and I hoped that my frozen fingers would be capable of catching the token. With a flurry of steam, a clatter and a roar, we passed under the road bridge and entered the station. A flash of steel, the smack of the token hitting the palm of my hand, my fingers curled around the cold metal and my other hand released the token that I was holding out ready for Fred. I looked down at his snow-covered figure as we passed. His grizzled expressionless face turned up to mine, the wad of tobacco was moved to the side of his mouth and then came Fred's usual and only comment, winter or summer: 'Nice now!'

Such was life on the country railway, and life was what it was all about. In its heyday, the railway needed the people and the people needed the railway. Then, unfortunately, the motor car came along and changed the whole pattern of life for everyone.

It seems to me that it was much simpler when the only worry was getting wet whilst walking to and from the station! No more the friendly chat with a neighbour as you wait on the platform, the excitement of going on a journey no matter how short, the solid clunk of a coach door, the brisk bark of a locomotive exhaust, the smoke and steam drifting past the windows. Another age, another time.

Tony Barfield was a locomotive fireman based at Kidderminster between 1952 and 1960. He is the author of When There was Steam *and* Panniers and Prairies.

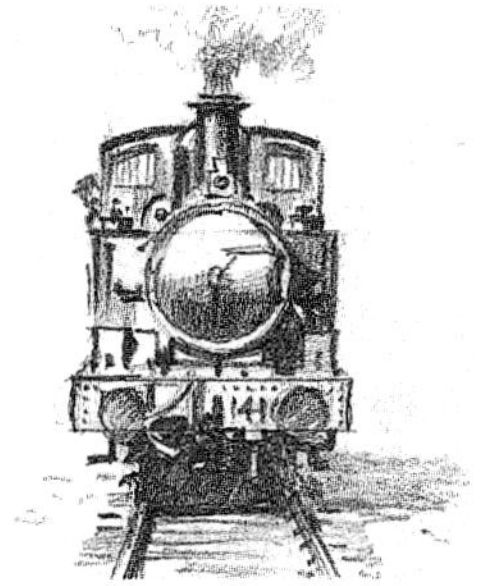

Ais Gill Viaduct

LMS Jubilee class No 5560 Prince Edward Island *heads the up Thames Clyde Express across Ais Gill Viaduct, about four miles from Ais Gill Summit, 1,169ft above sea-level. No 5560 was built by the North British Locomotive Company in 1934 and was withdrawn from service at the end of 1963.*

I had some reservations about undertaking this commission. It was for a Jubilee heading a London Midland Scottish (LMS) period Thames–Clyde Express on the Settle–Carlisle line. This would be a dramatic location with a fine train but since the return of steam locomotives to mainline operations on this route it has been much photographed and filmed.

The problem was to find some new aspect of the line, and as I searched through books and magazines it became clear that steam trains on the Settle–Carlisle had been covered very well and from every angle! I kept coming back to Ais Gill Viaduct, however, as it had a pleasing valley background and was one of the few which had a higher viewpoint, allowing the wheels of the engine to be seen without being obscured by the parapet.

Mulling over the numerous photographs of this location, it seemed to me that by extending the space to the right of the engine there would be a better feeling of movement and the expanse of the valley beyond would be emphasised. I knew that the composition would be rather unusual with all the action to the left-hand side, and as the painting progressed it became clear that something would be needed to restore the balance. Hence the introduction of the ganger leaning on the wall.

The location and the type of engine have a special meaning for me, which made working on the painting very enjoyable. I remember travelling with my parents by train to visit relatives in Scotland when I was very young. The train reversed at Leeds (this, to a small boy, was a complete mystery) and set off northwards. We came to what I now know to be the Settle–Carlisle stretch. Hedges became walls and 'mountains' loomed up over the train. Convinced that this dramatic scenery must be Scotland, I remember being very disappointed as it slipped away behind us and later, when we did cross the border, there was nothing to see but 'ordinary' countryside.

The Jubilee engines probably hauled our train to Scotland. They certainly became very important in my life a few years later when train-spotting became a serious activity. Expresses from St Pancras were headed by Jubilee or Black Five engines and only the former were of any interest to me – because they had names. All the names of countries and states in the British Empire, with a few warships and admirals, were there and anyone looking at our notebooks would have thought that we were in a geographical quiz. Hyderabad, Malay States, Hong Kong, Leeward Islands – where were all these places? We didn't know, but as long as we hadn't got it underlined in our books it was a 'cop'.

The Thames–Clyde Express was one of the few named trains on the old Midland line alongside the Waverley and the Robin Hood, and in British Railways days it carried a headboard which always made it look impressive. It is linked in my mind with, of all things, the Co-op bread round! In my later school years I had a holiday job with the Kettering Co-op as a bread-delivery assistant. It was a horse-drawn bread van, which was quite convenient because whilst the baker and I darted in and out of the houses the horse clopped slowly along the road. Unfortunately, if the horse picked up speed we had to do the same, and with a loaded wicker basket on the arm this soon became exhausting. It was often about this time that the Thames–Clyde Express pulled out of Kettering station and along the embankment. I only had time to give it a glance before pursuing the horse, but how I longed to be on that train!

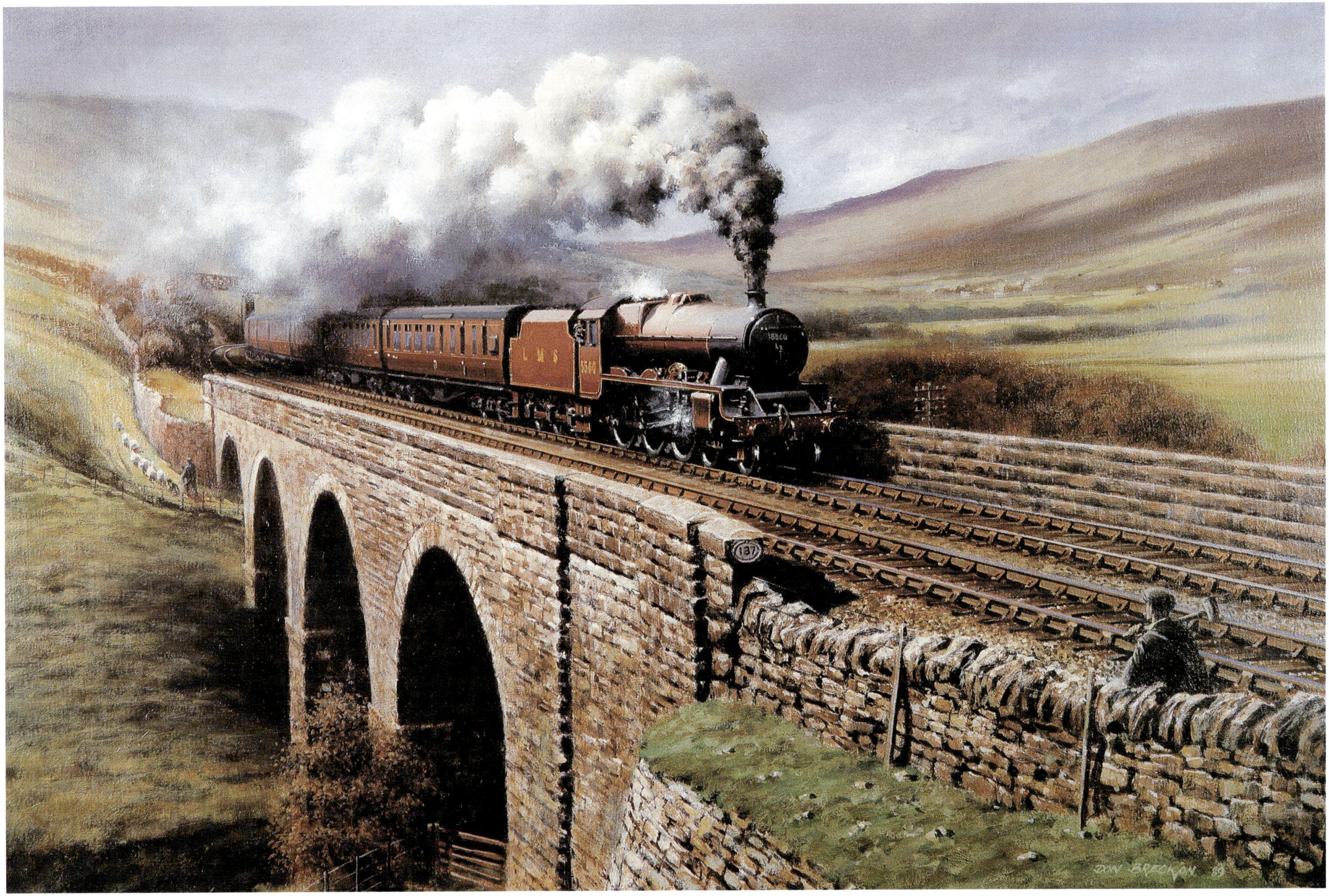
L M S
137
DON BRECKON

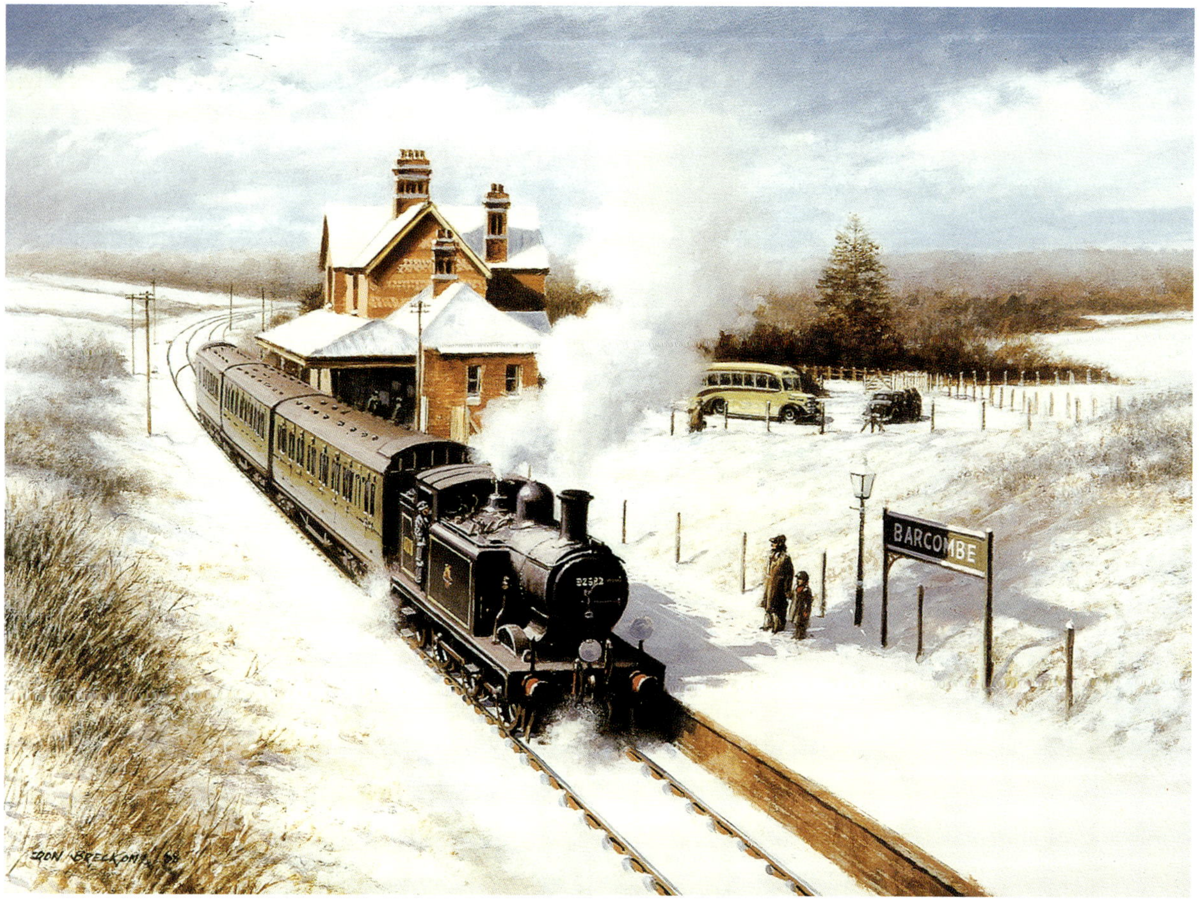

Winter at Barcombe (1988)
An ex-LBSCR class E4 pulls away from Barcombe with a train from Oxted to Brighton. Barcombe opened in 1882 and closed in 1955.

Talerddig
GWR Manor class 4-6-0 No 7808 Cookham Manor *heads an Aberystwyth–Manchester train up Talerddig incline on the Cambrian Railways line across mid-Wales. The Manor class engines worked the line from 1943 until the mid-1960s. No 7808 was built in 1938 and withdrawn in 1965. It has been preserved by the Great Western Society at Didcot.*

Talerddig Incline is on the main line of the former Cambrian Railways (later GWR) from Welshpool to Aberystwyth. The summit is 693ft above sea-level and for east-bound trains is the climax of the 14 miles from Machynlleth. The single-track line climbs at its steepest gradient of 1 in 52 for 2 miles before passing through a dramatic rock cutting near the summit.

This route was used by the Cambrian Coast Express but weight restrictions permitted only moderate-sized locomotives. The Manor class proved capable of taking up to eight coaches over the bank unassisted, though double-heading was common especially on the Machynlleth–Talerddig section.

The Manors were a Collett design, built between 1938 and 1950. In 1952 a series of tests was carried out at Swindon to improve the steaming of these engines, the visible results of which were the fitting of a different design of chimney.

I felt that the composition of this painting needed something extra and yet there was very little space in the foreground to work in anything significant. Then I remembered travelling on an HST when there was a sudden swirl of smoke past the window. Surprised by this echo of the old days of railway travel, I looked out and saw that the smoke was from a series of bonfires lit by workmen clearing undergrowth on the embankment. The speed of the train sucked up the smoke and it made wonderful patterns along the train for a few seconds.

I resolved to remember this – and then promptly forgot it until the Talerddig scene came along. Working it into the painting I was pleased with the contrast between the drifting grubby smoke of the bonfire and the powerfully-ejected white plumes of the engine.

Smoke and steam provide one of the pleasures of painting railway engines. The contrast between hard heavy metal and volumes of billowing steam which bring a feeling of power and animation to the machine, is a gift for the artist and photographer. Although loose and free, steam has patterns. In a hard-working engine, as in this painting, it blasts out of the chimney in tight compressed lumps which expand as they rise into the air. Enlarging and joining, they become soft-edged until they drift away, breaking up into straggly shapes which mingle with the trees.

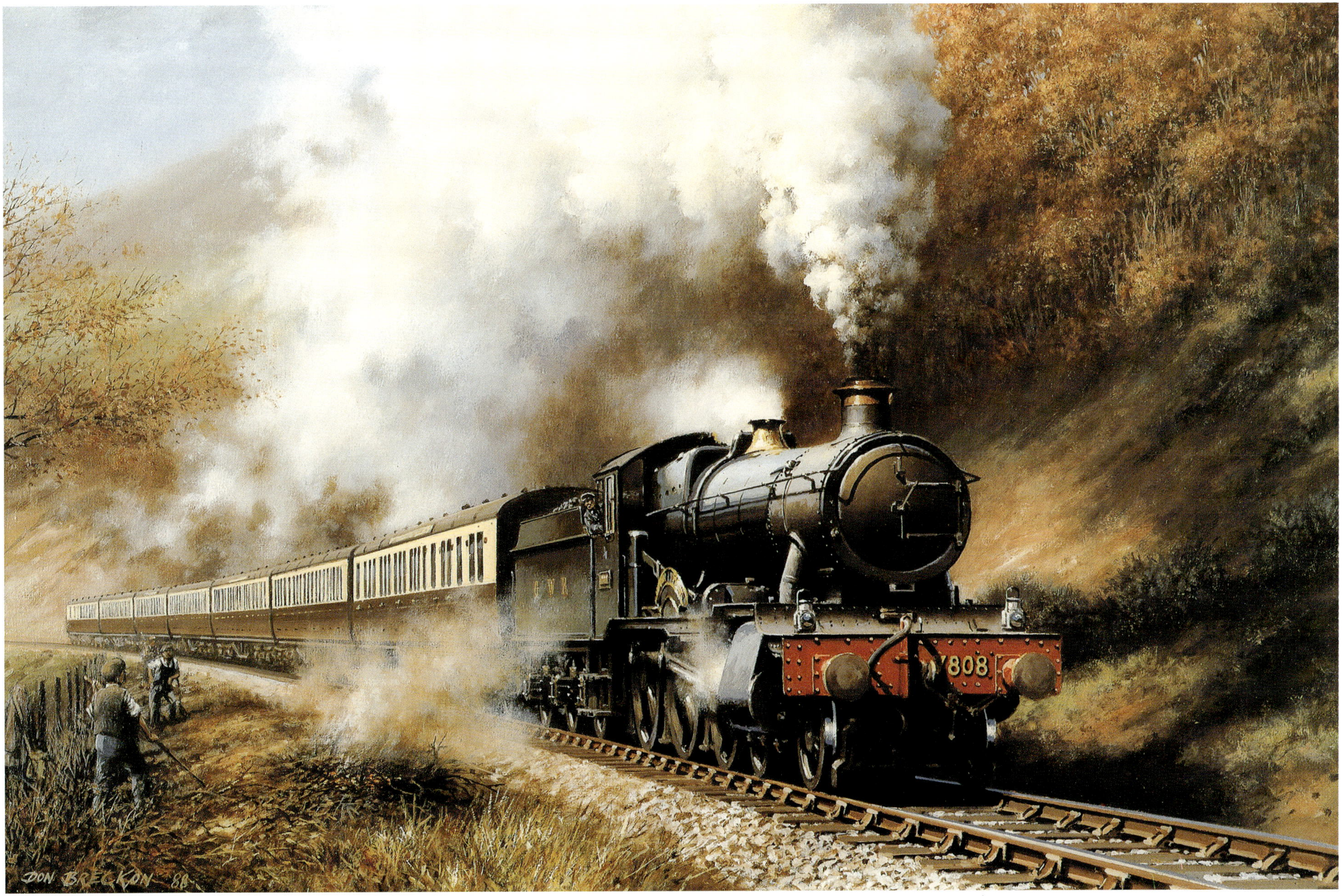
DON BRECKON 88
808

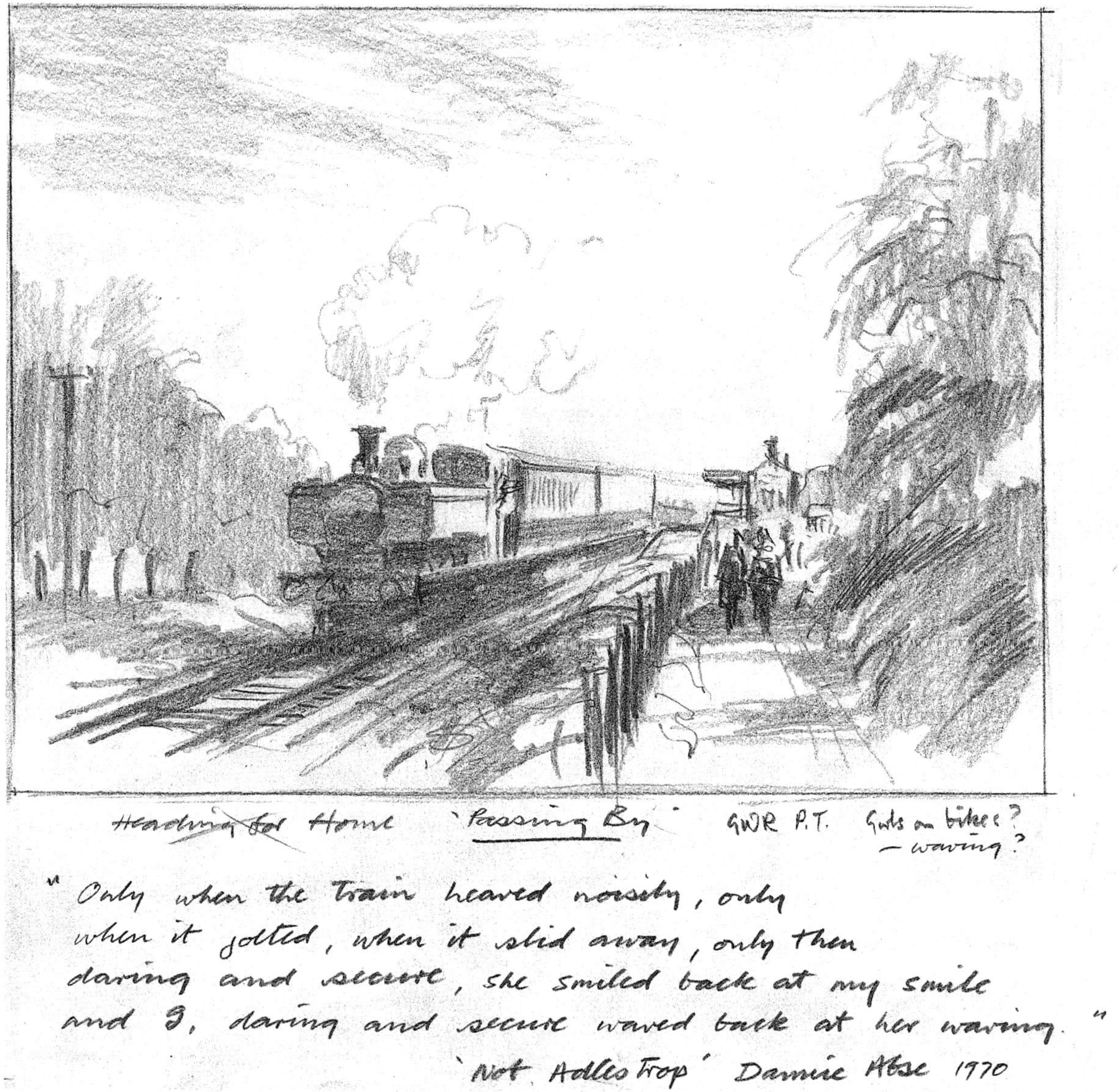

Passing By
As the local train pulls away from the station the young fireman waves to two girls cycling home beside the tracks. The engine is a GWR 0-6-0 pannier tank of the 5700 class. 9600–21 were built at Swindon between 1943 and 1945.

The initial rough sketches for this painting were based on an idea of passengers walking home along a road from a station as the train passed by. Seeking to link the engine with the people, I wanted the fireman, who would be on the left side of a GWR engine, to be waving to the group in the road as the train overtook them. But to be convincing there had to be a reason for his greeting. A small boy admiring the engine would merit an acknowledgement and to such a lad a wave from the crew of a steam locomotive would be like a gesture from royalty. But then the thought came to me that there was someone who would receive a much more enthusiastic greeting from a young fireman, and that would be an attractive girl!

The memory of a journey on the back of an open lorry to a Boy Scout camp in North Wales came back to me vividly. As we passed through towns along the way we were encouraged by the speed of the lorry and the fact that we were strangers in the area to shed our normal shyness and call out to every girl in sight. We were enjoying this hugely until the lorry pulled up at some traffic lights. A couple of girls who had just had the benefit of our bravado were now walking slowly past our lorry grinning with delight at our sudden discomfiture. We were marooned with our embarrassment as we willed the lights to change so that we could be somewhere else as quickly as possible.

This memory influenced my new layout for the painting with the two girls in a station lane, and on bikes to bring them closer to the pace of the overtaking train. Is the young fireman indulging in false confidence as he sweeps past, or does he know the girls? They are not obviously responding, so this question remains open to interpretation – which is all part of the interest of a scene within a scene.

The branchline stations served a well dispersed rural community and local people would be quite used to a long walk to and from the station. Bicycles, for those who owned them, could be left in the station cycle sheds for the day just as today's commuter will leave his car, but usually people settled for the long walk home.

Though homes were scattered, the sense of community was there. The station staff would know all the passengers and would be known to them. At some time or other most people would come to the station. It was a world regulated by the chiming of the church clock and the passing of the train.

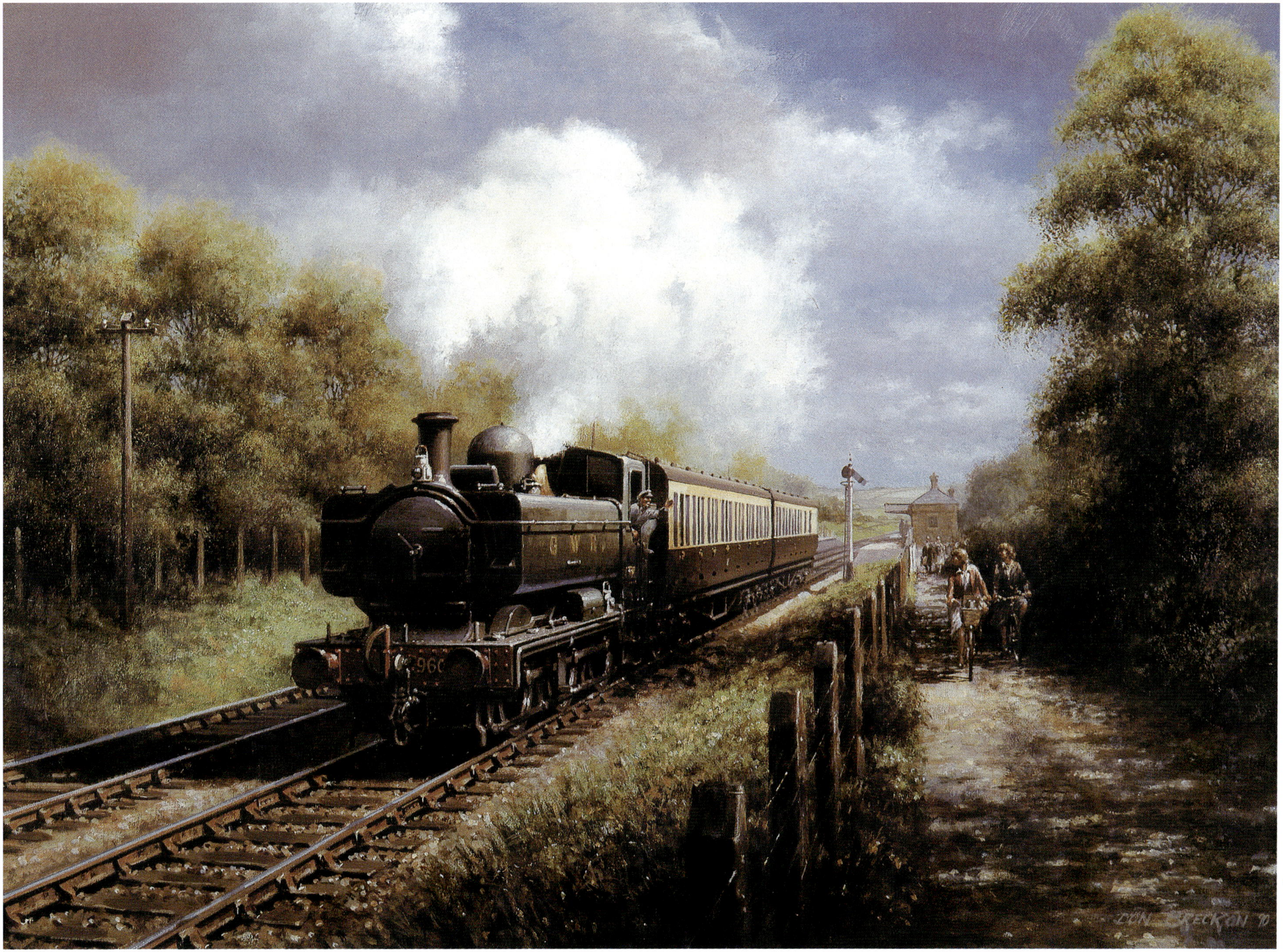

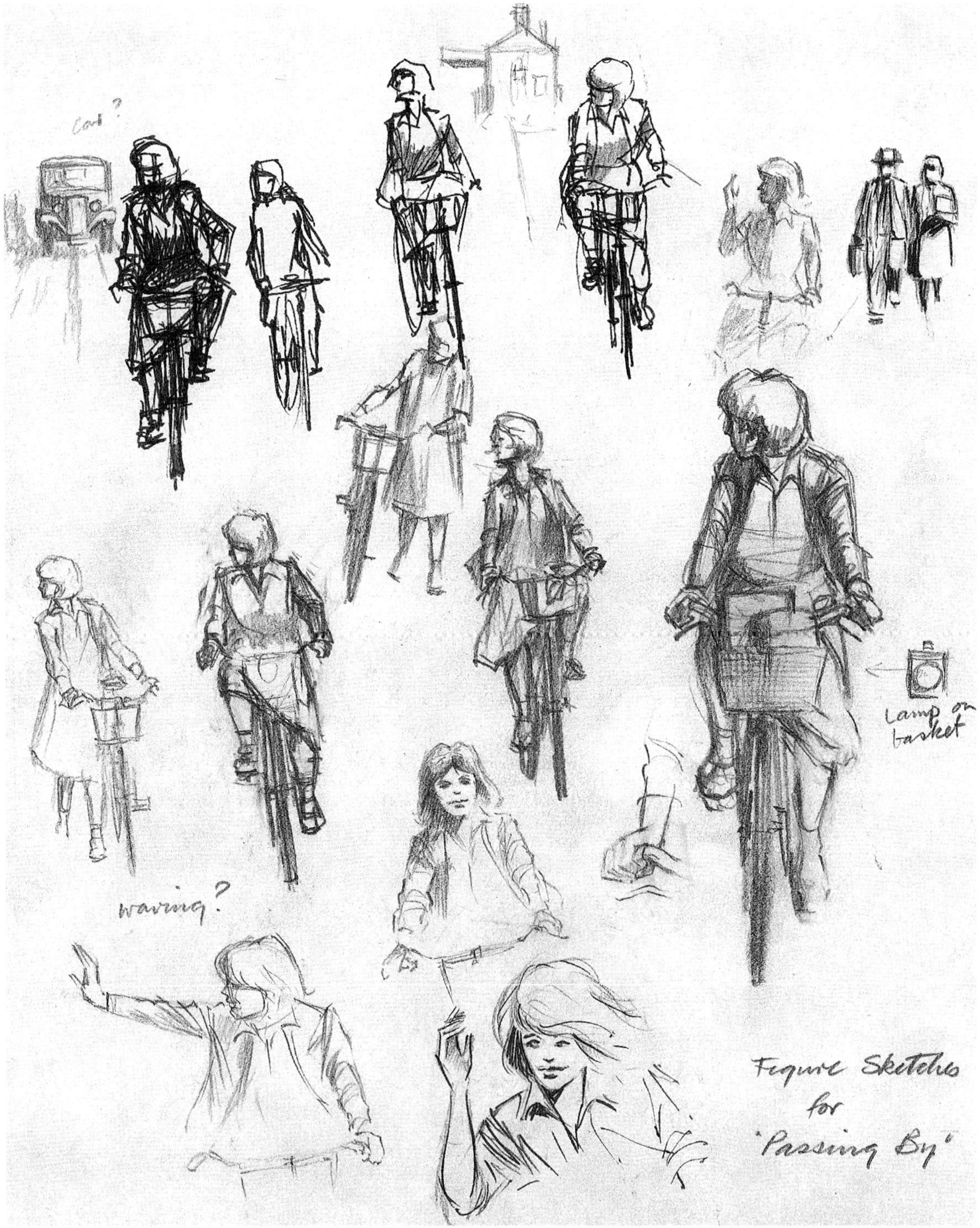

Winter Working
A GWR 2-6-2T Small Prairie locomotive heads a three-coach local train through a snow-covered landscape. A horse and cart bring a load of winter feed along the lane beside the track, and the farm dog lopes along leaving a trail between the wheel ruts.

Snow scenes open up new possibilities for creating contrasts within a painting. An obvious one is the contrast between the colours of the snow-covered landscape and the locomotive itself. The GWR green sits happily in the colours of a summer scene but when the snow covers the countryside the engine is highlighted in sharp contrast, which can be very dramatic. Also the soft nature of snow makes for an interesting comparison with the hard-edged metal of the locomotive.

With this as a start other differences present themselves which make for an arresting painting. Trees and hedges give the opportunity to bring in a touch of warmth and the shadows enable the form of the slopes to be defined. In fact, as the overall feeling is one of cold, finding warm colours to create a balance is important. The red buffer beam, of course, and the chocolate-brown of the lower part of the GWR coaches contribute to this, but the chance to use a faded red on the wagon wheel was not to be missed in this composition. Apart from a strong warm colour it echoes the red of the buffer beam to help the balance across the painting. The brown of the hedges spreads the warm areas into the landscape.

When a painting is the result of imagination rather than of a specific location the artist can develop the full potential of a composition, giving free rein to the 'narrative' of the scene as well as improving the balance of the work. In this case the barn was introduced for two reasons. Something was needed on the left to balance the shapes on the right, and by bringing in the barn with grouped cattle a connection was made with the cartload of hay. This was more obvious at a stage when I worked in an overbridge behind the train. Later, when things began to look rather crowded, the bridge was painted out.

Once again it was to be a case of the little things being important, or at least receiving all the attention. The dog was a late addition as I began to take an interest in the patterns of tracks in the snow. The thought of a dog padding along in the rear of the horse and cart came to mind, and it was to prove the key to the whole composition. Try covering up the dog and the whole picture is changed. Perhaps this is why, when people look at the painting, often the first thing they say is 'I like the dog'.

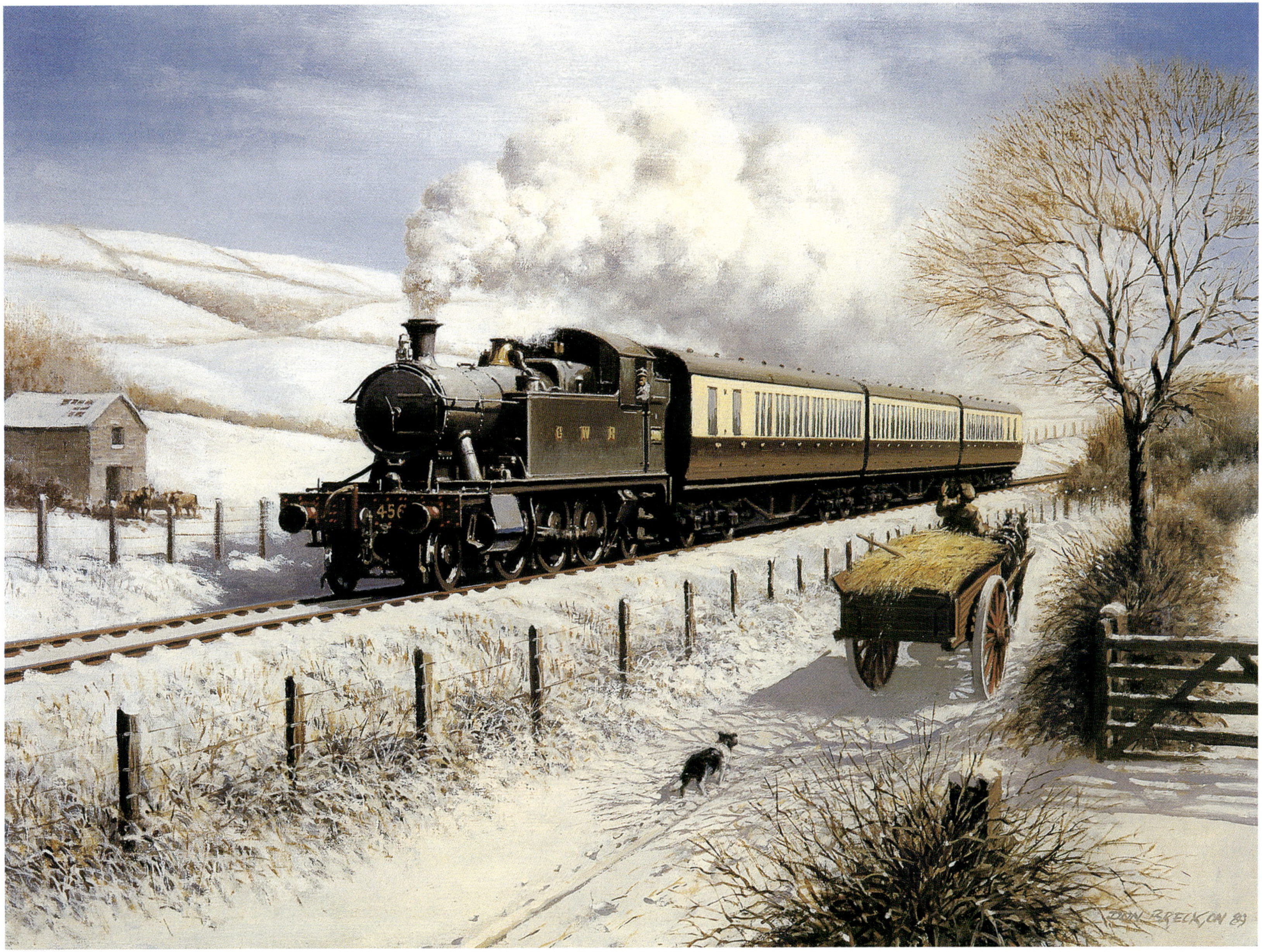
GWR
456
DON BRECKON 83

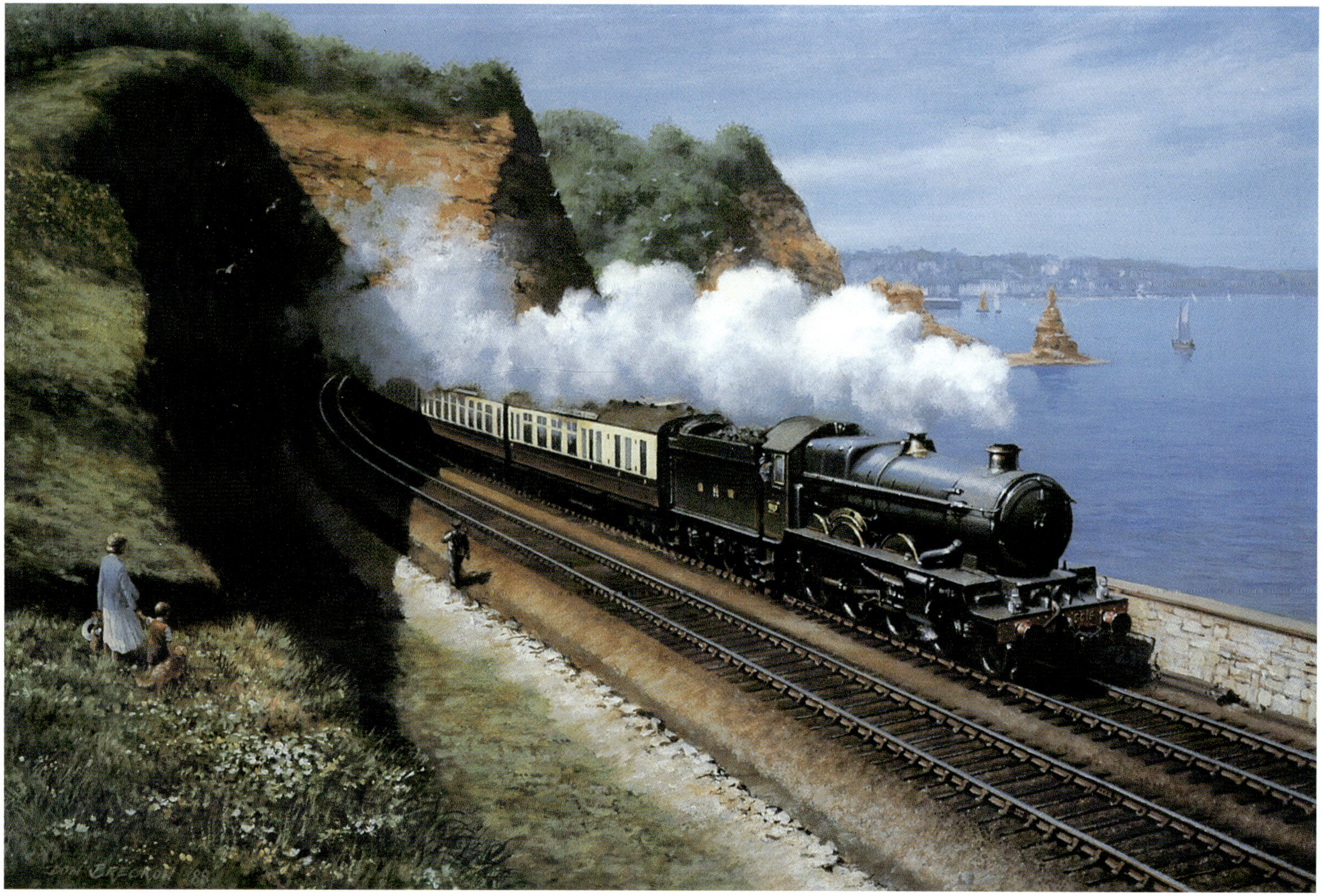

Devon Coast (1988)
GWR Castle class 4-6-0 No 5015 Kingswear Castle *heads the down Cornish Riviera out of the last of five tunnels near Pulpit Rock close to Dawlish on the South Devon coast.*

Along the Avon (1989)
GWR 2-6-2T locomotive No 4536 heads a local train from Bristol Temple Meads to Portishead along the southern side of the Avon Gorge. No 4536 was based at Bristol (Bath Road) shed and was built in 1913 and withdrawn in 1959.

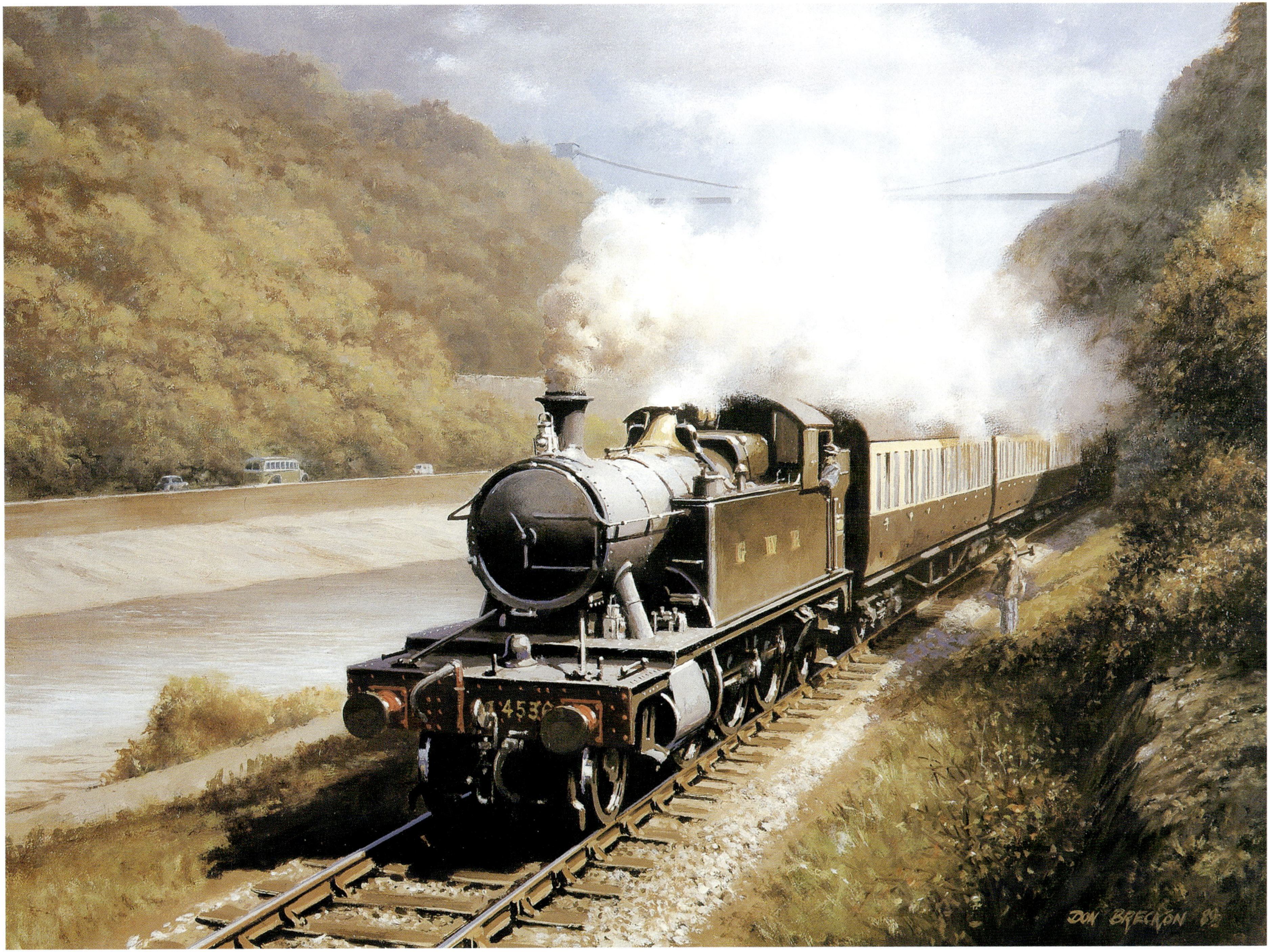
DON BRECKON

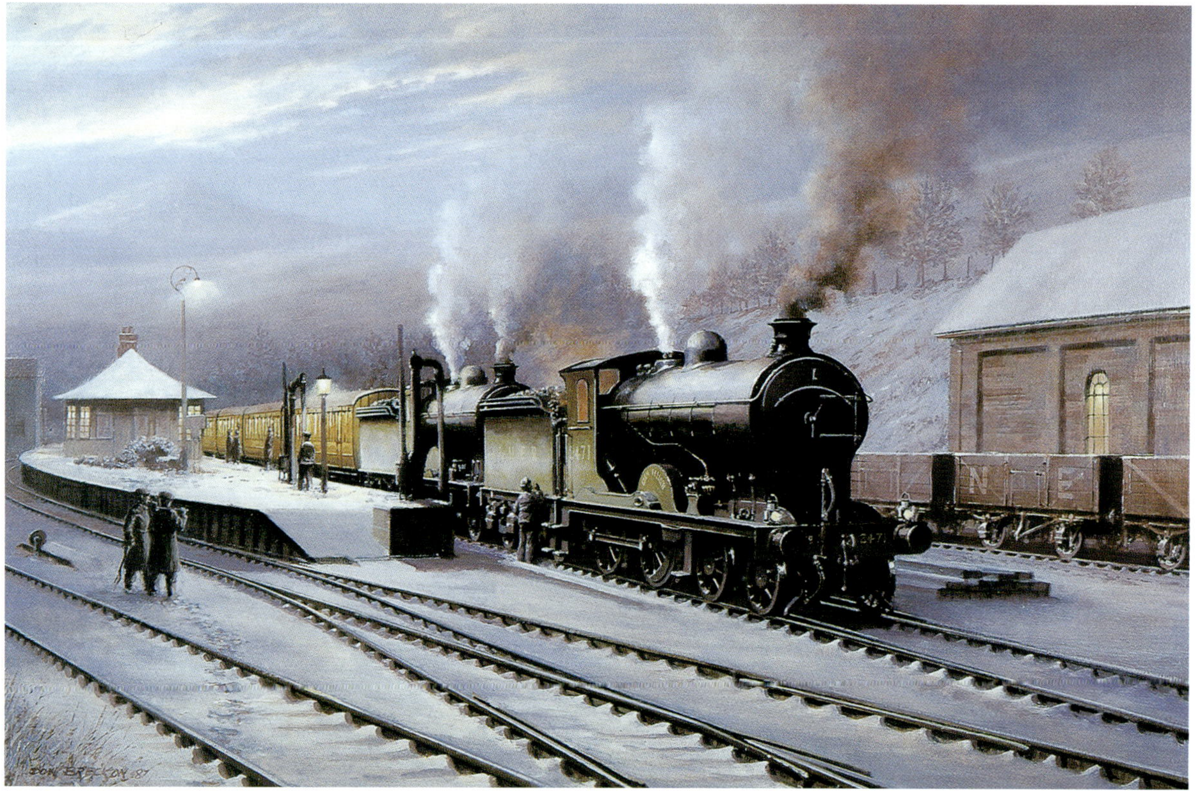

Waiting at Crianlarich (1987)
A Fort William–Glasgow express pauses at Crianlarich on a winter evening in the late 1930s. The train is double-headed by two of the D34 Glen class engines with 2471 Glen Falloch *leading.*

Waiting at Halwill (opposite)
A Southern Region class T9 waits at the head of a Padstow train at Halwill Junction in north Devon in the 1950s. The station nameboard states 'Halwill for Beaworthy, Junction for Bude, North Cornwall and Torrington lines'.

Jim Harries, who commissioned this painting, writes of Halwill Junction:

> Imagine a showery day with the prevailing south-westerlies pushing the clouds through to Devon, indicating that the surfing will be exhilarating along the north Cornish coast at Bude and Padstow.
>
> Halwill Junction was 500ft above sea level and had a middle-of-nowhere feeling, the railway no longer being in the lee of Dartmoor. Pictorially the damp platform and extensive sky reinforces the sense of wide open spaces.
>
> This is the 1950s with the elegant narrow-cab Drummond T9s with eight-wheeled water cart tenders still doing sterling service at the head of a down train. Also Bulleid Pacifics (Spam Cans) could be seen on the Padstow line and Maunsell Moguls and M7 tanks to Bude.
>
> An E1R 0-6-2 radial tank rebuilt from the Stroudly E1s would be in the short platform behind us with a coach or two for the Torrington line. This line had been built by Colonel Stephens of light railway fame and was run by the Southern Railway on completion in 1925.
>
> The station nameboard, posts and other obstructions retain wartime regulation black and white stripes in time-faded condition, but the platform edge has a fresh daily whitewash, the application being with a broom whose head was an inverted 'L' shape.
>
> As a child our summer holidays were spent at Bude and returning on the Atlantic Coast Express in September, father and I would get off at Halwill Junction to watch the ensuing activity. The locomotive from Bude would be detached and run round its carriages to recouple on the rear and then haul them back out of the station in the Bude direction – to the consternation of mother and sister on the train!
>
> Looking in the same direction the Padstow portion of the Atlantic Coast Express would appear from the cutting on the left and cross over the down line to reach the up platform. The Bude portion would then be propelled back into the station to be attached to the rear, and the family would be reunited to continue the journey to Waterloo with the West Country Pacific in charge.
>
> Soon after the closure of the line in 1966 the tall signal box, with the rest of the buildings on the up platform, were dismantled. The main down station bungalow, platforms, turntable pit, goods and abattoir sheds lay fallow for over twenty years. Then in 1989 all this was flattened in favour of a residential development. Of the station complex only the Junction Inn remains, with a new inn sign – 'Stirling Single of the Great Northern Railway'. Refreshment and sustenance are available inside, with interesting Halwill Junction memorabilia on view. Twenty years ago the front bar and the snug bar were in separate licensing authorities, the boundary between Okehampton and Holsworthy running through the inn. The front bar called 'Time' at 10.30pm and the snug at 11.00pm. Halwill Junction always was a place for sudden well timed activity.

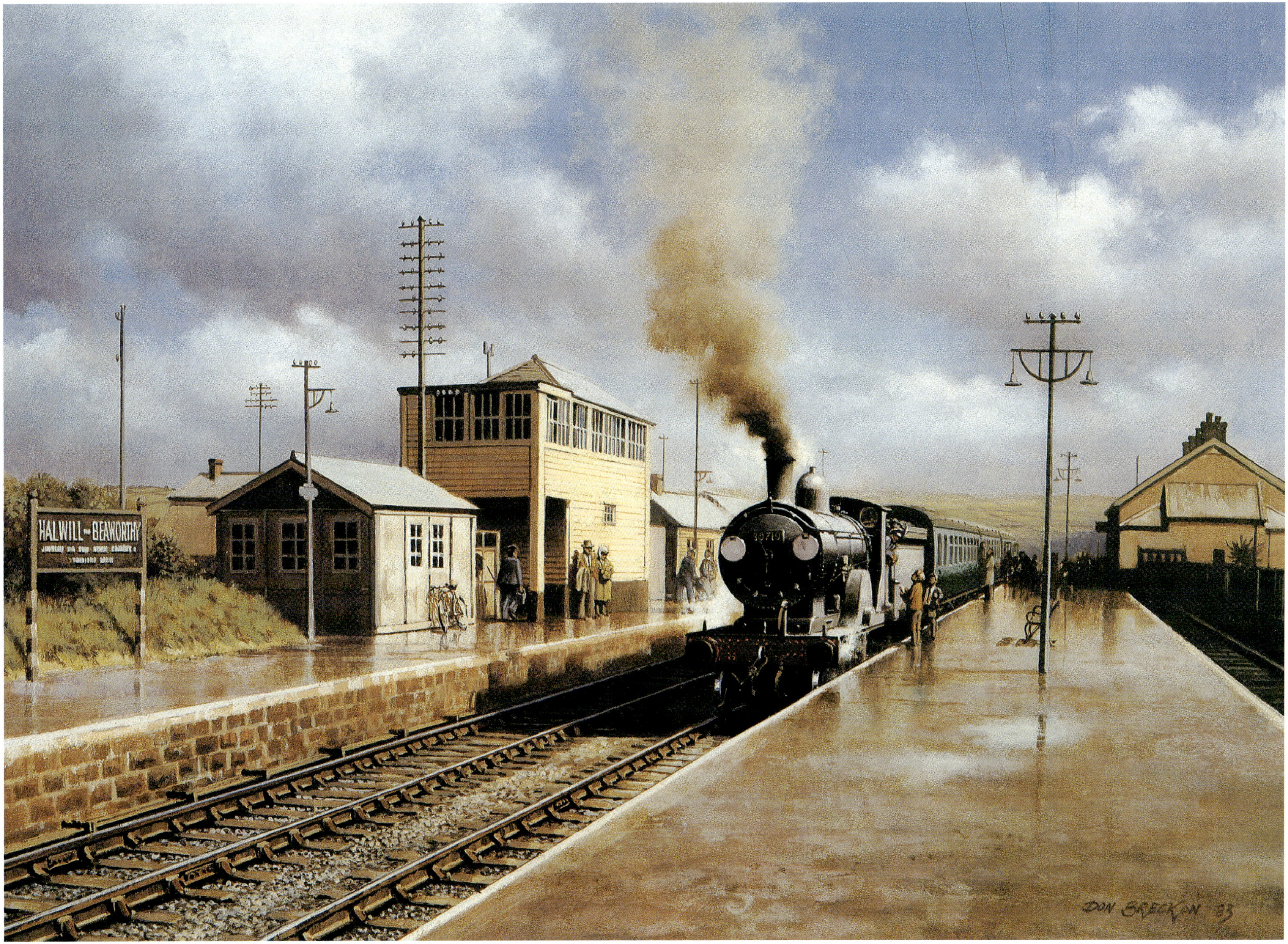
HALWILL BEAWORTHY
DON BRECKON '83

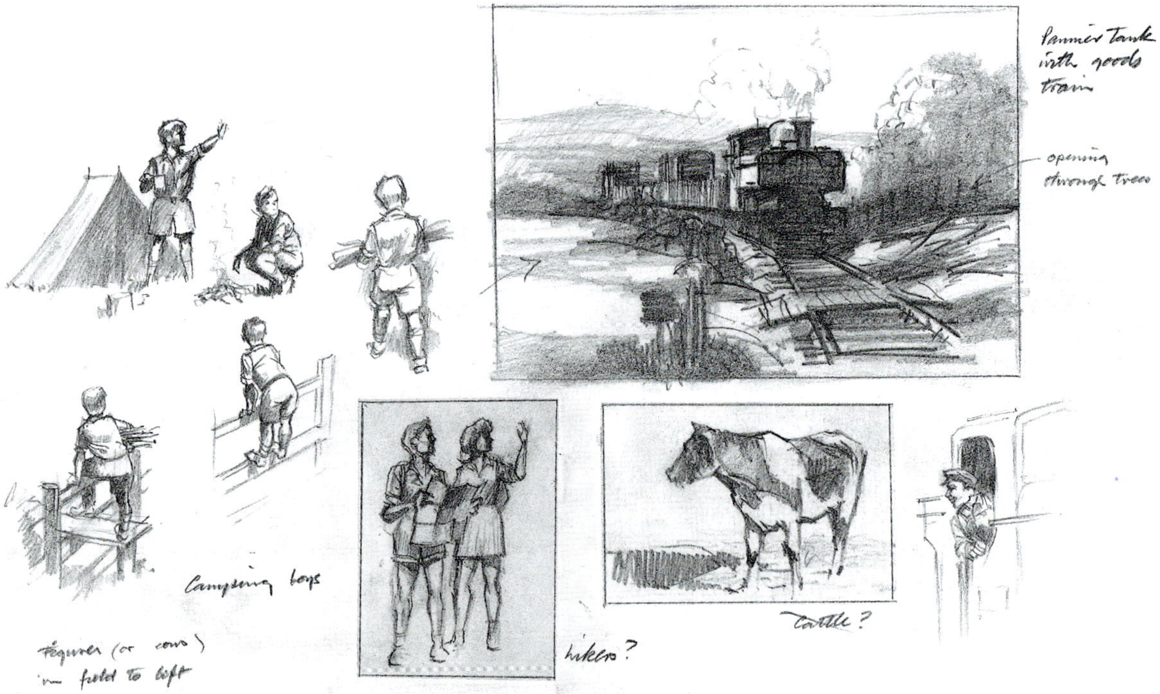

Sketches for 'Country Freight'

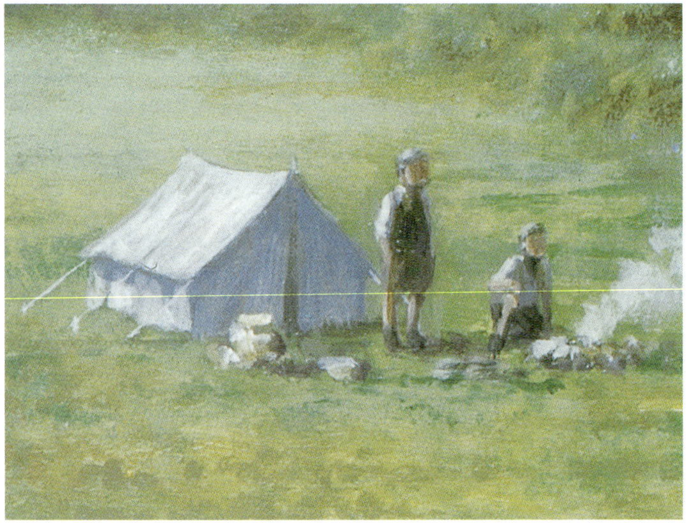

Country Freight
GWR 57XX 0-6-0 pannier tank locomotive No 3697 heads a branchline freight train around a wooded curve, admired by a trio of boys who have set up camp in the lineside field. No 3697 was built in 1941 and withdrawn from service in 1962.

This painting started out as a branchline freight train scene, but having sketched out the train I had no idea what to do with the surroundings! Actually this is not unusual because I find that paintings come in two categories, planned and unplanned. Sometimes a great deal of research and sketching is done so that the composition is fixed before I even pick up a canvas. On other occasions I am 'feeling the way in', looking for the happy accident and letting the painting run by itself for a while. This is a gamble which can be very frustrating while the thing refuses to work, but at other times new ideas come along which otherwise might not have occurred.

So there was this freight train . . . . The space to the left was the problem. It had to be open to show the curve of the train, so a field was the only option, but there had to be something in the field to balance the trees which I was working in on the right. I don't really know where the idea of the boys camping came from, but as soon as I decided on it I warmed to the feeling that they brought to the scene.

Everyone who experienced camping when they were children will remember it for the rest of their lives. Apart from the organised camps with the Boy Scouts or Girl Guides, there were those times with a few friends and a borrowed tent, a tin of beans and Dad's ex-army mess tins. Add the box of Swan Vestas and this was something different! We would go off like walking Christmas trees, with tin mugs clinking, into the vast unknown which lay at the bottom of the lane. Every field could produce a raging bull or an angry farmer and it was always a while before we could agree on a good spot to pitch the tents.

Lighting a fire was part of the fascination, and then cooking food on it – by now we were real backwoodsmen, even convincing ourselves that burnt beans and rock-hard baked potatoes were delicious. As it got dark we would build a bright fire to counter our apprehension about the strange noises which seemed to be coming out of the darkness around us. In our tents in home-made sleeping bags we felt cut off from the world and would talk most of the night away.

These memories came back to me as I worked on the painting but I was aware that, in terms of the composition, I had to open up this camping group to make it part of the whole scene. The boy bringing firewood was the key. With his bundle of wood suggesting where he had come from, his 'pathway' flows right across the foreground making a connection between the stile, the railway crossing and the suggested fields beyond the break in the trees to the left. The different elements of the painting could now relate in a curve from the tent through to the gap in the trees, thus opening up the space of the composition.

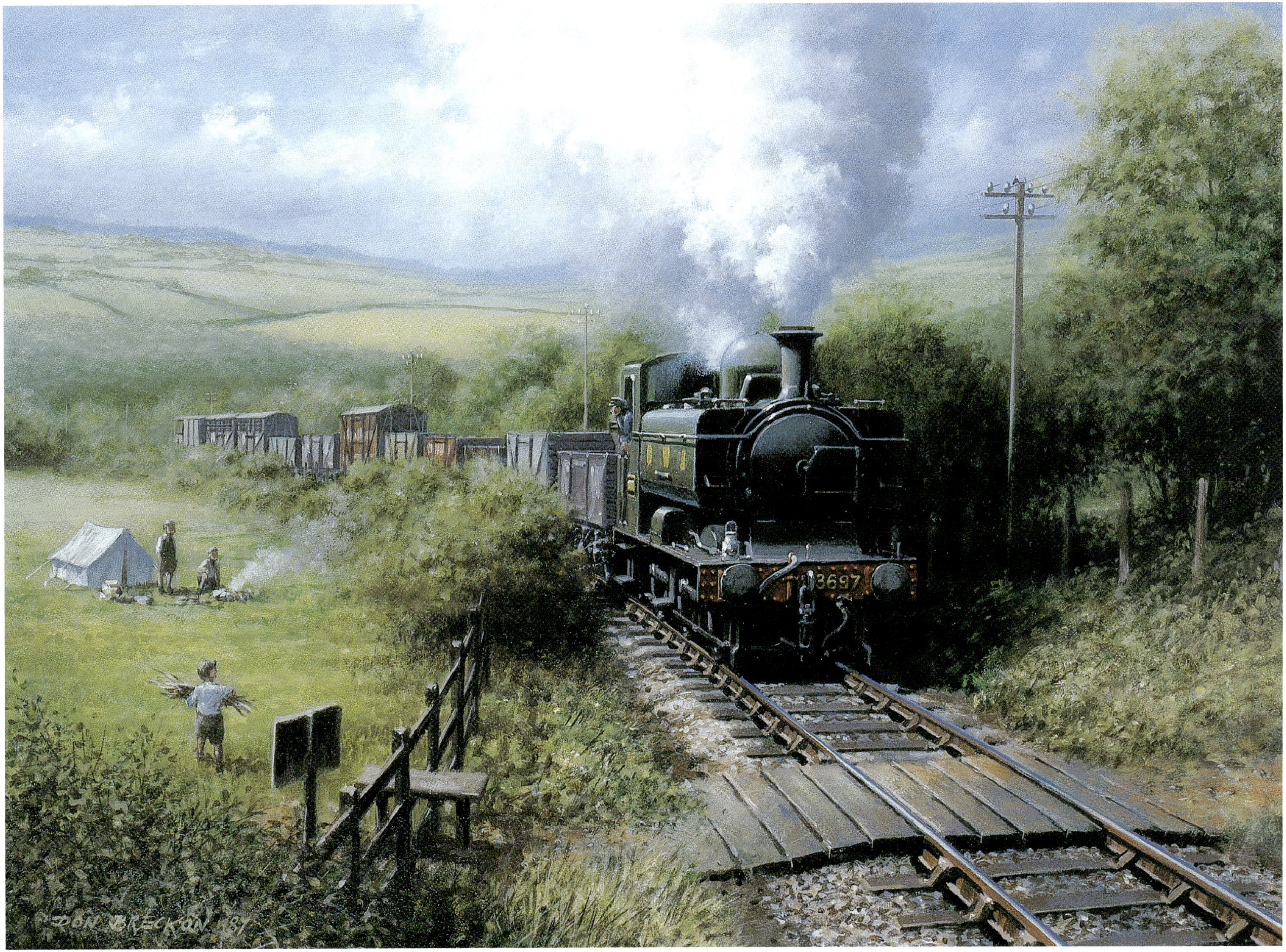
3697
DON BRECKON '87

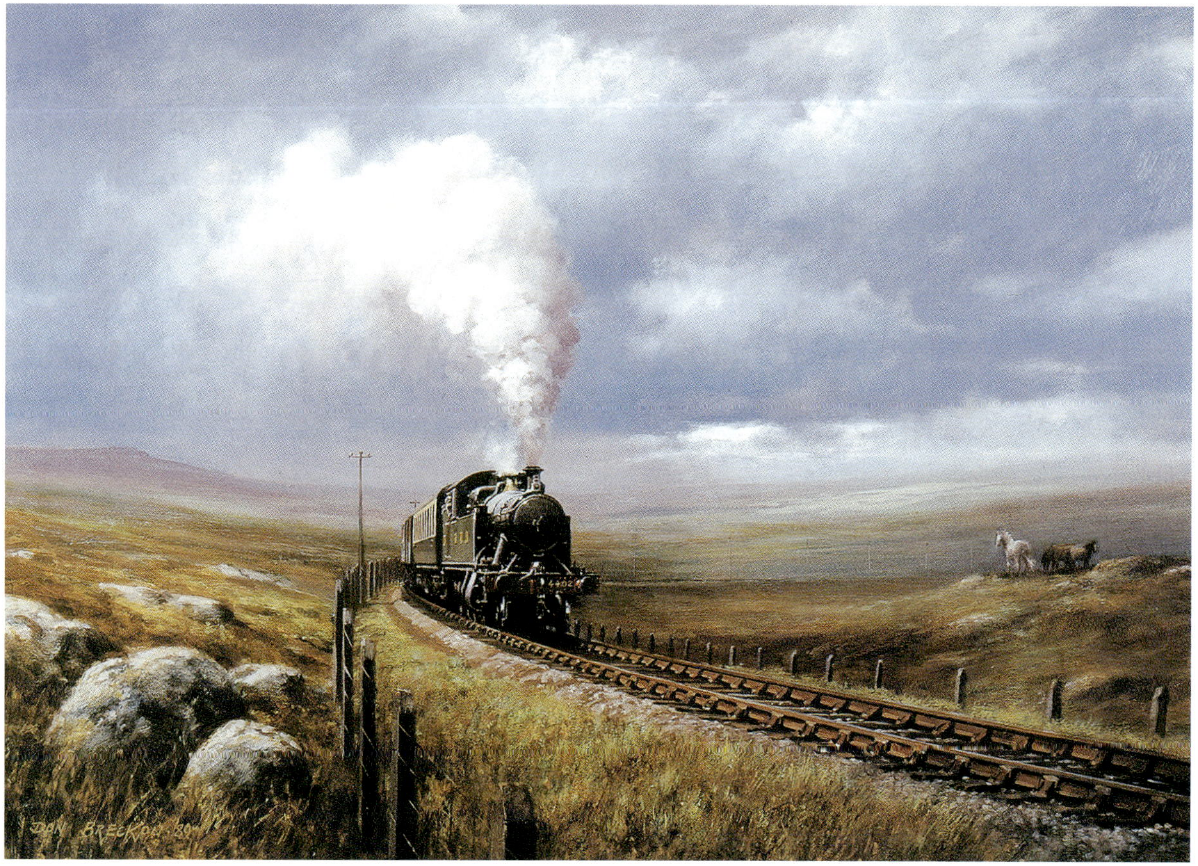

Across the High Moor (1989)
GWR 2-6-2T No 4402 brings the Yelverton train across Dartmoor nearing Princetown.

Heathfield (opposite)
GWR 1400 class 0-4-2T No 1427 stands at Heathfield station in Devon with a train from Moretonhampstead to Newton Abbot. To the right the train for the Teign Valley line to Exeter is waiting, whilst a two-coach auto-trailer train departs into the distance with a train for Moretonhampstead, on the edge of Dartmoor. The station was opened in 1886 and closed to passengers on 2 March 1959. No 1427 was built in 1933 and withdrawn in 1960.

David St John Thomas, who commissioned this painting, writes of the junction at Heathfield:

Though only a few miles out from Newton Abbot (reached partly along the bank of the Stover Canal which the railway replaced), Heathfield was in a quite different world. Changing from one branchline train onto another was always a thrill, and while the journey up to Moretonhampstead was rural enough, nothing prepared one for the utter railway-back-of-beyond that the Heathfield–Exeter train traversed.

For much of its life Heathfield had only the up platform plus bay, and crossing trains had to be done on the loop beyond the station confines. Once the GWR provided a separate down platform, the new-fangled illuminated panel in the signalbox (the first in south Devon) was more than justified. For in addition to the basic service from Newton Abbot to Moretonhampstead, and from Exeter to Heathfield, there was an amazing number of variations and one-offs. A few Exeter trains ran through to Newton Abbot, and for some years even to Bovey Tracey on the way to Moretonhampstead; there were also 'shorts' from Heathfield to Chudleigh Knighton Halt and to Christow on the way to Exeter. Several summers in the 1930s saw 'expresses' running non-stop to Bovey Tracey, one from Torquay not even pausing at Newton Abbot.

There was a daily freight to Moretonhampstead and another from Newton Abbot to Christow. Since the route via Christow was used as an emergency alternative when the sea wall was blocked at Dawlish, another daily freight ran that way, usually non-stop, for crew-training purposes. But lignite was mined on an extensive scale at Heathfield in the years after the war, and these through freights then normally picked up a full payload here . . . and extra lignite specials had to be run as well. So busy indeed was Heathfield that sometimes a freight would have to be held at the next signalbox in the Teign Valley, Trusham, for several hours to wait for a path through the station.

The really hectic days were naturally those on which expresses were diverted this way, and during and immediately after the Second World War there were also ambulance trains which parked on two sidings just off the Teign Valley line. Excitement there may then have been, yet the country railway was never more fascinating than when just looking after the needs of the locals, and the morning get-together of the three auto-cars was always a Heathfield highlight.

The picture shows that scene. The auto-car for Moretonhampstead has just left the down platform and a few passengers are making their way to the Teign Valley car in the bay; on this day the up from Moretonhampstead to Newton Abbot comes in locomotive first, instead of the auto-car being propelled as would normally be the case.

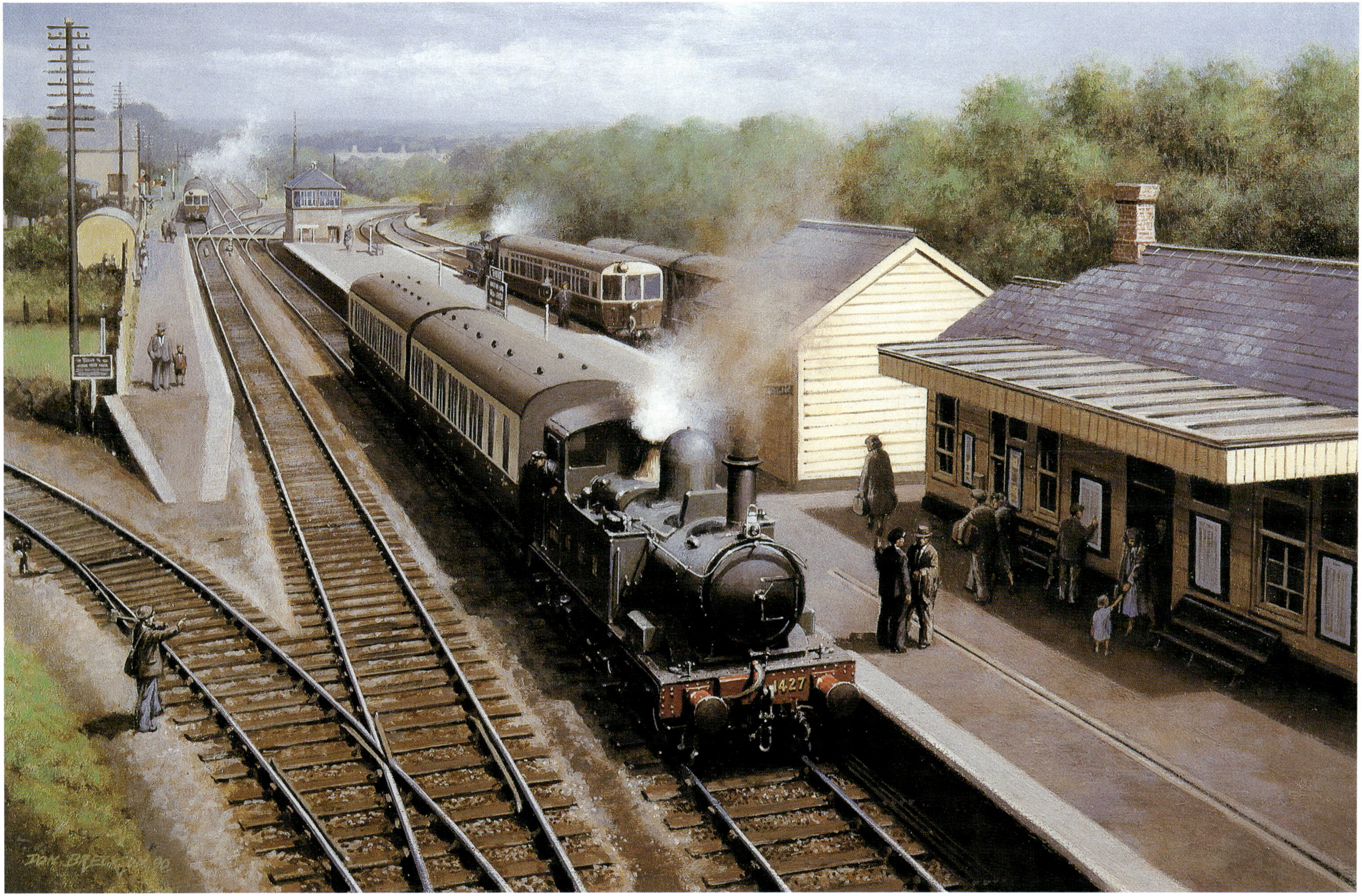
1427

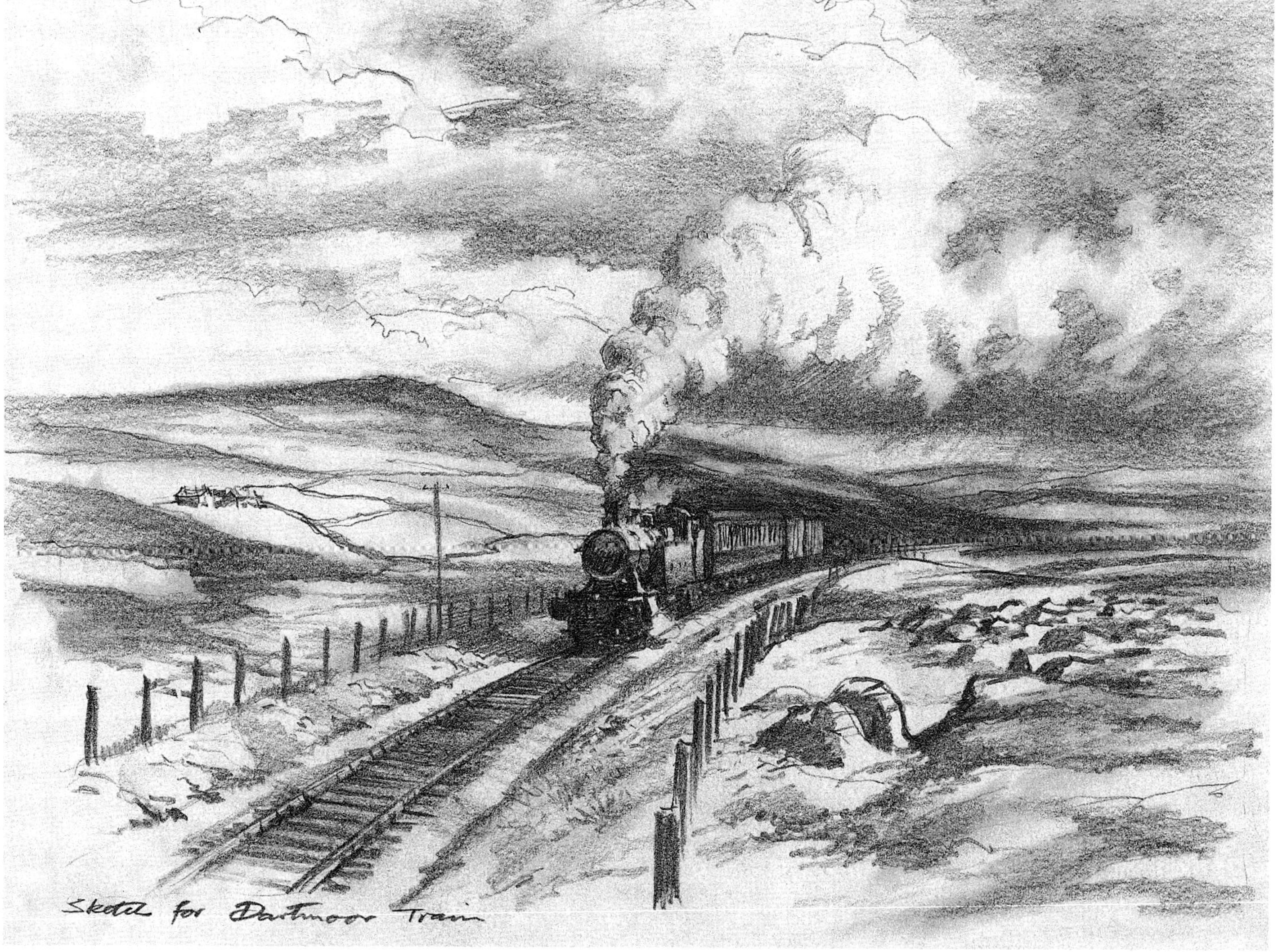
Sketch for Dartmoor Train

THE COUNTRY BRANCH LINE

Tony Kingdom

The day is sunny; the outside air is hazy and still, whilst inside the auto-coach there is the soothing murmur of quiet, multiple conversations. There is a general atmosphere of peace and tranquillity as other sounds add themselves to the scene. The gentle hiss of steam from leaking joints, the sound of the fireman shovelling and applying the blower to the fire, forcing the emission of semi-transparent, blue, sulphurous fumes which spiral upwards from the chimney.

Suddenly the driver ceases to chat to the guard and the small group of station staff. Their last words to each other louden as they drift apart to attend to their respective duties. There is a lurch as the brakes are released, the creaking springs protest in answer, the home starter drops and we are slowly pressed into motion, the driver's hand easing the regulator open.

Our branch line train gathers momentum and other sounds begin to be heard, the staccato bark of the exhaust, the whistle's shrill farewell, the hard rumble of steel wheels upon equally hard steel rails, the clatter of points and the rattle of rail joints as we pass by. Back streets and allotment gardens give way to greener pastures as the train leaves the town behind and heads for the country. Now and then quickly evaporating 'smoke' wafts by the window as we proceed on our holiday. At last those long, long weeks of waiting are over, and we are on our way. The journey itself is a highlight for me.

Such were my fond childhood memories during the Second World War, and since, of our short holidays in the country, often only ten to twenty miles from home, just a few minutes' car ride for the child of today. How often must that short scene have been played out by countless thousands of children, to say nothing of their parents – not only for holidays and the odd Sunday School outing and visit to distant relatives, but for more mundane and less happy trips such as going to school or work.

To sum up, the rural branch line was a way of life, now sadly passed into history. My own part of England is known as the West Country but, to be more accurate, is really the South-West Country. It is blessed with some of the most spectacular scenery in Great Britain, but the changing seasons show the land in very different moods and types of beauty. Through them all the branchline train continued to run, come what might, even in the deepening snow of mid-winter.

In general, the country branch line could be divided into two types. Firstly, the very familiar passenger line, which also carried freight. Secondly, the less familiar goods or freight-only line whose usual raison d'être was to cater for a particular type of freight, such as the clay lines of Cornwall or the coal lines of South Wales.

The ubiquitous passenger branch line was the most varied and unique of railways. Each company, and later each region of British Railways (BR), had its own mixed type of locomotive power and rolling stock, sometimes peculiar to individual branches. Examples of this were the Princetown branch in Devon with its 44XX tanks, which were versions of the 45XXs equipped with smaller wheels to enable them to negotiate the severe curves of the line; the fondly remembered Adams tanks of the Axminster to Lyme Regis branch; and the tank *Fair Rosamund* which ran on the Woodstock branch in Oxfordshire during the 1930s.

Coach stock could also be tailored to a branch. For example, four and six-wheeled coaches were used during the early days of the Tiverton Junction to Hemyock branch in order to negotiate the tight bends and limited clearance of the line. The Southern Railway (SR) used exclusively the old gate-type London & South Western Railway (LSWR) coaches right up to the end of operations on the Plymouth, Friary and Turnchapel branch, delighting children by allowing them to ride between the enclosed portions of the coach, out in the open and hanging onto the iron gates.

Goods lines too had their special locomotive and wagon requirements. Examples of these were the Beattie well tanks of the SR's Wenford Bridge clay line in east Cornwall. These were replaced later by the ex-GWR 1366 class 0-6-0PTs, also well known for their appearances on the Weymouth Quay line in Dorset. The two lines differed, however, in rolling stock. The Weymouth line could accommodate mainline coaches but the Wenford Bridge 'specials' for passenger traffic were forced to use Toads and other brake vans, such were the tight bends and limited clearance.

It seemed that both before and after the regrouping of the railway companies, right up to the ultimate demise of the steam-operated branch line, each company or, later, region used any little oddment of tractive and rolling stock it may have had available at the time for its essential traffic feeds to main lines.

Of course, that is a generalisation. Many branches were worked by stables of good standard fleets of locomotives and rolling stock. To name but a few, the GWR's 45XX and 14XX tanks and 57XX and 64XX pannier tanks; and the SR's 02, A1X 'Terriers', and M7 tanks. Coaches were often GWR B sets or normal mainline corridor stock, while the SR used non-corridor coaches or LSWR gate-type stock; mainline corridor coaches also were accommodated on some lines.

Later BR replaced ageing locomotives and stock with its own Ivatt class 2 tanks and BR MK 1 coaches.

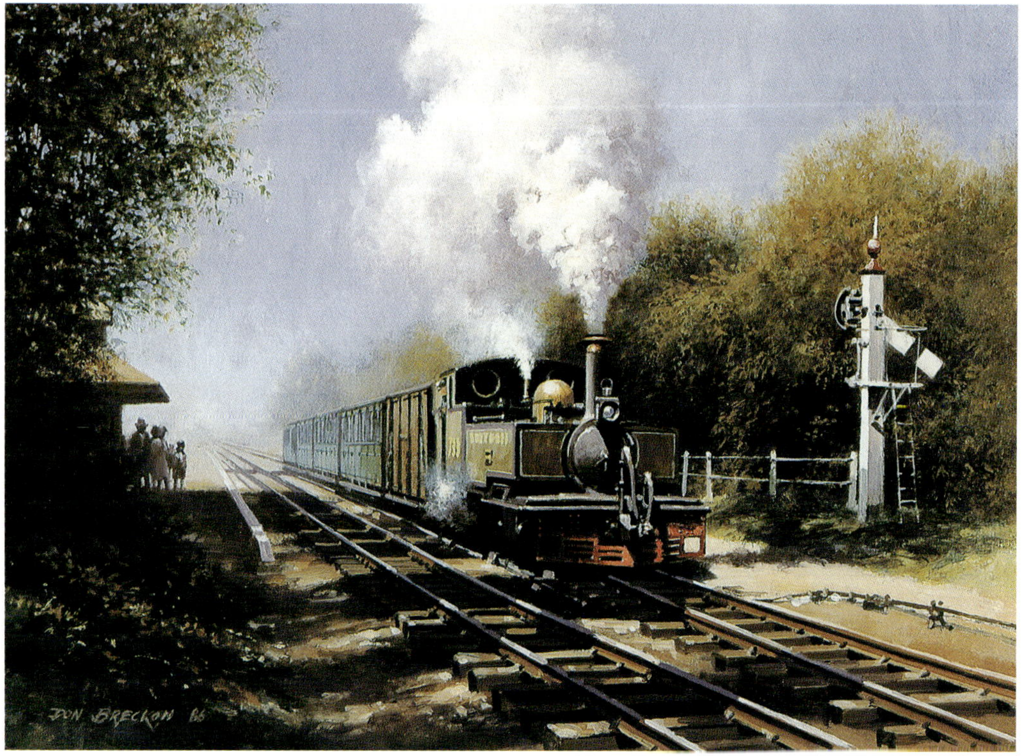

Lynton and Barnstaple (1986)
2-6-2T No 759 Yeo *heads a train for Lynton away from Woody Bay station.* Yeo *worked on the 1ft 11½in gauge railway from its opening in 1898 to the close in 1935.*

The Forest of Dean (opposite)
GWR pannier tank 0-6-0 No 7723 shunts wagons for Cannop colliery during the Second World War. On the road below a group of Italian POWs are being marched towards the colliery while a farm cart and lorry are engaged on coal delivery service. No 7723 was based at Gloucester shed and spent much of its working life in the Forest of Dean area. Built in 1930, it was withdrawn in 1960.

The Forest of Dean is an area that I have visited only briefly, so its atmosphere is unknown to me. When Mr Williams commissioned this painting I was therefore very grateful for the following description of the scene and its wider setting which he wrote with such obvious pleasure.

> The Forest of Dean is that strangely isolated corner of Gloucestershire sandwiched between the River Wye and the River Severn. During the 1930s and 1940s, the period of my boyhood, it was a truly magical place to play, roam and explore. It was also GWR country. The Forest of Dean was criss-crossed with a cobweb of mineral branch lines serving the numerous collieries and quarries. The scars of industrialisation were never very prominent, however, for the foliage and undergrowth wrapped around all the man-made scenes. I was forever fascinated with the railways, with the single tracks snaking in and out of the glades and the rattling pannier-hauled trains of wagons shooting in and out of the trees.
>
> One particular scene is etched on my memory. Cannop colliery had close connections with my family and was well sited for me to visit on my cycle during the weekends and holidays. I would cycle through the woods to the colliery sidings and watch the fascinating variety of activity. The whole complex was engulfed by trees, set at the bottom of a steep valley. The main approach road was straddled by a double-track railway bridge which carried the branch line serving the colliery. It was below this bridge that I would stop and watch the pannier shuffling the coal wagons to and fro. To complete the scene and fix the date of the 1940s, I recall the columns of the Italian prisoners of war marching under the bridge to the local saw mills. They would be dressed in dark chocolate-coloured battle dress and forage caps with the distinctive marks of the POW – yellow, red and orange circles and triangles patched to their trousers and tunics.

I prepared the sketch from old photographs of the scene because today the bridge and most of the embankment have gone. The additional information, that farm carts had been pressed into service for the colliery during the war, was splendid because it gave me the opportunity to bring in an interesting foreground object to balance up the figure of the boy who would be looking back and up at the locomotive.

The line of prisoners was a problem. There wasn't room for them on this side of the bridge and if they were on the far side they would be too far away to distinguish what they were. Playing around with ideas on scraps of paper I saw that they could actually be used to carry the eye through the bridge, the shadow of which was rather strong, almost framing the scene beyond. Taking the line of men from sunlight, through the shadow of the bridge, and into the light beyond served to traverse this frame quite well and opened up the space on the far side.

Perhaps the colour of the wagon is rather bright for wartime coal carrying but it serves to pull out the foreground and provide a contrast to the multitude of greens in the picture.

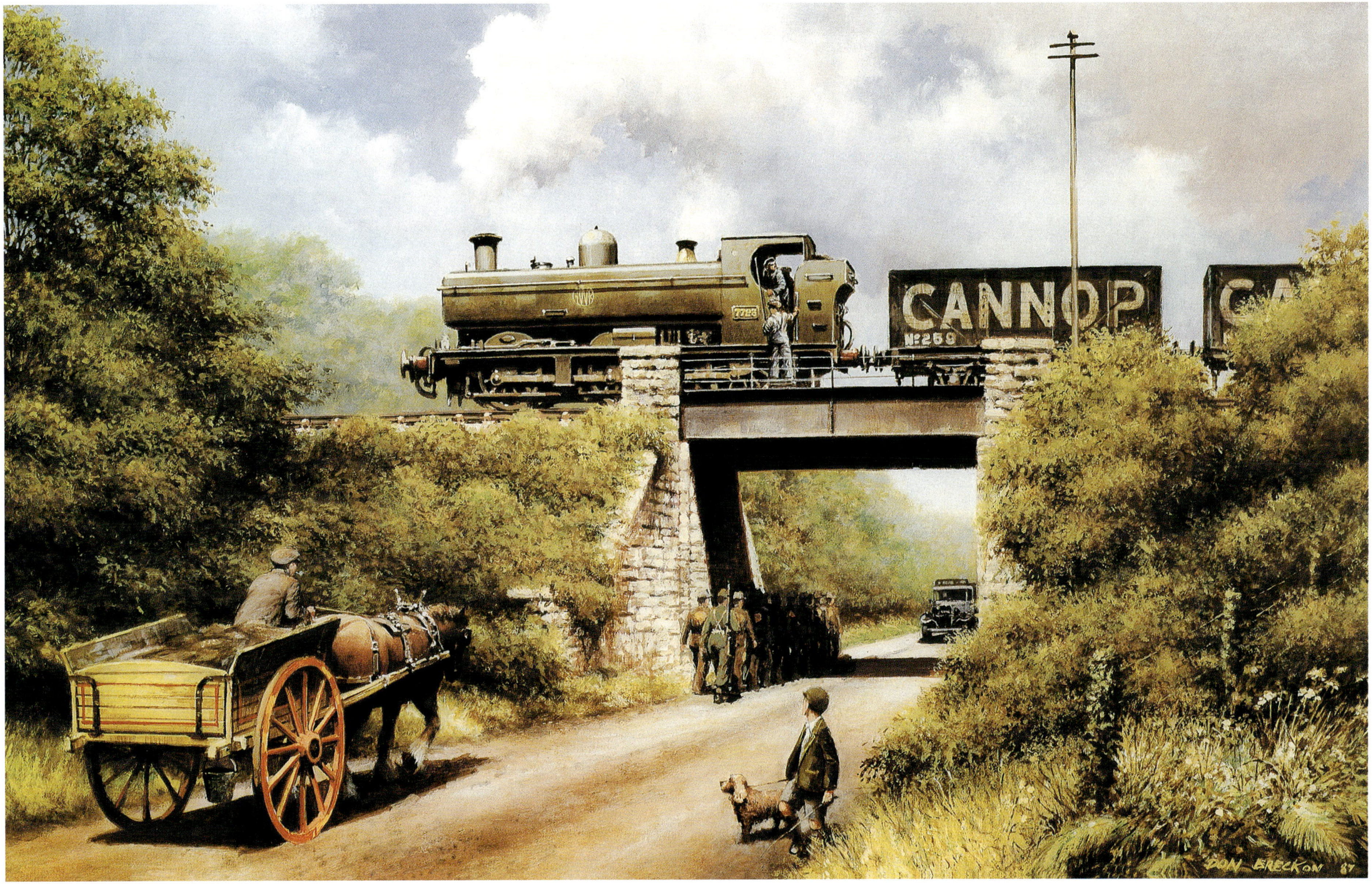
CANNOP
Nº258
DON BRECKON 87

Passenger trains were what one might call the standard or typical traffic, with the aforementioned journeys for school, work and holidays. There were branch lines, however, whose traffic was occasionally of a special type, separate from the general public. For example, the Princetown and Portland branches regularly carried prisoners and their warders. Transfer of the offenders from the courts to prison, and sometimes from prison to prison, by rail were a common sight before the advent of road transport and the subsequent demise of the branch line.

Branch lines serving rural areas accommodating MOD establishments had, over the years, heavy passenger traffic generated by servicemen and women. During the First and Second World Wars this traffic increased dramatically and in some cases extended itself to lines hitherto unaffected. Secrecy was paramount in those times: trains often ran at night, cameras were banned, film was unobtainable by the public and we were constantly reminded that 'Careless Talk Costs Lives'.

Wartime also saw the transfer of German, Italian and other Axis Powers prisoners of war to camps in Wales, Scotland and the north of England. Southern England too had its prisoner of war camps, but mainly for the softer element. Geographically, it was too near the continent for the harder types who might make escape bids; and so, SS and other undesirables were sent by train to the remoter parts of Britain.

A lesser known and rarer type of wartime passenger traffic was VIPs. The most famous such journey was on the Brent to Kingsbridge branch during early 1944, when General Montgomery and General Eisenhower inspected the D-Day landings practice area in south Devon. A large part of the coastline east of Kingsbridge and Salcombe was used as a training area for American troops preparing to invade northern France, due to the geographical similarity of the two coasts.

VIPs of a more civilian nature, namely royalty, were also at times special travellers on the branch lines. In 1902 King Edward VII on his visit to Dartmouth Royal Naval College, used the Newton Abbot to Kingswear branch for his royal train, although the train was not used as sleeping quarters for his Majesty. Not so, however, for the visit of their Majesties King George VI and Queen Elizabeth during their West Country tour on 28 and 29 August 1947, when the royal train was used as both living and sleeping quarters. It was housed, under strict guard, at the lower end of the Totnes to Ashburton branch, between Ashburton Junction off the main line and Buckfastleigh.

Earlier this century and before, VIP dignitaries who lived in the great country houses often used to hire their own trains to remove their complete households to London for the winter season. Special trains were made up of first, second and third-class coaches together with horse-boxes and other freight wagons, which picked up their cargoes at the nearest station to the manor. This invariably meant travelling over a branch line.

One of the most nostalgic scenes that has now passed into history was that concerned with goods traffic. It was that much loved train, the pick-up freight. General freight of all types was catered for on a wagon-for-wagon and station-for-station basis, thus serving the individual needs of the farmer, the businessman, and indeed all members of the community. Loads would consist of anything that could be moved: livestock of all kinds, animal feeds, fertilisers, fuels of all types solid and liquid, parcels of any size, building materials, and many other things. Traffic over the branch lines for these materials was too varied to describe in detail, but in general the up and down movements worked as follows (p. 50).

The Racing Ground

Between Cheltenham and Gloucester the LMS and GWR lines converged, resulting at times in trains of the two companies running side by side. LMS Jubilee class No 5682 Trafalgar *on a Bristol express, and GWR Hall class No 5993* Kirby Hall *with a Wolverhampton to Ilfracombe train, are taking advantage of the racing ground. 5682 was built in 1936 and was withdrawn in 1964. 5993 was built in 1939 and withdrawn in 1963.*

As the LMS and GWR main lines crossed Gloucester they converged. Between Cheltenham and Gloucester, and then between Tuffley and Standish junction to the south-west, it was possible to see trains of the two companies running side by side. To spirited engine crews this became a real racing ground and was a chance to show 'the other lot' the superior speed of their engines. The timetable did not take this rivalry into account and officially such activities were frowned on, but when trains did find themselves within sight of one another the race was usually on.

Ray Gwillan describes such an encounter in his book *A Loco Fireman Looks Back*:

> Sure enough a plume of exhaust steam shows from behind the cutting and therefrom emerges a Black Five on a passenger train. The Midland men see us too late for with our foreknowledge of his existence we have a head start over him. Slowly we draw ahead and leave the Midland men pounding in our wake until at the parting of the ways at Standish we are half a length ahead, and we leave them to go sailing on down to Bristol, with a cuckoo or two from our whistles. We cannot hear his reply but see the steam from his whistle and with a wave we disappear from each other's sight.

To be at the lineside on such an occasion and witness two expresses approaching at speed, with the tingle of competition in the air, must have been an unforgettable sight. Having missed the real thing I looked forward to the imaginary experience in a painting, so I sketched out the composition. Partisan feelings were not involved as it became clear that the left-hand engine would have to be further forward for it to be seen.

At the painting stage I darkened the sky to the top right to contrast with the billowing smoke, which needed emphasis to convey power and speed. It also helped the atmosphere by making the smoke first darker then lighter than the sky. The landscape is played right down in this scene, with only the figures on the embankment and the telegraph poles suggesting a stillness in contrast to the rushing trains.

The rivalry between the railway companies of the Big Four – London & North Eastern Railway (LNER), SR, LMS and GWR – was very fierce from footplate to boardroom, and even today feelings can be quite strong among enthusiasts though forty-two years have passed since nationalisation. The GWR was 'God's Wonderful Railway' to its admirers, but to rivals it was 'The Gas Works Railway' or the 'Great Way Round', a disparaging comment on the early tendency to take the indirect route. The Somerset & Dorset (S & D) passed through attractive countryside between Bath and Bournemouth but to a few disgruntled passengers the S & D became the 'Slow and Dirty'. The LMS got the 'Ell of a Mess' label from some, and the LNER in East Anglia was referred to by American servicemen during the war as the 'Late Never Early Railway'. The prize for the most demeaning translation of company letters was probably earned by the early Oxford Worcester and Wolverhampton railway – the OWW. Despairing travellers labelled it the 'Old Worse and Worse'.

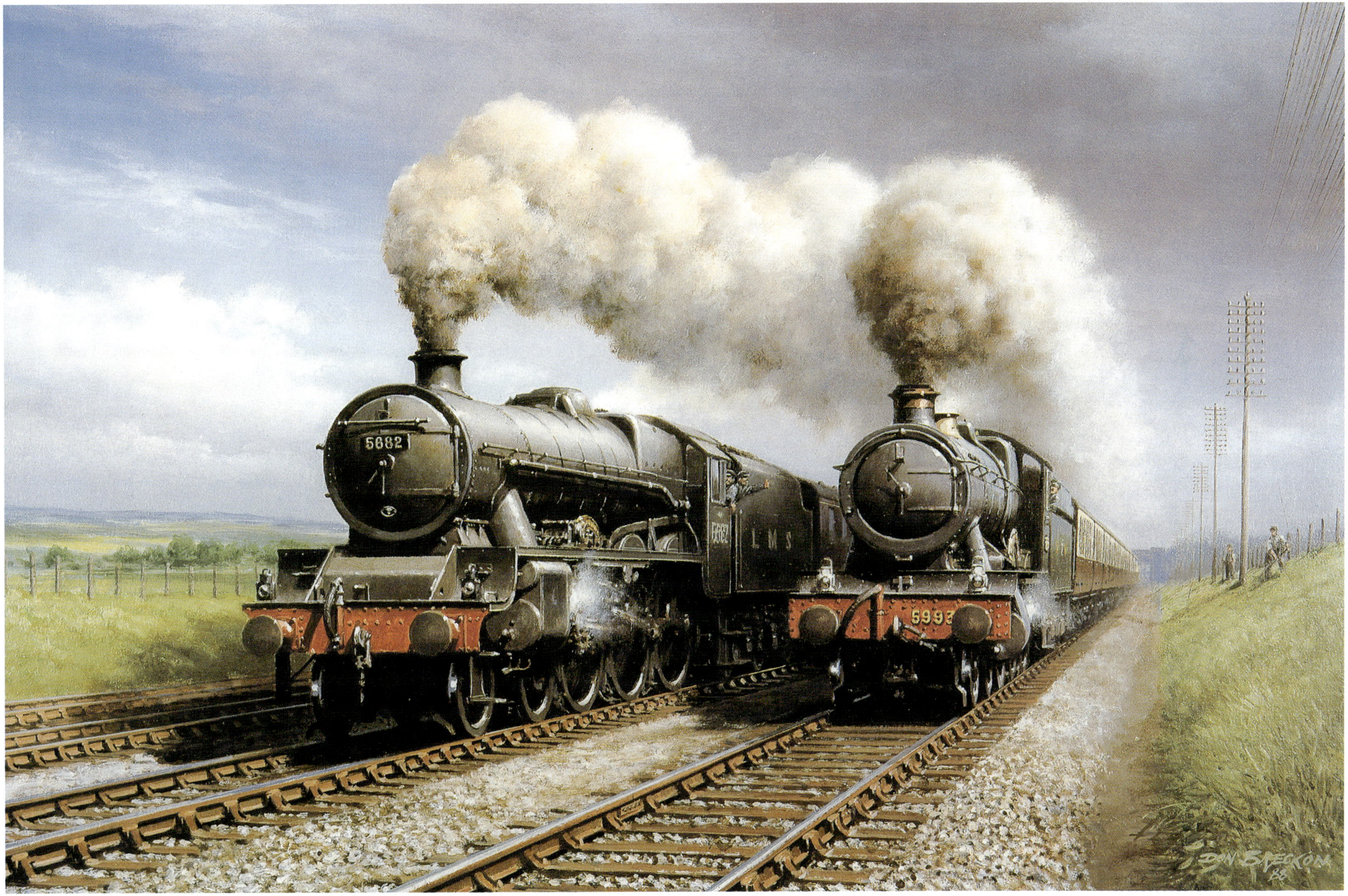
5682
L M S
5993

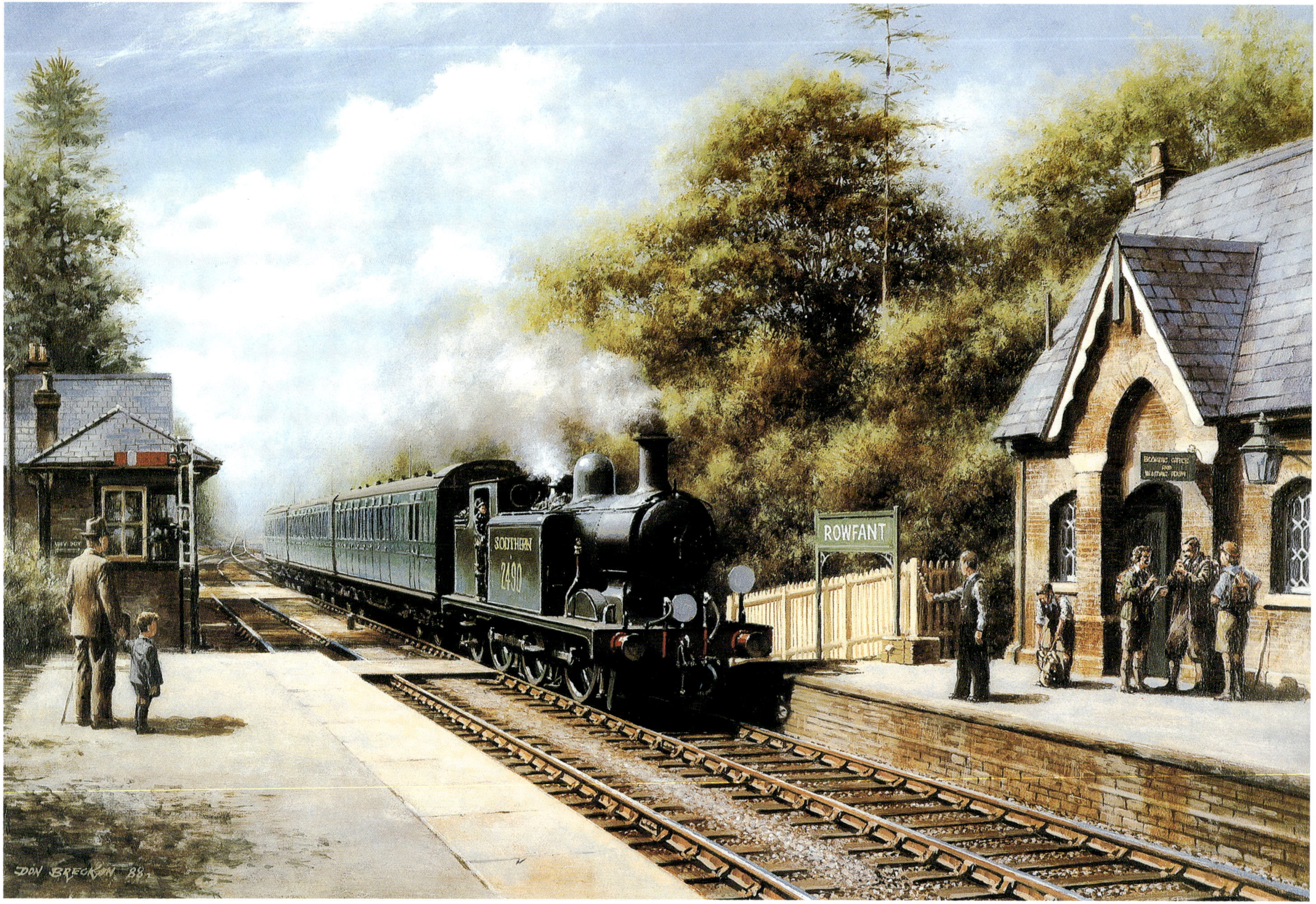
ROWFANT
SOUTHERN
DON BRECKON '88

Ramblers at Rowfant (1988)
Southern Railway Class E4 0-6-2T No 2490 runs into Rowfant station with a local train from Three Bridges to East Grinstead in the 1930s.

In 1855 a branch line was constructed to connect East Grinstead, an established market town, with the London to Brighton main line. The connection was at a locality known as Three Bridges, no village existing there until after the railway connection was made. The new line passed through a mixed landscape of woods and agricultural land and Rowfant station was the only original halt. Why was such a distinctive and grandiose design used for a halt apparently in the middle of nowhere?

The answer to this question seems to be one which applies to many such rural anomalies throughout the developing network of railways in Victorian times. Local landowners were frequently required to give permission for routes through their properties and they reacted in different ways. Opposition sometimes resulted in lines being delayed for years and often concessions were made to landowners which defined the progress of connections and the development of the locality forever, with occasionally bizarre results.

Rowfant House was a quarter of a mile from the route of the new line and it is almost certain that permission to cross the land was given by the head of the family on condition that a station was built to a design befitting the family's status in the area. The downside building featured in this painting had a porch included in its structure where the family could shelter whilst the carriage arrived to drive them home, or where the coachman could wait for his master to arrive on the train.

The line survived for more than a hundred years and latterly was known by the locals as the Jungle Line, because of the profusion of plant and animal life around it. Often the construction of a branch line created its own natural habitat by making cuttings and embankments, and by introducing materials foreign to the local environment. In this case chalk was brought in to build up embankments and now shrub species associated with downland habitats grow profusely in an area of natural sandstone and clay.

Ramblers at Rowfant was set in a period when the branch line was still active but was being used increasingly by people seeking access to the countryside for their leisure. It seems appropriate that after the line was closed in 1966 it was acquired by West Sussex County Council and eventually opened as the Worth Way, a six-mile route where walkers, horse riders and cyclists can discover the interesting and varied wild life peculiar to the old Jungle Line.

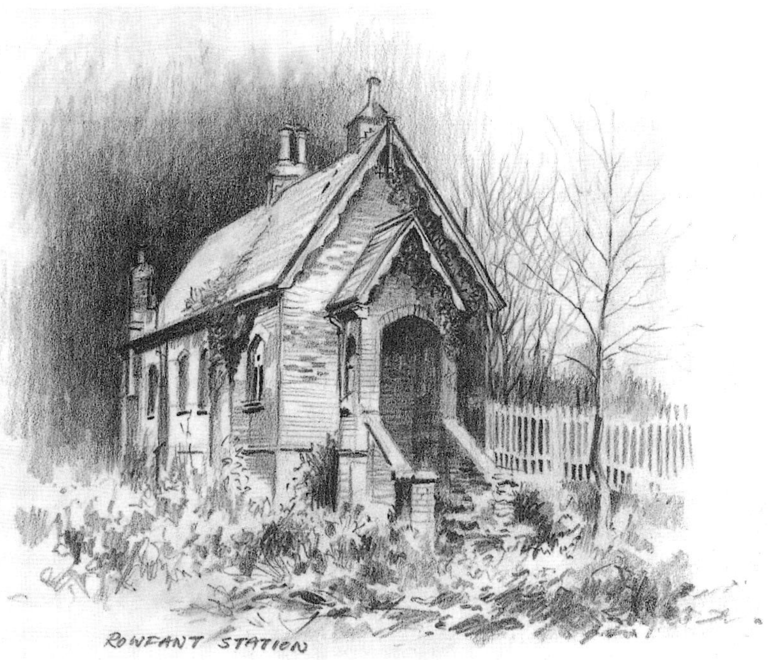

Sketches for 1930's hikers – 'Ramblers at Rowfant'.

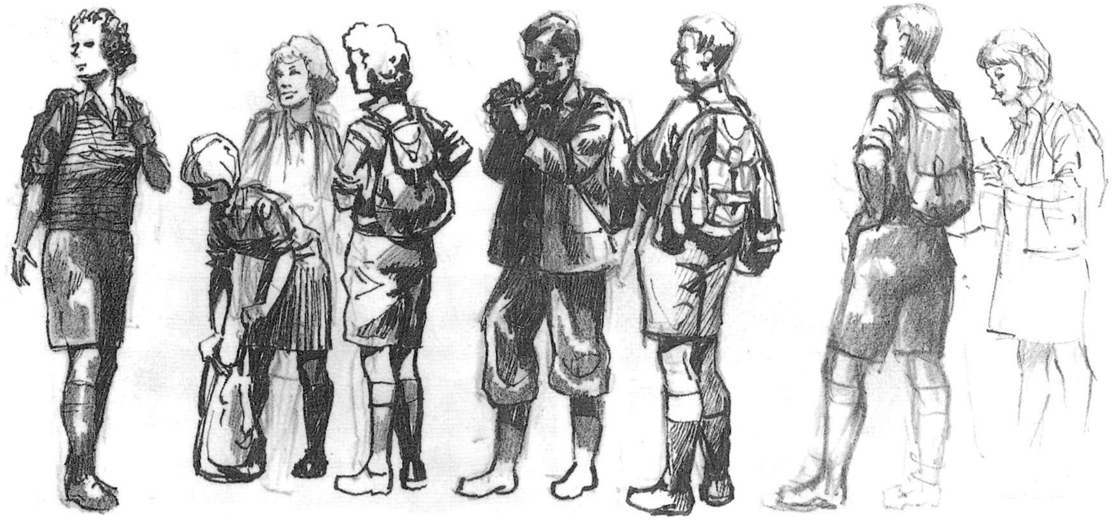

Outward freight from farms, factories and general public was taken to the nearest station and stored in the goods yard to await dispatch. Two or three times a week, as a general rule, a small locomotive would appear hauling an incoming train from the city or town and distant rural areas, with a wide array of wagons appropriate to their individual loads.

It would commence its run down the branch, stopping at each and every station with goods handling facilities. Here it would unload small loads and then engage in a leisurely shunting of wagons, dropping off those which had reached their destination. It would continue this ritual to the end of the branch. Its arrival there would signal another shunting session, which would include picking up wagons with destinations in other parts of the country. These, together with any 'empties' from previous trips, would then constitute an up train whose final destination would be the nearest main-line marshalling yard. First, though, it would return up the branch picking up further wagons and part loads as it made its way back to the main line, and hence the name of the train. This quaint and historic practice is often demonstrated during public open days on preserved railways such as the Severn Valley Railway.

It is also worth noting that removals were a feature of freight traffic along the branch lines. Complete loads of household and farmyard effects were transported in a single or part trainload when a family decided to shift from one part of the country to another.

Special freight loads such as coal, clay, quarry-stone etc could also form such trains, supplementing passenger traffic. Many lines built originally for specific freight loads became passenger lines in later years.

This fact is a good lead into my final subject, narrow gauge lines. The most famous of these are the now preserved 'Little Trains of Wales', many of which started life as slate or quarry lines. Others of particular note are the famous Romney, Hythe & Dymchurch Railway in south-east England and the Ravenglass & Eskdale Railway in Cumbria, both fortunately preserved. Sadly, in the West Country the Lynton & Barnstaple Railway and the Bideford, Westward Ho & Appledore Railway have long since gone.

And so, with due consideration given to the many and varied types of country branch lines, even those with very light traffic which ran mixed trains to economise, we realise that these faithful servants of public transport were truly a way of life for all of us who knew them and now, thanks to preservationists who maintain some lines as working museums, are a valuable history lesson for those unfortunate enough not to have known them.

Tony Kingdom *is the author of books on the Yealmpton, Princetown, Turnchapel and Ashburton branch lines and of a book on the Plymouth, Tavistock and Launceston Railway.*

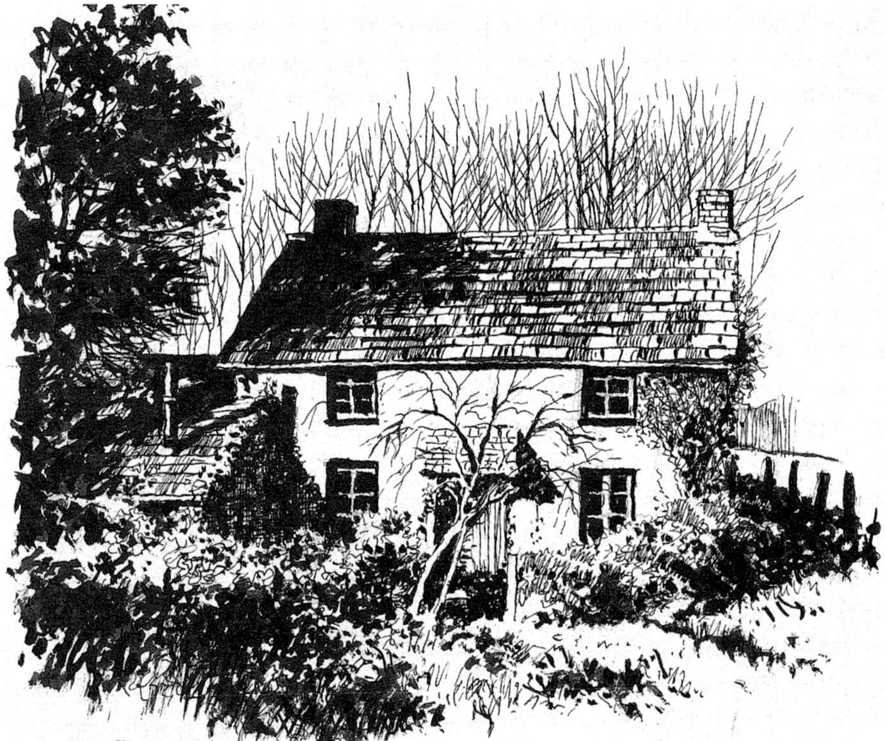

COTTAGE IN CORNWALL

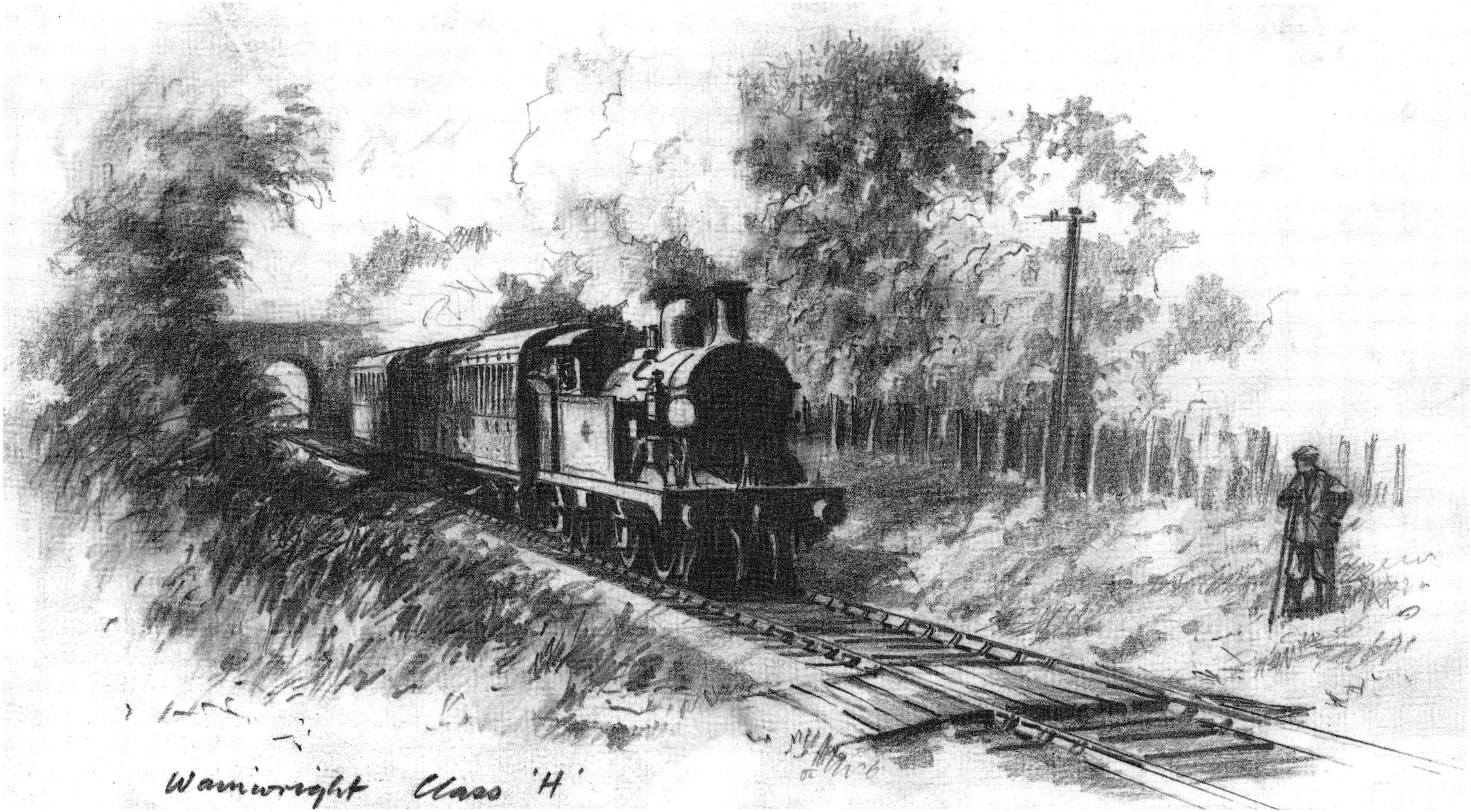

Wainwright Class 'H'

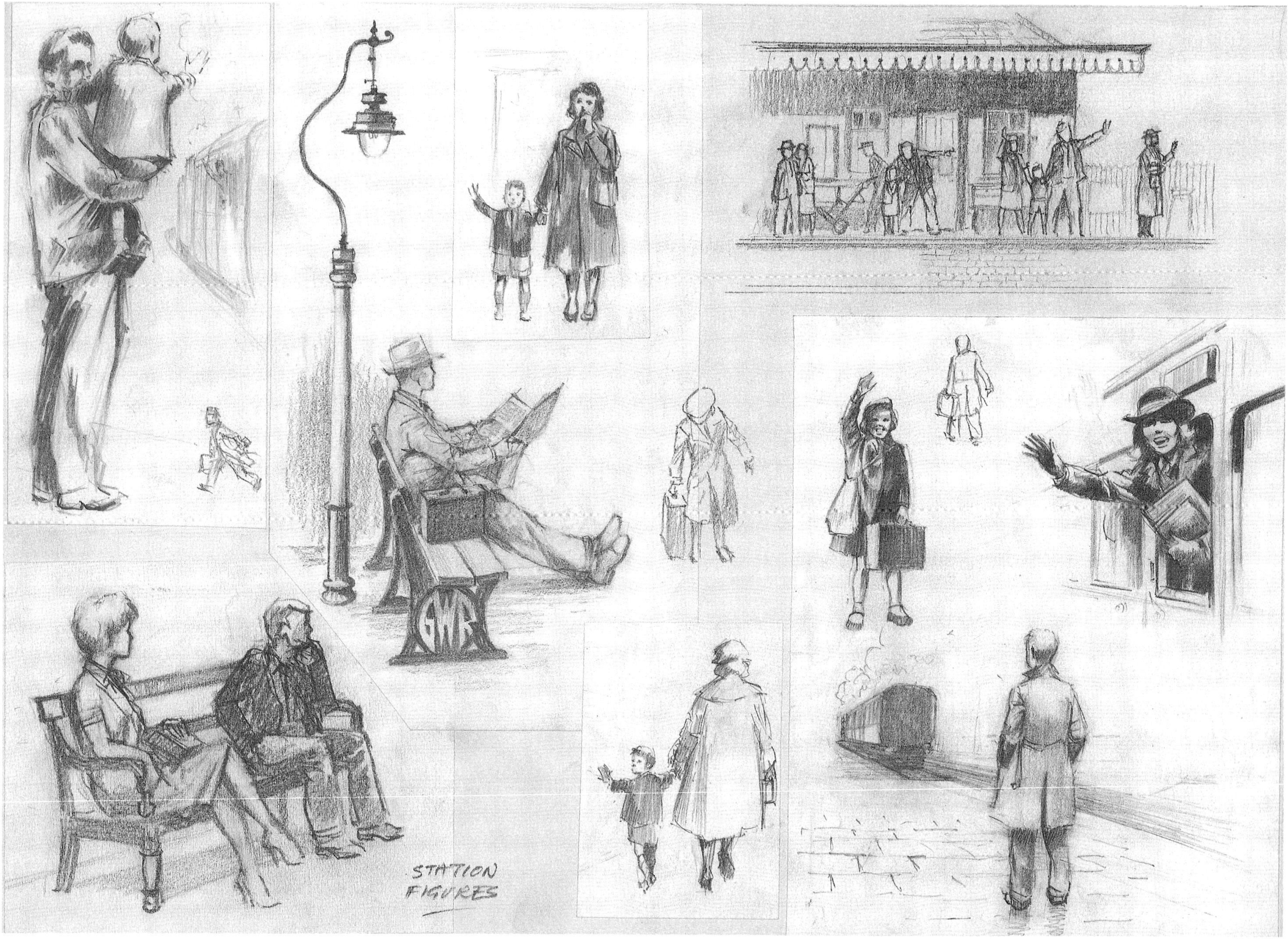
GWR
STATION
FIGURES

A BRANCH LINE REMEMBERED

Guy Pannell

The cat idly lowered the paw he was washing and peered out from the shade of the pampas grass which was conveniently planted on the garden bank above the station platform. The rails shimmered in the afternoon heat. Where they passed under the road bridges that marked either end of the station limits they seemed to vanish altogether into a sea of dancing light. Those bridges marked the boundary of this, the real world: the junction. Beyond them the tracks led to towns and cities where men sweated in factories and shouted in offices and women struggled with the shopping. But here those things were unimportant, only imaginings or half-forgotten memories.

The cat sniffed the air. To the familiar scent of engine oil and tar from the sleepers, and the perfume of the cypress trees in the cemetery just across the road, was added a new element – the yucca plant on the island platform was in flower again. The drone of the bees collecting pollen from the proudly tended plants was punctuated by a sudden 'ting-ting' from the signalbox. Moments later came the sound of the train it heralded – the familiar bark of the Great Western prairie tank at its head stirring the heavy air as it pounded up the branch. The carriage wheels squealed their time-honoured protest as they rounded the curve at the junction and then the noise subsided as the driver shut off steam and the train coasted into the island platform.

The arrival galvanised the station into action. Above the sound of hissing steam and slamming doors porters shouted 'All change, all change.' 'London train, m'dear? Over the bridge.' And over the bridge the passengers trooped, an army of feet thudding on the wooden stairs: sunburned families making the reluctant trip home from a salt-spray holiday, travelling salesmen travelling back to

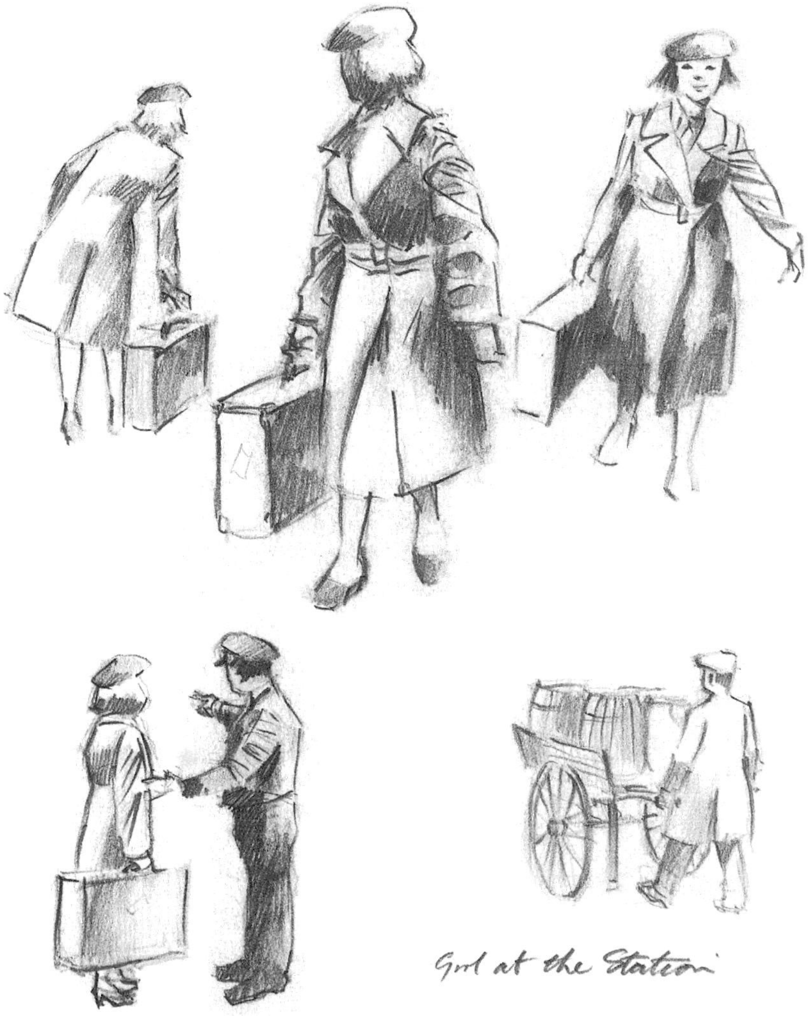

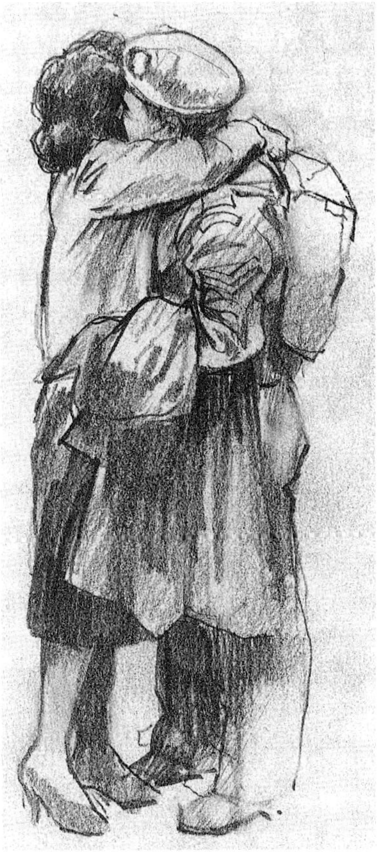

Birmingham, country gentlemen on their way to do business in the city, and servicemen making the painful trip back to duty after a well-earned leave.

The porters cursed under their breath as they struggled to wheel their luggage-laden trolleys over the timber crossing and up the ramp onto the far platform. They had to look sharp: the London train was due in three minutes and there was still a woman with her pram and baby to see safely over the crossing. They never minded helping. What they did object to was the way the guard off the branch train always collared the smartest luggage – and the best tips.

'Hang on, Jack. There's a down fast coming!' The porter paused, pram in hand, at the top of the ramp while the express whistled her way through the station. The drivers of *Eastbury Grange* and *Spitfire* liked to make their presence felt as they hurried their charge on her way from Wales to Penzance. As the signal clattered back to danger and the dust began to settle the porter was off with pram and over the crossing – to be rewarded with a handsome sixpenny tip.

Now the London train was running in, a single Castle class at her head. She was allowed to pause for only two minutes – two minutes for the station staff to load a hundred passengers and their luggage, the parcels for up the line, and the idiot who arrived in the booking office demanding a return to Paddington with just thirty seconds to spare. They managed it, as they nearly always did, gave the Right Away and heaved a satisfied sigh of relief as the driver of *Swordfish* gave a brief toot on the whistle and opened up the regulator.

By the time the last coach had cleared the end of the platform the porters had disappeared to brew a well-earned cup of tea. Over on the far platform the prairie tank simmered quietly in the sun, her crew exchanging local gossip with a shunter who'd strolled across from the goods shed. Otherwise the station was again deserted, apart from the cat. Exhausted by the burst of activity he settled his head on his paws and dropped into a slumber, lulled by the fading beat of the Castle's exhaust as it lifted its train out of the valley and on towards the world outside.

For more than a hundred years this schizophrenic stop-go activity was an essential part of daily life at country stations the length and breadth of Britain, from St Erth (change for St Ives) in the far west of Cornwall to the very north of Scotland, from the Weald of Kent, the open acres of Norfolk and the wooded byways of Leicestershire to the harsh moors of the Pennines and the craggy Lake District. For many communities it was the railway that opened up the delights and drawbacks of civilisation. They brought coal to heat Victorian villas, books for the new Victorian schools, and an increasing flood of trippers and tourists. They opened up new markets for local produce, carrying away corn and vegetables and livestock from the country to the cities. They also bore away families in search of work and new homes, and young men to the wars.

Our cat could have been a watcher at any number of country junctions. Only the proud names of the locomotives and the sharp smell of Welsh steam coal betray the Great Western, here at Brent in South Devon – the stepping-stone to the Kingsbridge branch. It was a line that in its short twelve miles seemed almost a gateway to heaven, flirting constantly with the delightful River Avon as it wound through secret wooded combes and remote stations on its way down to Kingsbridge and the tang of the sea, sparkling in the Salcombe Estuary.

In a pattern that was commonplace across the country, this branch line became a vital part of everyday life. It provided jobs for scores of hungry families. The stations needed porters and clerks, shunters and signalmen. Out on the line the gangers toiled in the heat, the snow and the drenching rain to keep the track in good fettle for the safety of the trains. And the trains themselves couldn't run without the guards and inspectors and the envied footplatemen.

Porter Jack's family from Brent was typical of so many who devoted their labours to the company with fierce pride over several generations. His father James Garland was a ganger on the Great Western. During the First World War he went to France to use his skills so that the railways there could carry men and horses, guns and ammunition to the Front – and bring the wounded homewards.

Back home, his three sons followed him into the company. Jack became a porter at Brent, and up in the wilds of Dartmoor; Harry travelled down the line to Kingsbridge to be a porter, met and married a local girl and settled down; and brother Gilbert went only half as far, to Loddiswell to be a ganger. He found digs, married the landlady's daughter, and for fifty years kept his length of track in prize-winning condition. His rewards were a gold watch for his long service, and the quiet satisfaction of a job well done.

Their sisters still remember how the railway provided almost the only link between Brent and the outside world during the first half of the century. Times could be hard. There were no holidays and few outings for ordinary folk then. Almost every child in the town would look forward for weeks to the Sunday School outing. Just about every family would go. Sudden conversions were made from Chapel to Church just so the children didn't miss this special treat.

For most of the families involved this was their only day away from Brent in the whole long year. When it came, the station platform would be crowded from one end to the other, the hubbub growing as the shouts from excited children mingled with the voices of anxious parents, until an imperious whistle heralded the arrival of the special train which would take them to the seaside at Teignmouth.

Later the enterprising school staff arranged trips by train to open their pupils' eyes: they ventured to Exeter and Torquay for singing competitions, dancing displays and hockey matches. These were trips that helped the eager youngsters to 'see a bit of the world'. And as the youngsters matured, the railway came to play a vital role in their courting. From five until midnight on a Saturday was their time for fun, and there was no better way to spend it than by taking the evening train to Millbay station in the heart of Plymouth. The city's theatres and cinemas were waiting to welcome the crowds who'd travelled in by train from many miles around. At the end of the evening the visitors would pile back onto the midnight train, carrying fish and chips and bottles of beer for the snug journey home, cuddled up with their sweethearts in a corner of the carriage.

During the week the trains would bring passengers from the villages in the Avon valley up the branch to do their shopping in the grocer's, the Post Office, the draper's and the shoe shop. And by train would come the fresh stock for the shops, and the newspapers that brought tidings of coronations, disasters, and distant threats in far-off countries.

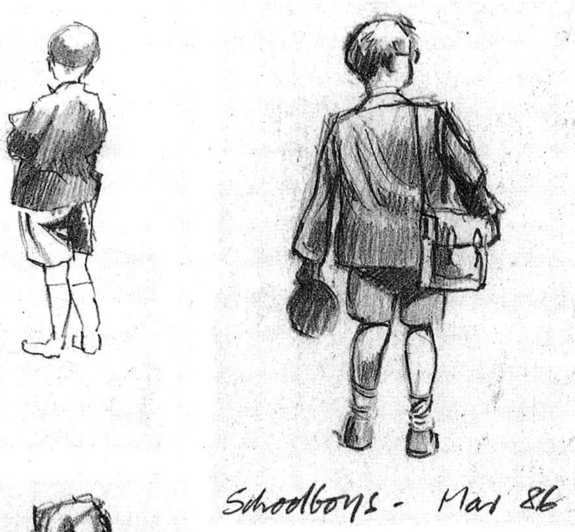

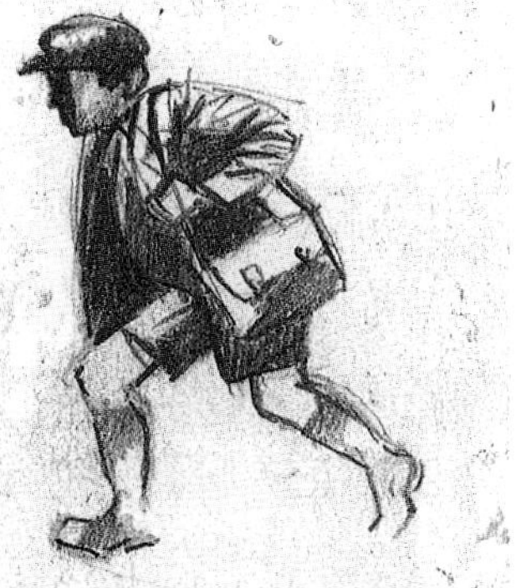

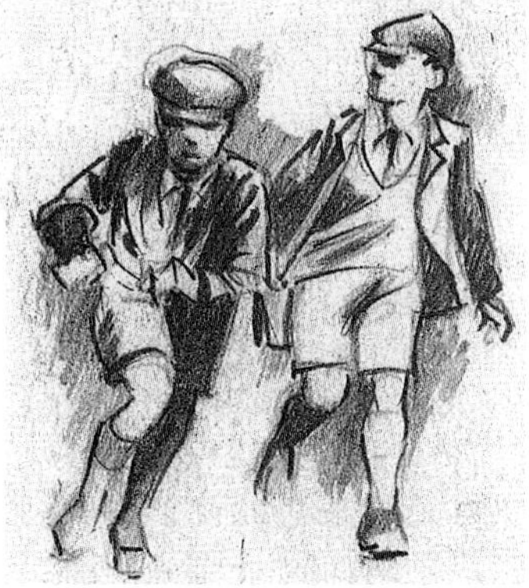

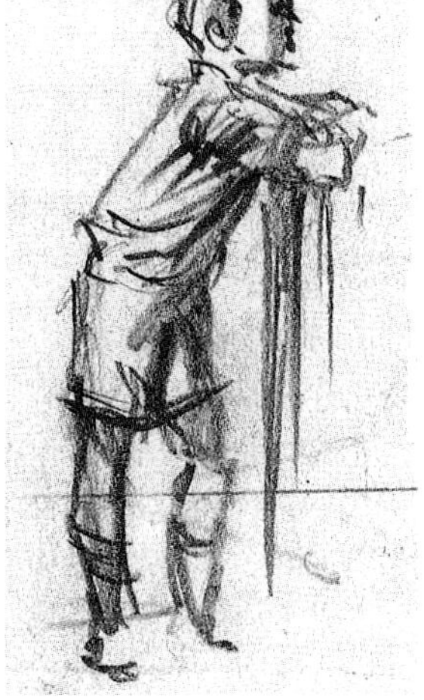

There would be visitors too. At first, the gentry from up-country for a spot of shooting, or sailing at Salcombe. But as times got better the trickle of holidaymakers grew into a flood. The Saturday trains would be crowded with families bound for Kingsbridge, or the excitement of a spell in a camping coach. And Brent station would give them a welcome as they waited for the connecting train. There were always fires in the waiting-rooms, except in the very hottest of summer weather, and the gardens looked a picture. Roses and pampas grass covered the banks, while on the platforms there were the exotic yuccas suggesting climes more favoured than this outpost of Dartmoor, and neat borders with rows of annual bedding plants.

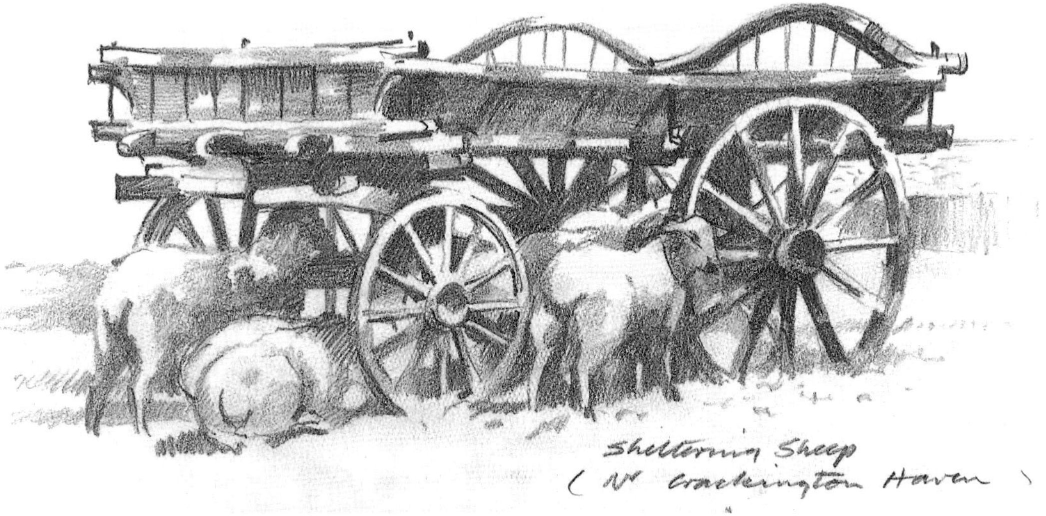

World War II also brought human cargoes. Thousands of American servicemen came to train for D-Day on the south Devon beaches. For a year the branch groaned under the weight of the personnel and ammunition needed for the task, building to a hectic crescendo in May and June 1944 as units departed for the airfields of Wiltshire and more troops arrived to join the seaborne invasion fleet.

When it was all over the railway picked up the pieces of its daily routine. Once again men cycled three or four miles from the moor to catch the early train to work in Devonport Dockyard. Commuters would hurry down at eight o'clock to be carried off to work in Plymouth offices and children boarded the local train for Totnes, bound as unwillingly as ever for school.

Well into the 1950s the goods yard was a lively place. The morning freight down from Newton Abbot would bring in coal, cattlefeed and farm machinery, much of it bound for the branch. And up from Kingsbridge would come flour from the mills, day-old chicks, sugar beet, sheep and cattle. On Brent Fair days the pens would be choked with cattle and ponies waiting to be shipped as far away as Northumberland. In some weeks up to 25 tons of rabbit would be dispatched to the Midlands and Yorkshire. The rich seas worked by the fishermen of Hope Cove and Salcombe provided another 25 tons of lobster and crab for market. When the water board was building the Avon dam on Dartmoor it arranged for sand to be brought to Brent by rail. In the yard the contractor's men sweated to shovel it into the waiting lorries.

Summer Saturdays saw the station and the branch at their busiest, in terms of people carried.

Gara Bridge Crossing

GWR 2-6-2T No 4561 moves over the level crossing at Gara Bridge station in Devon as it leaves with a train from Kingsbridge to the mainline junction station at Brent. Gara Bridge, opened in 1893, was the only passing station on the Kingsbridge branch. It was closed in 1963. No 4561 was built in 1924 and withdrawn from service in 1962.

Level crossings are an interesting aspect of railway working. In Britain there are fewer than in most other countries relative to the volume of railway traffic, which is surprising considering our multitude of roads and lanes. The ups and downs of the British countryside probably made bridges a stronger option.

The double-gate crossing would be controlled from a signalbox by means of a large wheel turned by the signalman. The smaller crossings on branch lines were manually operated by a man or woman living in a gatekeeper's cottage beside the track – echoes of the lodgekeeper's house at the entrance to the country estate. Often branch lines would also have several occupation crossings on roads to farms, or other private properties, which were under the control of the user. Here there would be reminders from the company not to open one gate and drive onto the track before opening the second!

On level crossings the railway took precedence and when the gates closed everything came to a halt. It was rather like that old radio programme *In Town Tonight* where the sounds of the street and traffic were instantly silenced by an authoritative voice calling out 'STOP'! Sometimes the minutes would tick by at the gates with no sound of an approaching train, and a few malevolent stares would be directed at the signalbox. The signalman seemed to enjoy this feeling of power as he wandered about behind his shiny levers ringing bells or making tea.

At last the train would sweep through the gates, looking large and majestic, and passengers would glance down at the assembled throng which their train had imposed upon so effectively. Now and then it would not be an express but a goods engine shuffling through with a single brake van. Then the multitude would mutter in discontent, 'To think we've been waiting here for that!'

The possibilities of level crossings have been well explored in films, both from the dramatic and humorous angles. In one of Buster Keaton's films he manages to strand his house on a crossing whilst towing it along the street – with inevitable results. In Stephen Spielberg's *Duel* the hero's car is being nudged steadily into a passing freight train by a large menacing tanker lorry which is intent on his destruction.

I chose the level crossing at Gara Bridge on the Kingsbridge branch because there was a pleasing balance of trees, and because the station platform could suggest the train just pulling away. The fencing along the side of the road was limiting as it obscured most of the vehicles which I hoped to include. Finally I decided to use it as a perch for the children watching the train. I moved the tractor from one side to the other. There wasn't much of it to be seen but it did contribute to the composition, and finally I settled it on the right with the trailer introduced to give a touch of light brown colour against the trees. The 45XX tank engine sat well on the smooth 'road' area, thus increasing the feeling of movement.

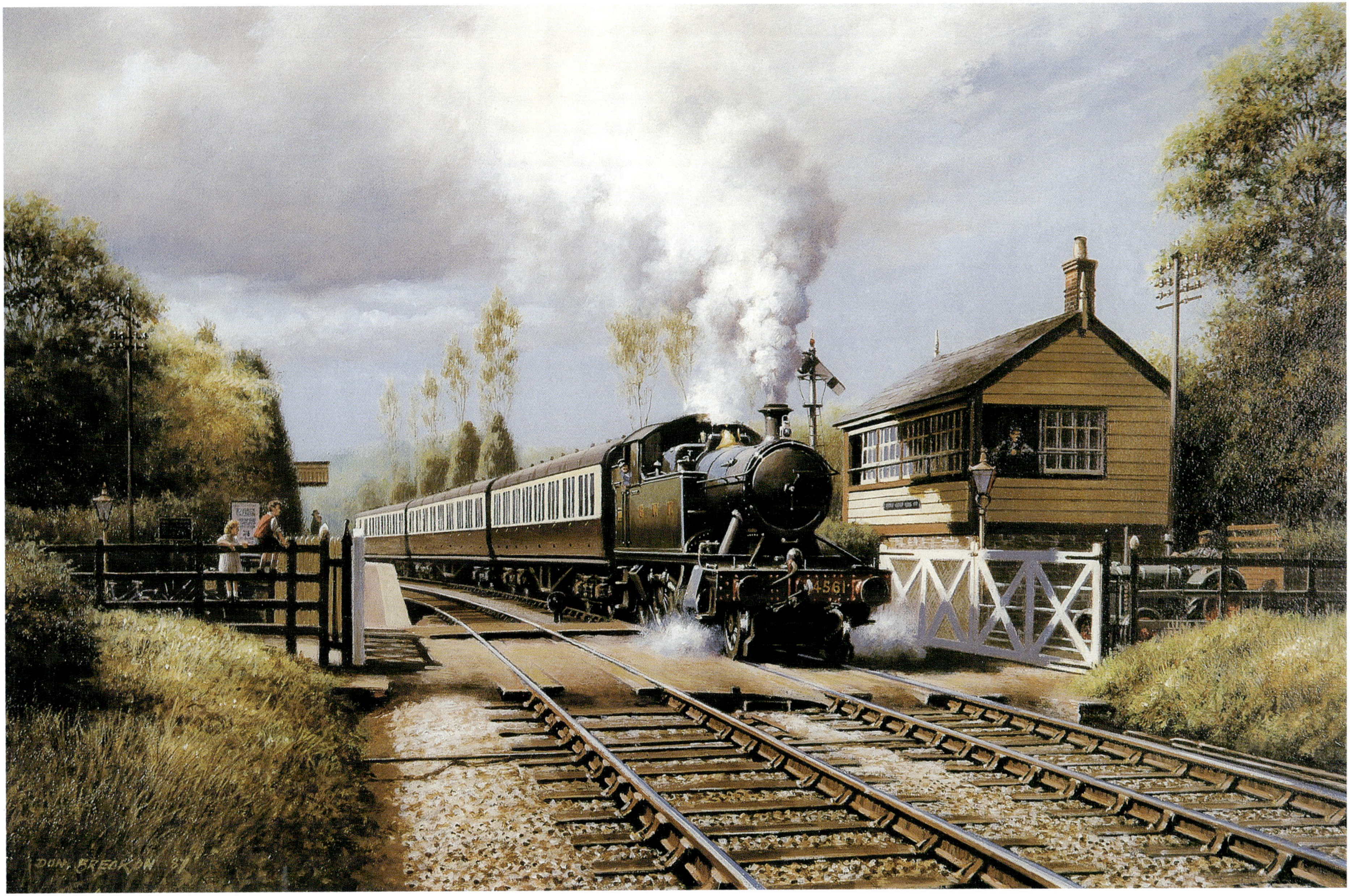
DON BRECKON '87
4561

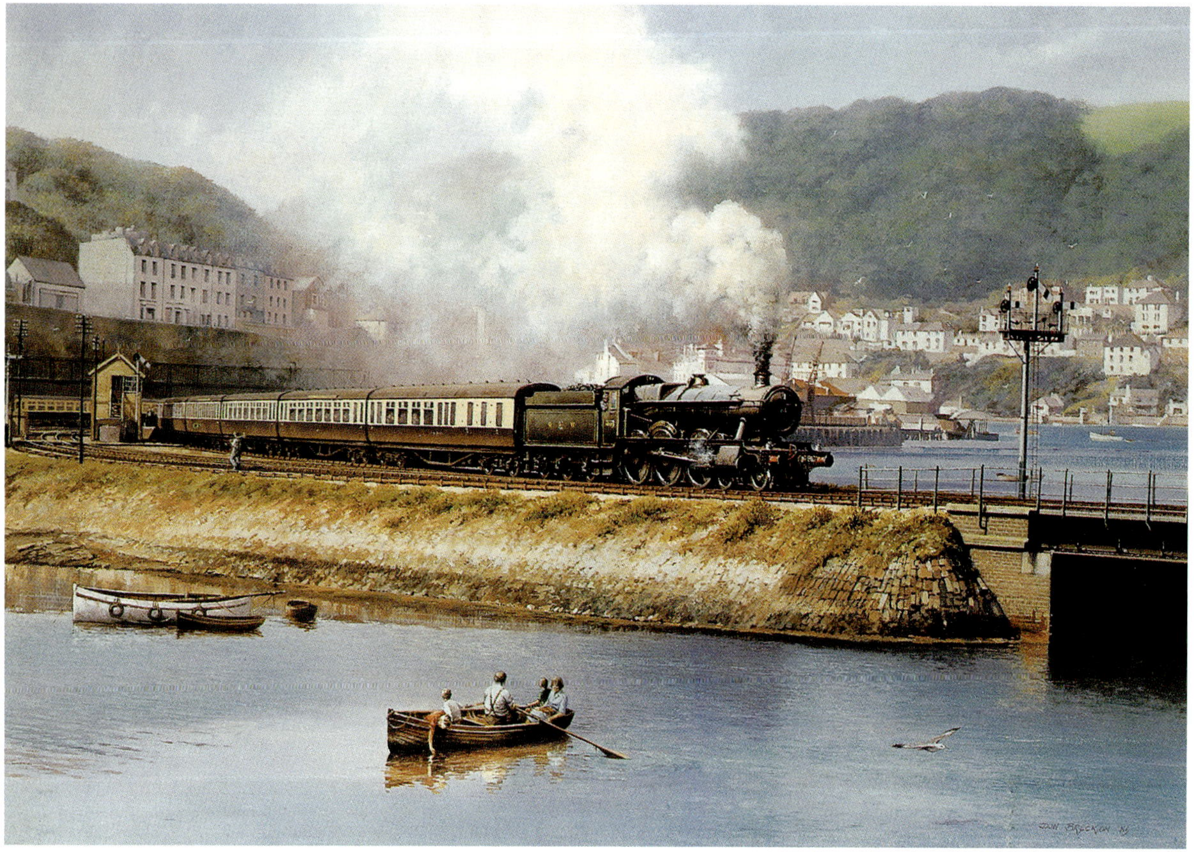

Dumbleton Hall Leaving Kingswear (1983)
GWR Hall class 4-6-0 No 4920 Dumbleton Hall *leaving with an express for Paddington.*

Nearing Padstow
Southern Region West Country Pacific No 34017 Ilfracombe *opens up as it clears the girders of Little Petherick creek bridge with the down Atlantic Coast Express from Waterloo. The final part of the journey runs alongside the River Camel from Wadebridge to the terminus at Padstow.*

I first saw this bridge on a chilly Sunday afternoon. The track was long gone and the entrance to the bridge was barricaded to prevent anyone from walking across. There was a rumour that it would not be demolished because it was intended to open the old line between Padstow and Wadebridge as a footpath. As it turned out, it was eventually opened up as the Camel Trail for both walkers and cyclists to enjoy, offering a flat and scenic route skirting the coastline and crossing the creek as it flowed out into the Camel estuary. My sons and I were able to cycle over this bridge and it was a strange feeling to imagine the rumble of wheels and the clank of connecting rods echoing among the girders. Now there are just bicycles and strollers where the Atlantic Coast Express once passed.

When I was commissioned to paint the scene I looked forward to starting work on recreating the line as it had been in earlier days. A friend of mine mentioned that he used to fish from the bridge when it was still in use. Apparently when a train crossed over it created 'quite a shake'. No doubt the fishing must have been pretty good!

The Bulleid light Pacific fitted into the picture well because of its association with the Atlantic Coast Express, and the rather square profile echoes the angular lines of the bridge. In fact the streamlined casing earned these locomotives the nick-name of 'Spam-Cans' – spoken with affection of course! Most of the class had the casing removed from 1957 onwards but many remained in their original condition until the end of steam railways.

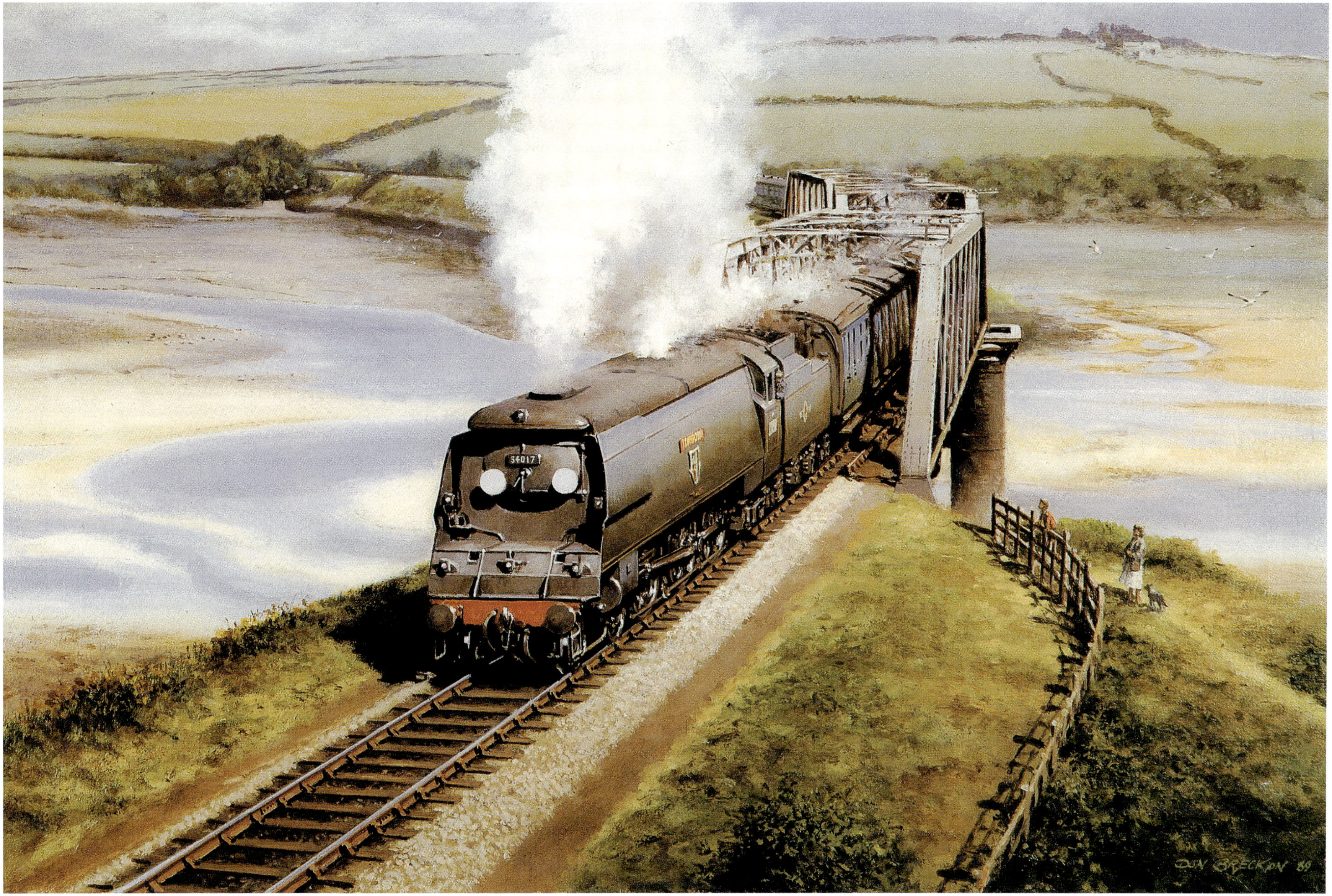
34017
DON BRECKON 89

One express from Paddington would include a rake of three or four through coaches packed with holidaymakers for Kingsbridge. And from Bristol, Wales, the Midlands and the North came hundreds more. As the two little tank engines panted up and down the line, crowds of two or three hundred people would have to wait on Brent platform.

It was a hectic time for the station staff but there weren't too many grumbles, as one former station master recalls. 'I soon learned not to let a connecting train set off down the branch if the people on the incoming mainline train could see it. That was guaranteed to make them hopping mad. But what their eye couldn't see they couldn't grieve over.'

Once on their way down the branch the holidaymakers entered an enchanted world of buttercup meadows and scattered farms. The line followed tree-shaded stretches of the River Avon and it crossed and recrossed the river ten times as the flashing water made its way to the sea. Five miles down the valley the train plunged into a narrow combe, through thick woods, and then hurried back into the sunlight as the valley opened out at Gara Bridge. Here the river was crossed by an ancient hump-backed bridge that carried the road from Plymouth to Dartmouth.

The train rattled over the level crossing and into Gara Bridge station, as perfect a country setting as you could find anywhere in England. This was the only crossing place on the branch, so it was granted the extra status of two platforms. On the left, the down side, stood the main station buildings and the bay that housed two camping coaches. On the up platform, conveniently close to the crossing gates, was the signalbox, adorned by a large rose bush with scented white blooms.

The train would pause here on busy summer days to enable another coming up from Kingsbridge to pass and this gave their passengers just a few minutes' glimpse of a secret paradise. For a handful of holidaymakers every year their stay was lengthened to a week or two, if they'd booked a holiday in a camping coach. Stepping off their train and onto the platform, the visitors found themselves in a haven of tranquillity and beauty, nestling in the fold of a thickly wooded valley. There was just space for a few small fields before the tree-hung hillside climbed up towards the sky.

Inside the chocolate and cream coach the thoughtful staff would have a kettle boiling, the table laid for tea and fresh linen ready. Milk, bread, groceries and newspapers came down by train, ordered over the telephone by the friendly signalman. Even fresh water arrived by rail. Nearby were a sandpit, swing and skittles for the children, and there was a lawn and flower beds around their coach. The vehicles had almost every convenience, but perhaps one was lacking – a bath or shower. However, in fine weather the river was at hand for a dip, and in bad weather the station staff might invite campers to their homes for a bath.

There were camping coaches on the line for nearly thirty years, but the sound of laughter from happy campers was to die with the summer of 1963. The end came with a swift and brutal swing of the Beeching axe, which lopped off the branch. *Trains Illustrated* of February 1958 opined: 'It is extremely unlikely that this line, with its incessant stream of holiday traffic during the summer months and its all-year-round freight traffic, will be closed, since it can hardly be a financial burden or an uneconomic proposition.'

The British Railway Board thought otherwise, and in 1962 published notice of its intent to close the line. The community fought hard to save it, but were powerless against faceless officials who had redrawn the timetable to provide a much poorer service, and provided ambiguous and incomplete accounts to support their case for closure. The last trains ran on 14 September 1963, watched by one local resident who had witnessed the first train in 1893. Brent station closed the following year.

A valiant attempt to preserve the line was thwarted by railway officials who, even as the enthusiasts negotiated to buy it, sold the rails for scrap. And so the Kingsbridge branch fell silent, to be reclaimed by nature, a victim of the all-conquering motor car. But the railway may yet fight back. A campaign carries on to reopen Brent station, and other stations on the main line to Plymouth. The car is in danger of being strangled by its own success, and people again see rail as a sensible and civilised way to travel.

From St Erth to Leicestershire, from the valleys of South Wales to the heart of Scotland, with park-and-ride schemes and commuter halts, communities are working to breathe fresh life into their country stations.

Guy Pannell has been a journalist for 23 years and is now news editor for TSW. He has always been a railway enthusiast.

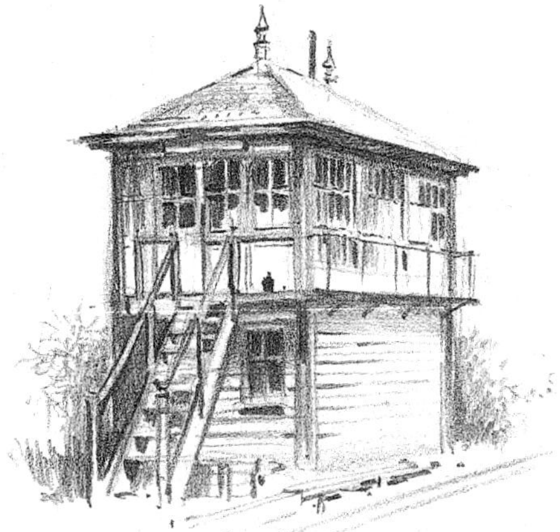

Midland Signal Box

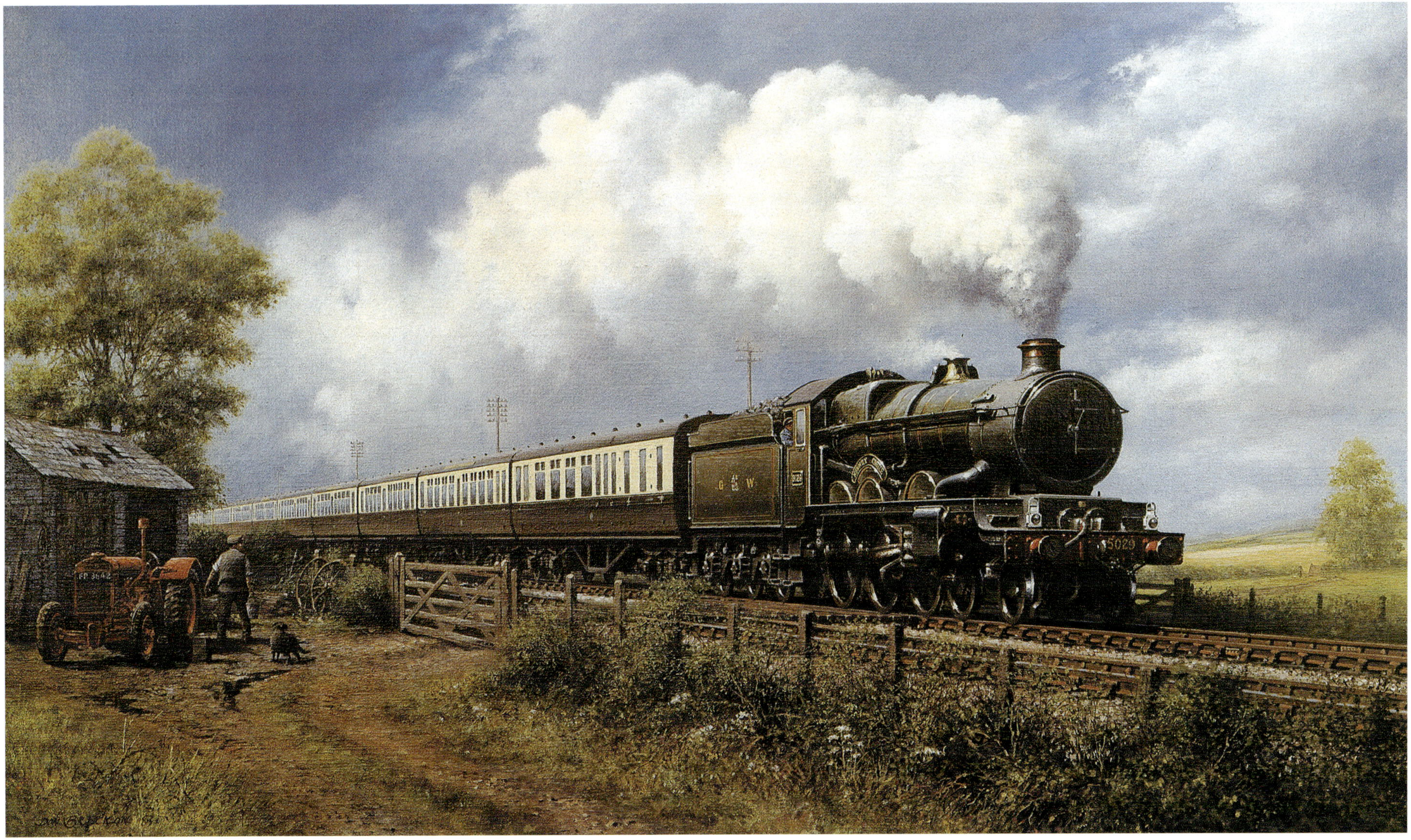

Nunney Castle (1983)
GWR Castle class locomotive No 5029 Nunney Castle *with an express in a country setting.*

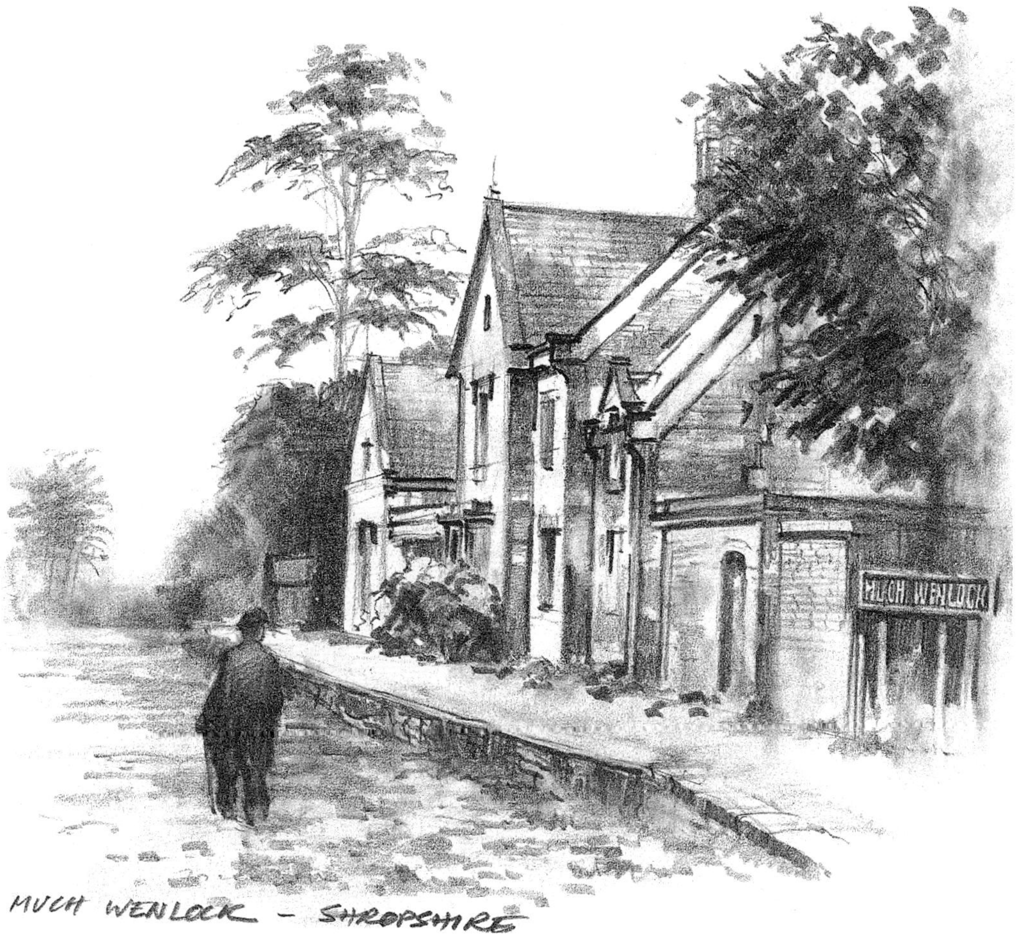

Much Wenlock
GWR 2-6-2T No 4401 brings a local train into Much Wenlock station on a summer's day in the late 1940s. Much Wenlock was on the line from Wellington to Craven Arms in Shropshire and opened in 1862. After 1951 passenger trains terminated at Much Wenlock, until in 1961 the line was closed completely. No 4401, one of a class of only eleven engines, was built at Wolverhampton in 1905 and withdrawn in 1954.

I have taken Much Wenlock station as a subject on two or three occasions. The stone building and surrounding trees create a very pleasing scene, and even the name has a ring of the English countryside.

Several photographs of the station showed interesting shadows of the trees across the tracks, giving dramatic horizontal bands to the composition and setting off the stonework of the station building. As the rails ran through the shadows a light-dark, light-dark pattern built up, carrying the eye more slowly into the distance and enhancing the feeling of space. It definitely had possibilities!

The problem, as in all paintings of stations, was where to put the train? In this case if the engine was in the foreground it would obscure most of the building. Pushed into the background the feeling of the train's movement might be lost, affecting the contrast with the stillness of the setting. The answer was, as in most cases, a compromise. A little of the building was lost behind the engine but the majority was visible, to give the impression of the train slowing down along those last few yards.

Country stations were often a clutter of details beloved of those who have an affection for such things. Name boards, posters and fire buckets were hung on the main building and gradually extra huts for bicycles, lamps, and other items were added over the years. The scene was never complete without milk churns, porters' barrows and interesting parcels or boxes waiting to be loaded onto a train when someone had time.

Figures in a painting are very important even though they may be quite small. Because the viewer can relate to a human figure the eye will keep returning to it. The porter and the cyclist set against the light building are especially noticeable and must be convincing in the way they stand. For instance, the cyclist leans forward with his elbow on the saddle. Perhaps this evokes memories of standing in sunshine doing just that, and a link is immediately established which gives conviction to the whole painting.

In 1989 *Much Wenlock* was published as a limited edition print. Not long afterwards I received a letter from Mr R. L. James saying that he had presented a framed print to his father on Christmas Day. 'His delight in receiving such a present is explained by the fact that he was station master at Wenlock from 1953 to 1958, a period he recalls as the happiest during his long railway career.'

It gives me great pleasure to know that my interpretation of a scene is appreciated by someone who was so personally involved in its reality.

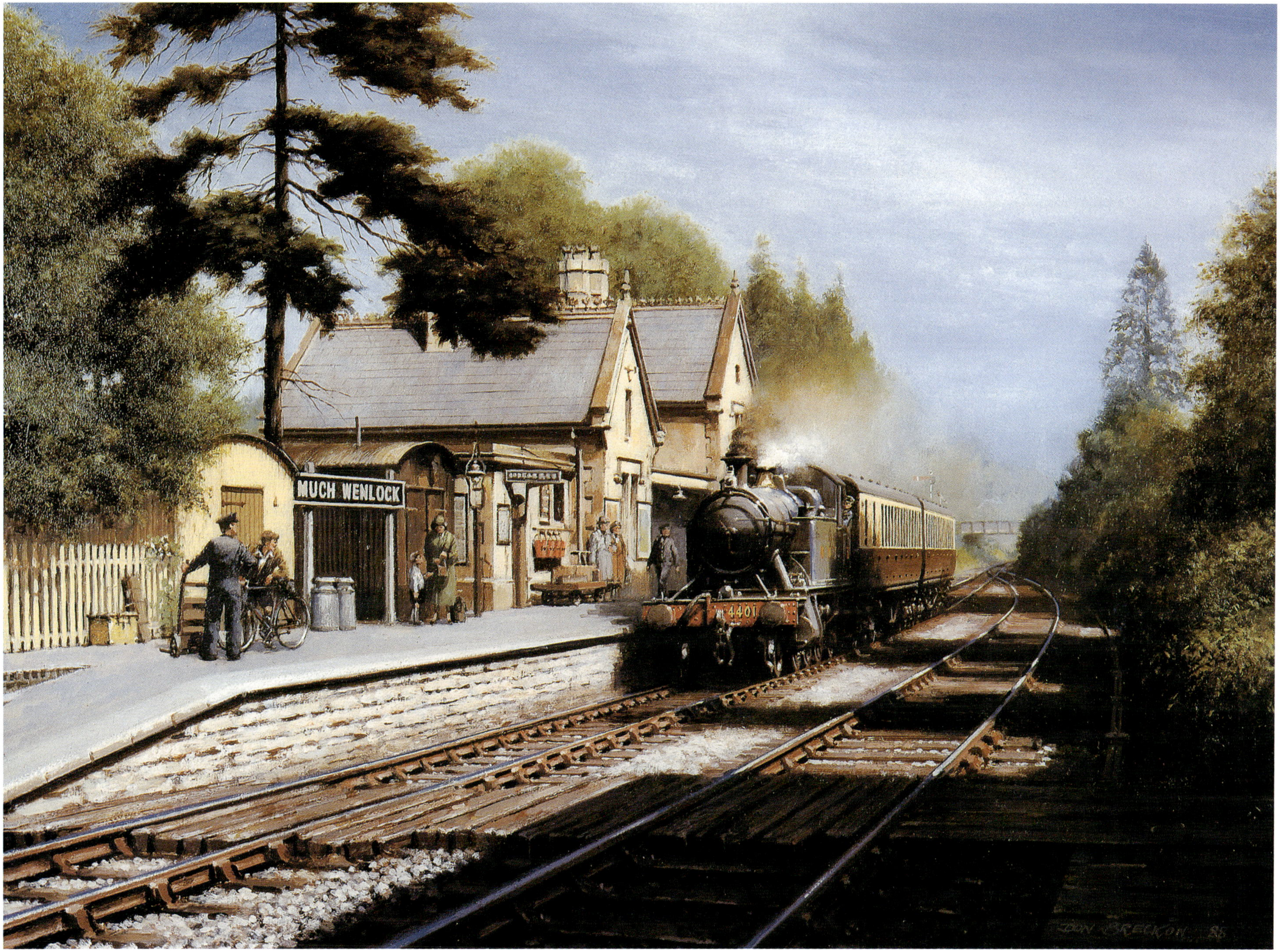
MUCH WENLOCK
4401

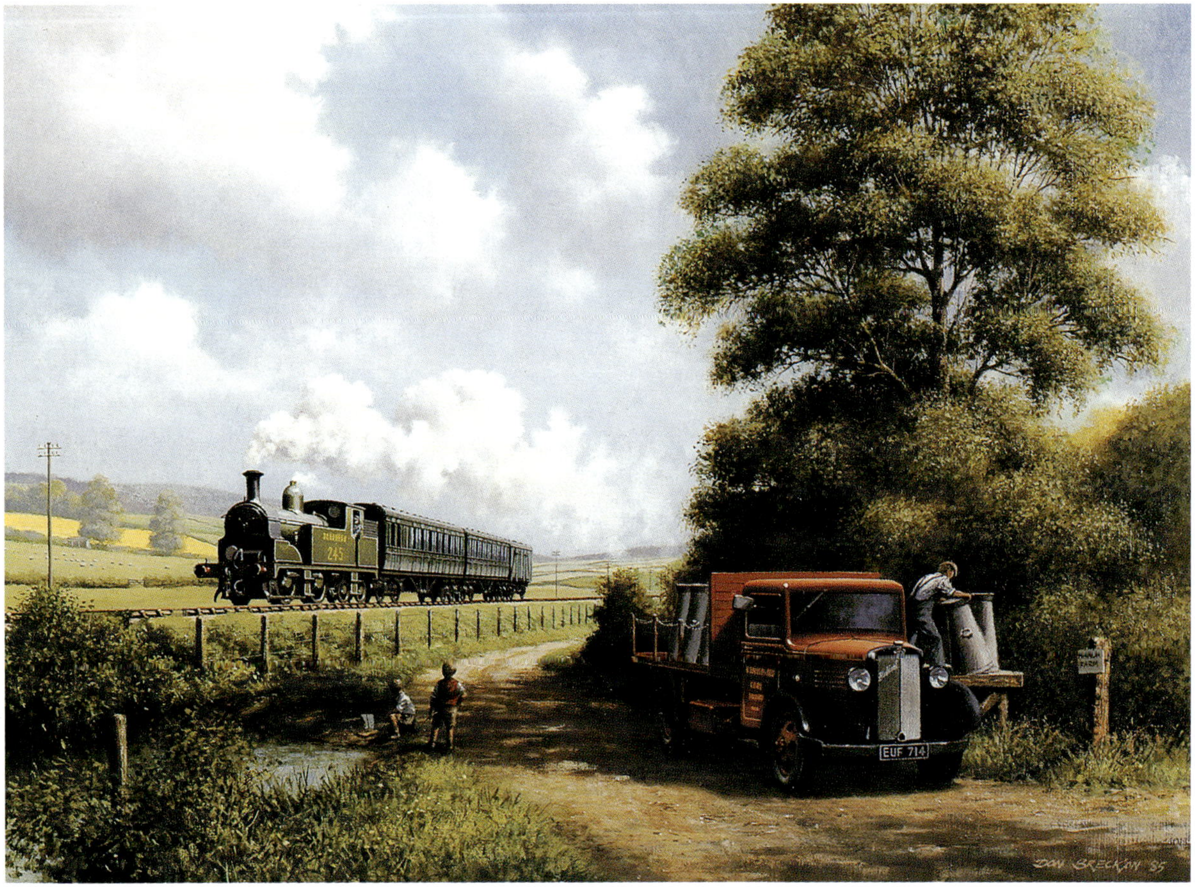

Collection at Manor Farm (1985)
A Southern Railway M7 tank locomotive passes with a local train as farm milk is being loaded for the dairy.

The Milk Train
GWR Hall class 4-6-0 No 5997 Sparkford Hall, *with an up milk train on Bruton Bank in Somerset, overtakes a farmer on a Fordson tractor pulling a trailer loaded with churns. No 5997 was built in 1940 and withdrawn from service in 1962.*

With the coming of the railways to assist distribution, the milk market changed from local trade to the beginnings of a whole new industry. At first the milk was carried in churns in bogie vans codenamed 'siphons'. In 1927 the GWR began to use tank wagons for bulk carrying, but churns continued in use and were to be a part of the railway scene until the 1960s. Therefore it was common for siphon vans and tank wagons to be in the same train.

Hygiene was always a problem. As early as 1881 there was a report concerning the opening of churns on Paddington station. Apparently this was common practice but considered undesirable. Much later the tanker wagons gave rise to anxiety as passengers noticed their often dirty exteriors, acquired through constant use. Much care, however, went into cleansing the glass lined interiors to make the wagons fit to carry the milk from the branchline stations to the delivery points.

Mr Longman, who commissioned this painting, had more than a passing interest in the milk trains. Longmans' Farms had kept 'large herds on Richest Pastures of Somerset' in Sparkford near Yeovil. In the 1930s the Farms used the advertising slogan 'Quickest possible service, 4 hours from Cow to London.'

Mr Longman recalls:

> Before the war we had Guernsey and Jersey cattle for high-quality milk and also Shorthorns for a dual purpose – milk and beef. Milk from the latter was made into cheese on the farm. The high-quality milk went to London by train.
>
> The morning's milk was cooled into churns which were then placed in a large tank fed by cold spring water to a depth of approximately three feet and left all day. The evening milk was also chilled in churns but did not go into the tank, as all the churns were then loaded onto a trailer pulled by a tractor and taken to Sparkford station. There they were loaded onto railway trolleys to await the overnight train to Paddington. The churns went into covered wagons with slatted sides.
>
> There was also a local creamery at Sparkford – The Sparkford Vale Creamery – where milk from other farms was taken and made into Cheddar cheese, whilst milk destined for London was put onto the train. The Creamery had its own siding and a GWR tank engine was often to be seen.

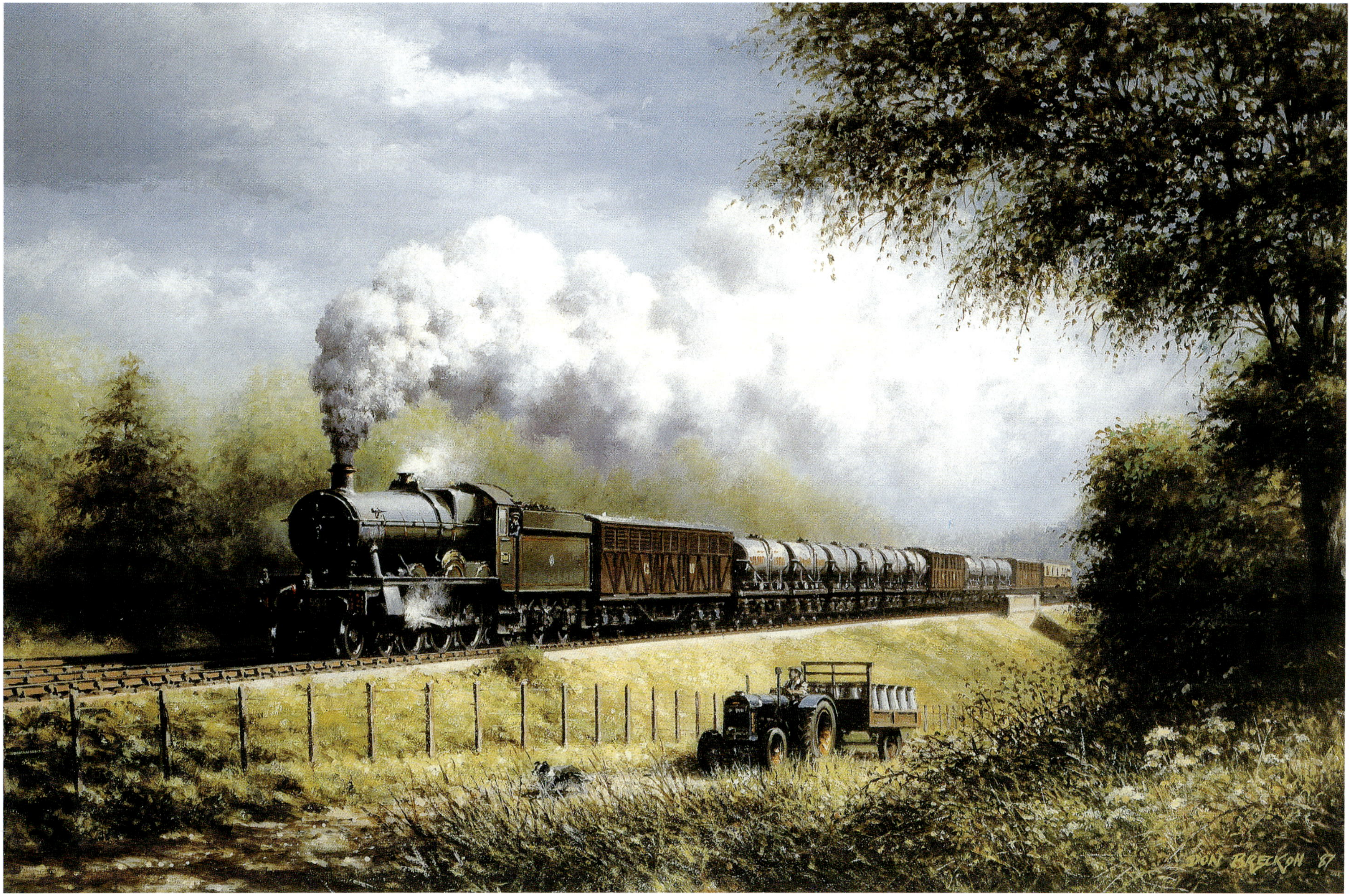
DON BRECKON '87

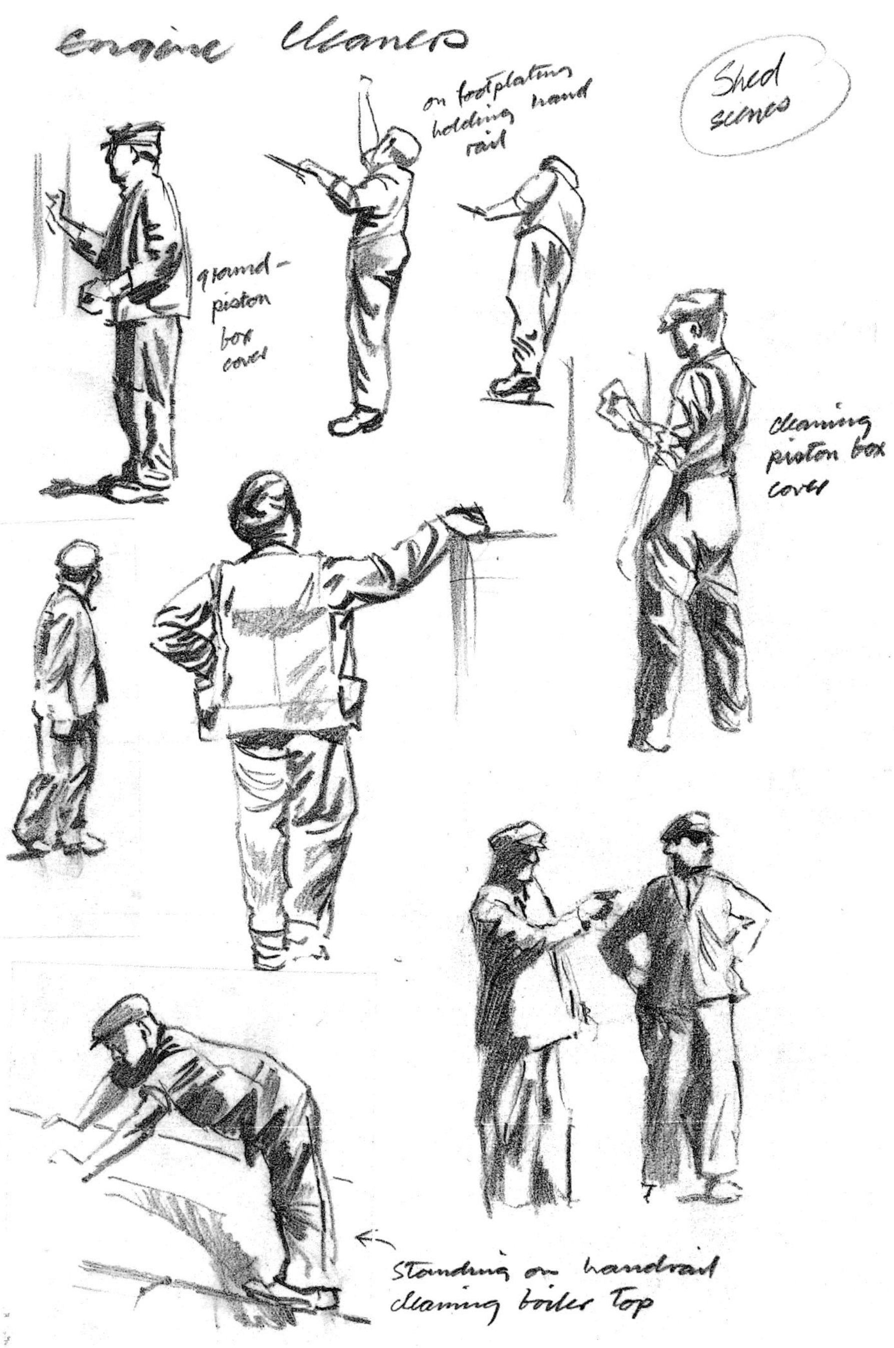

Engines at Peterborough (New England) Shed
Four Eastern Region Pacifics stand outside the engine shed at Peterborough. They are class A1 No 60130 Kestrel, *class A3 No 60044* Melton *and class A4 No 60017* Silver Fox. *In the background stands class A3 No 60100* Spearmint.

One may look in vain for anything which has a 'Country Connection' in this painting! When I realised that there was no representative of what had been the LNER in this particular collection of paintings, I decided to include this recent work as a salute to that railway and because it is a shed scene.

Engine sheds were only seen from a distance by the travelling public and what they saw probably didn't seem very inviting. To a youthful trainspotter squeezing through a gap in the fence it was heaven on earth, with the added thrill of knowing that you were not supposed to be there. Those who have done it will still have vivid memories of scuttling around among the gritty puddles, scribbling down numbers in notebooks until that loud shout 'Hey!' triggered a panicky rush for the exit.

The A4s were impressive engines, especially when running at speed. At the end of my trainspotting days we decided to have a look at the LNER and cycled over to Tallington, north of Peterborough, on several occasions. It was foreign territory to us but I remember that we were impressed by the speed of the expresses. There was much muttering about only having time to glimpse the numbers and having to look up the names afterwards.

Of all the A4s, *Silver Fox* looked the most impressive to me, with the galloping fox emblem on the side. I recall a time during my teaching career when the school hired the film *Elizabethan Express* for the railway club. The commentary was a bit quaint but there were dramatic shots of the engine at speed. The music grew more insistent as the train went faster until the commentator broke in with 'She's over the border . . . and she's running on time!' I must admit to a tingle down the spine at that moment – almost as if I'd built the engine myself!

When working on the painting I decided to make the sky stormy to heighten the drama of the scene and to pick up some of the colours in the foreground. Fortunately the shed is open at the far end so I could create a little distance between the nearer engines, thus avoiding a shut-in feeling to the scene. A3 Pacific *Melton* is fitted with German-style smoke deflectors which were introduced for these engines during the final years of steam. In my much earlier trainspotting days one nickname for smoke deflectors was 'blinkers' and the version on *Melton* certainly seem to merit the name more than most! Without the blinkers and with a single chimney, plus the LNER apple-green livery, the sole surviving member of this class of engine is the much travelled *Flying Scotsman*.

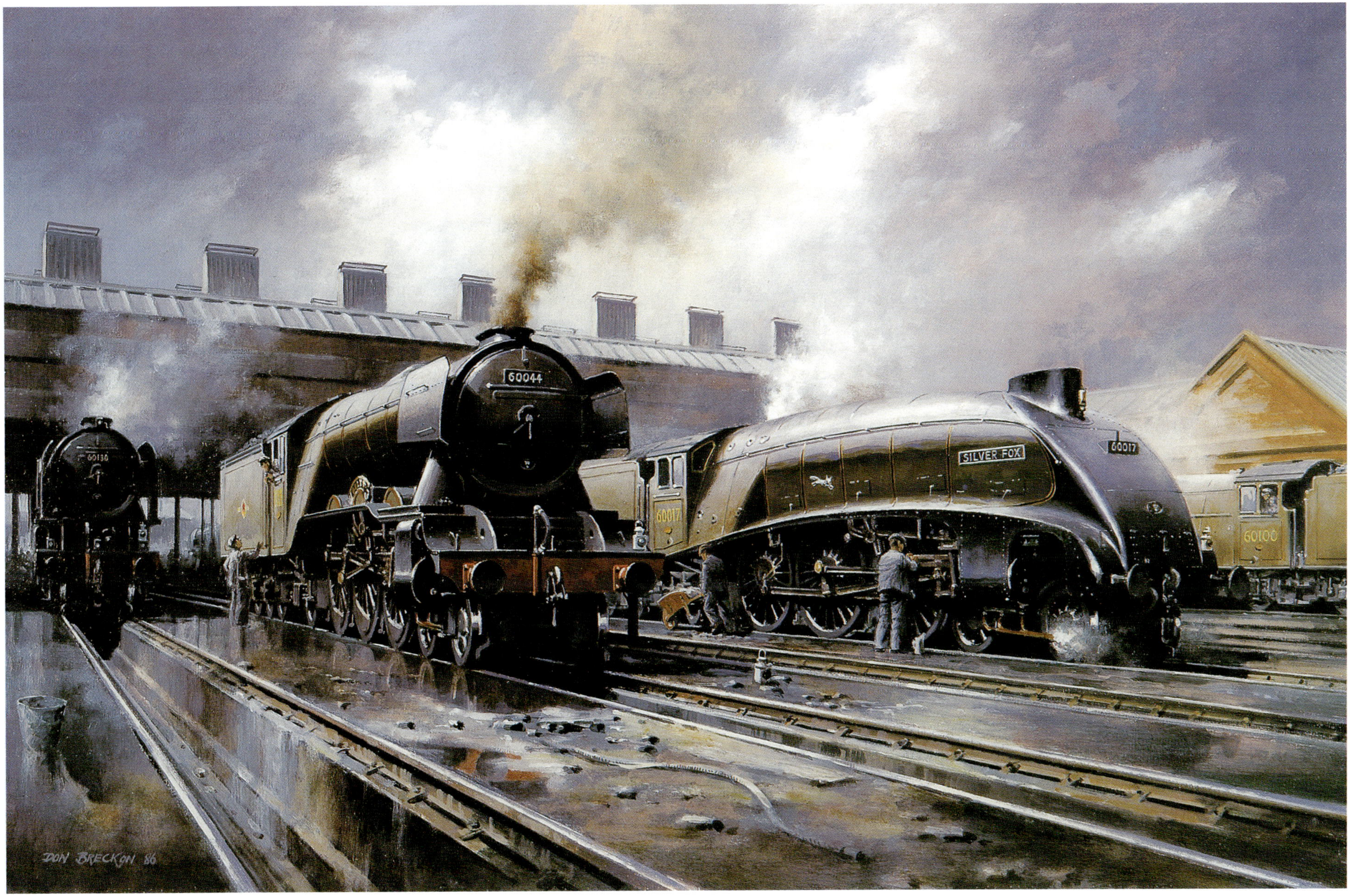
60044
SILVER FOX
60017
60017
60100
60130
DON BRECKON 86

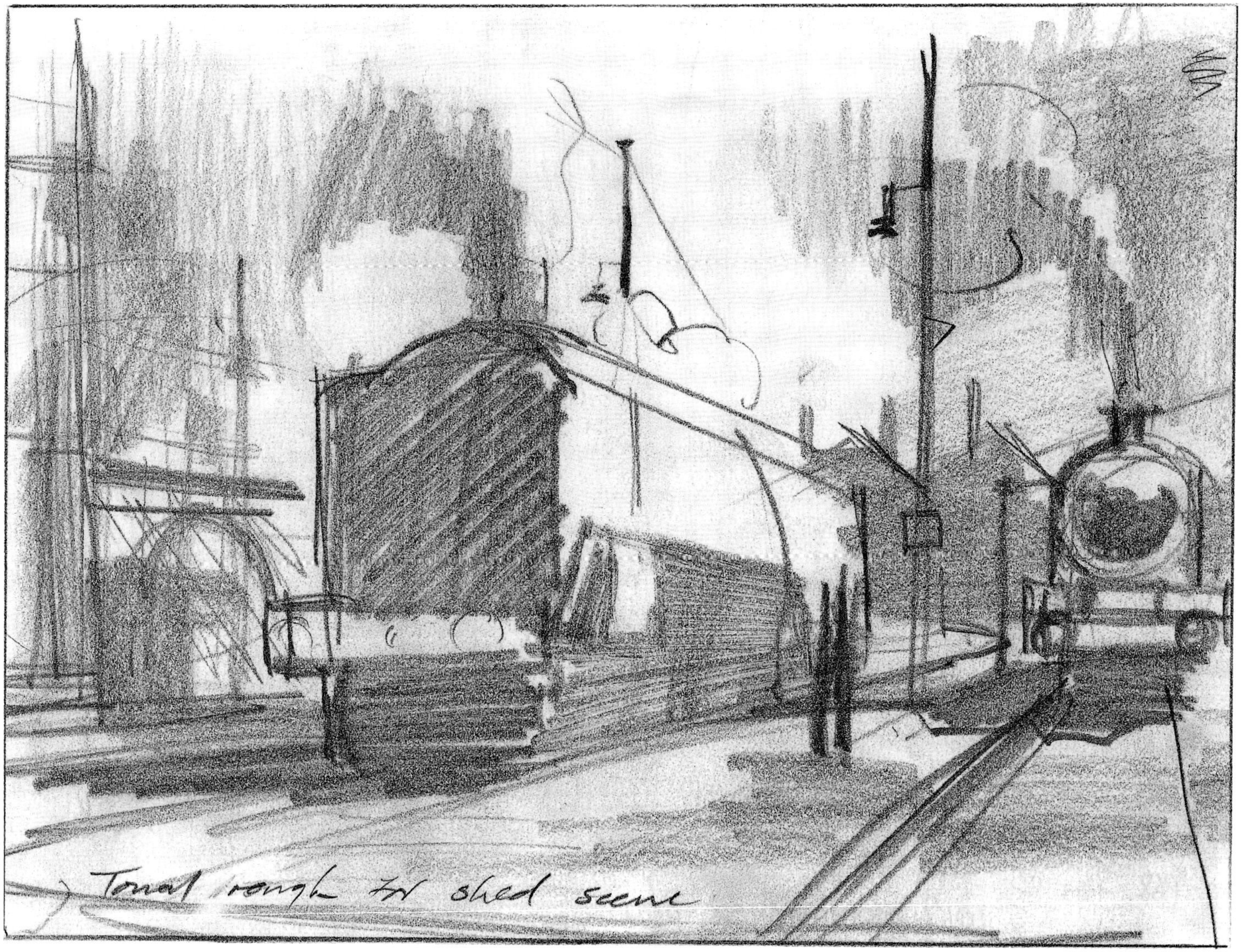
Tonal rough for shed scene

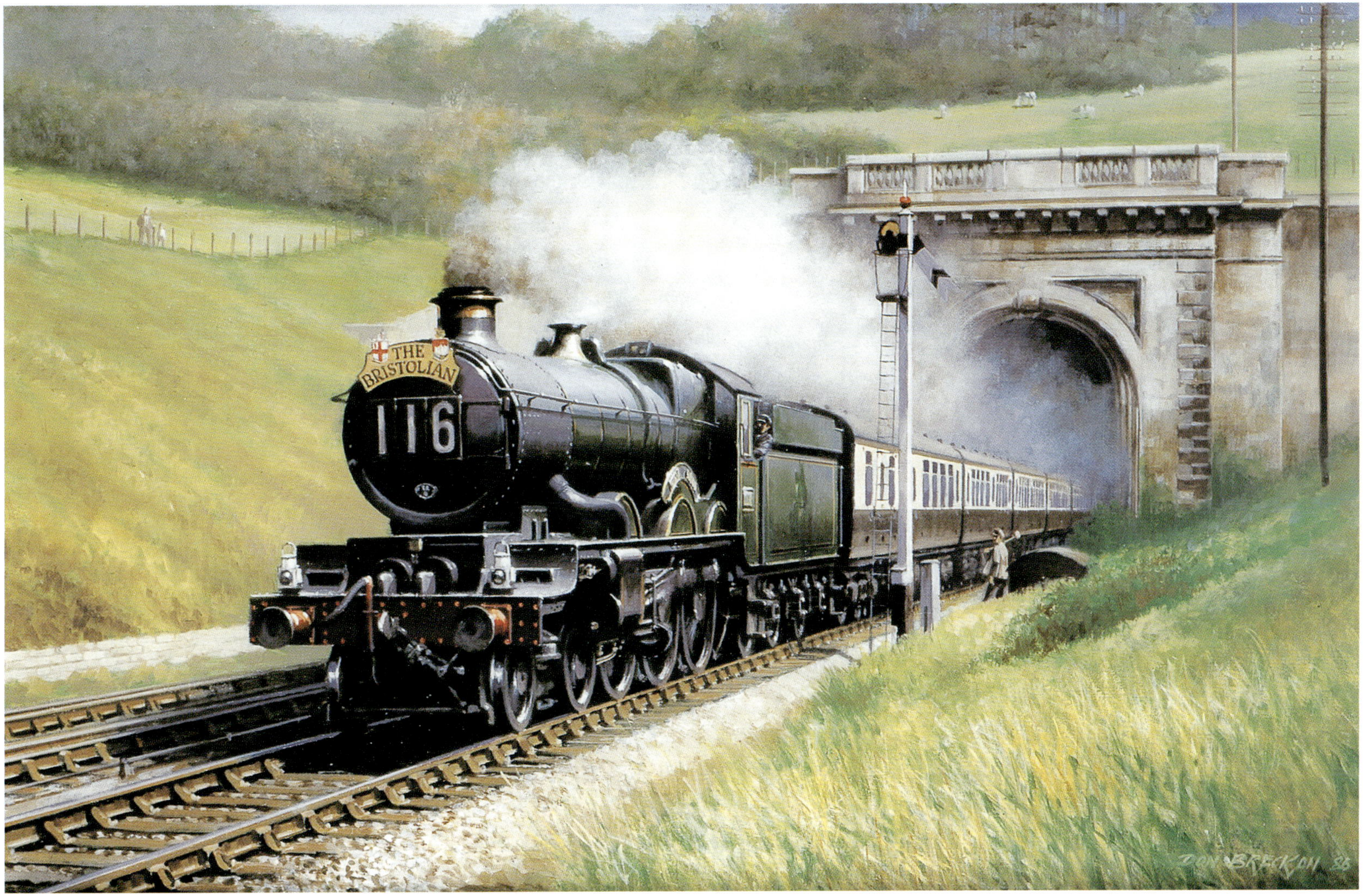

The Bristolian Leaving Box Tunnel (1986)
Castle class No 7034 Ince Castle *leaving Box Tunnel with the Bristolian in the 1950s. The Bristolian was inaugurated by the GWR in 1935, suspended during the War and restored in the Festival of Britain, 1951. It was steam hauled until 1959 when the Warship class diesels took over.*

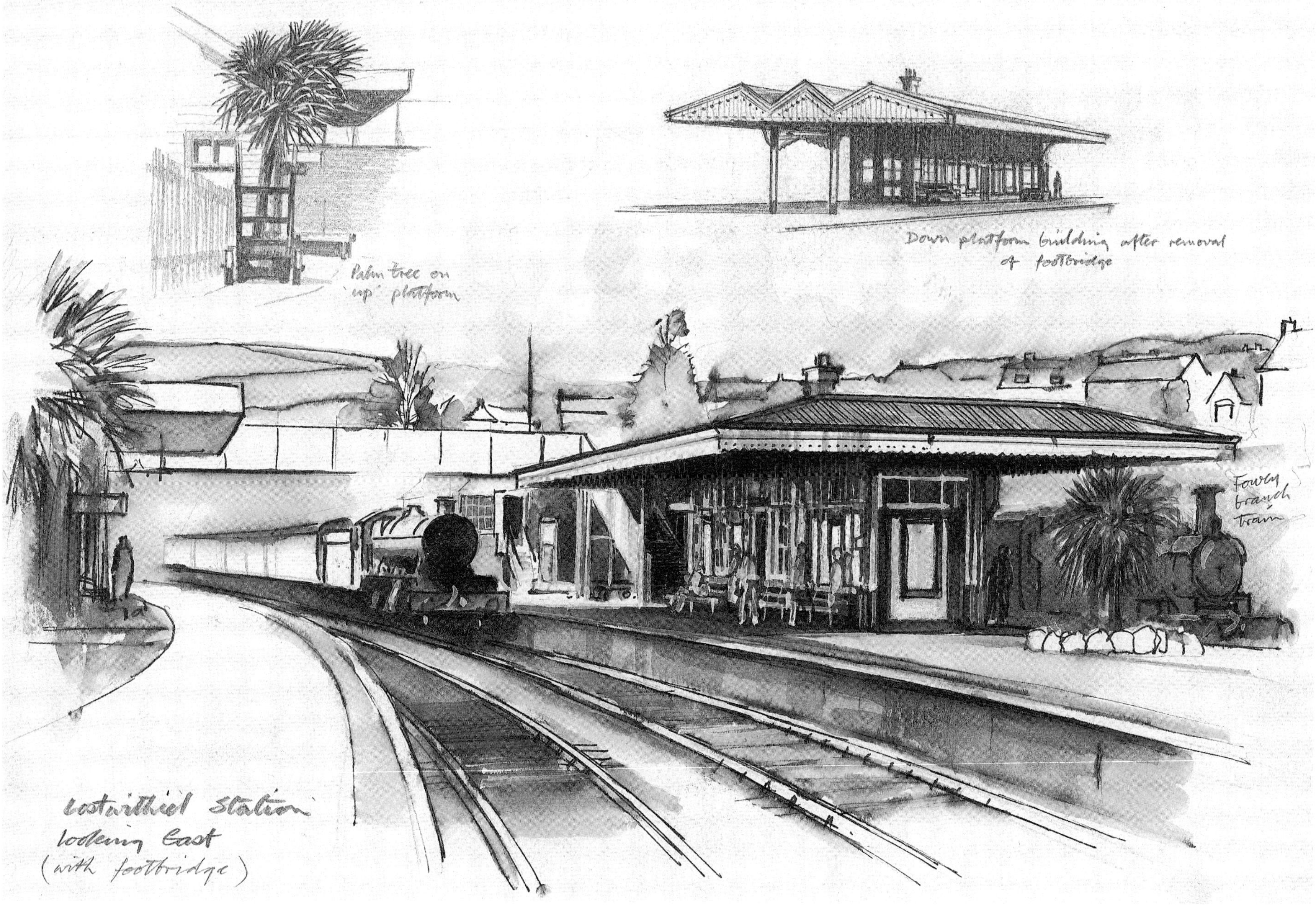
Palm tree on 'up' platform
Down platform building after removal of footbridge
Fowey branch train
Lostwithiel Station looking East (with footbridge)

CHANGING TIMES: LOSTWITHIEL STATION

Don Breckon

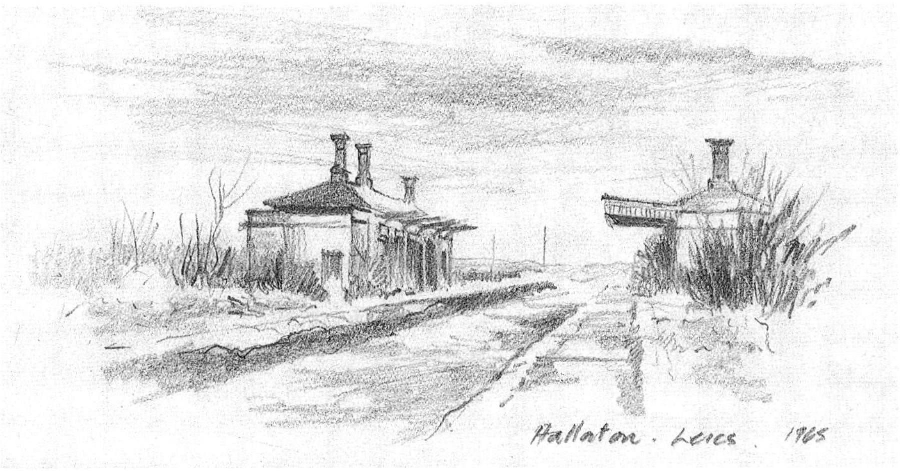

The 1960s was such a decade of change that new ideas, attitudes and lifestyles were seized upon in a riot of euphoria. But behind the excitement and frivolity of the times were some who were saddened by the passing of the old ways.

Mass production of the motor car after the Second World War brought a new, individual mode of transport within the financial reach of ordinary people, and just as one hundred years before the railways had meant the mobilisation of the masses, so the age of the private car resulted in the demise of the whole railway system. Even the carriage of freight was affected, as road transport provided door-to-door accessibility to markets and could be tailored more easily to customers' needs.

It was the branch lines that would suffer most. With ageing rolling stock and out-of-date work schedules, heavily subsidised by public money, they were soon recognised as being economically unviable. In the countryside the railways were torn up as the villages lost their branch lines, and the steam engines which had been so much a part of Britain were drawn up in silent queues in the breakers' yards. Whilst the locomotives awaited the cutter's torch, in villages throughout the land the station buildings crumbled into decay. Where the rails had once been, weeds grew quickly and choked the remains of carefully tended gardens. To those who loved railways and trains it was a depressing time, as they witnessed the apparent destruction of what they had thought to be a permanent part of life.

What an opportunity was missed when branch lines were closed and so many country stations were demolished! The course of the track was sold off in job lots or was left to become overgrown. A few precious trackbeds were turned into footpaths and cycleways, giving a hint of what might have been. A whole network of access routes to the countryside, away from traffic, could have been developed if there had been a policy of retaining all these lines as country trails for walkers and cyclists. Old stations might have become hostels or restaurants. We lost a unique chance to create a wonderful facility for generations to come, and to preserve buildings which were an important part of local history.

At first the effect on these small country towns and villages was not too catastrophic, as for another decade the motor car, the lorry and the bus replaced the train for local journeys. But these new forms of transport gradually brought profound changes which at the time few people could have foreseen.

The quiet streets of villages where families were once content to grow and play have now become servants to the needs of the motor car. Narrow streets do not satisfy the urge for speed, the need for ever-increasing mobility, and buildings are therefore torn down in the name of progress. The distant sound of the train which occasionally intruded into the country silence has gone, but the noise of the traffic is never-ending, and reaches further and further into previously untouched communities. Even in towns and villages where the railway still survives, local use has been curtailed, and the benefits of the station are no longer of much consequence to the community which the railway was once built to serve.

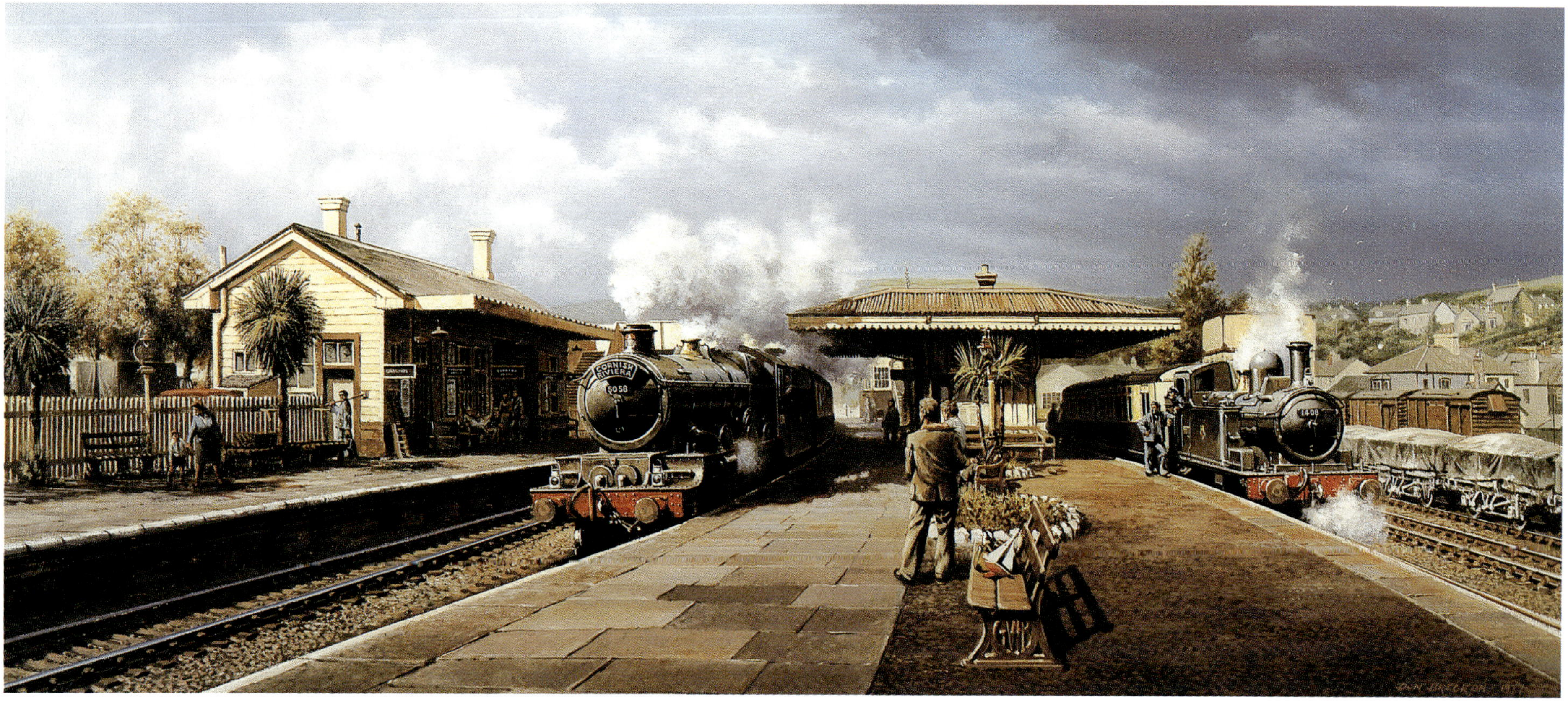

The Cornish Riviera Passing Lostwithiel (1977)
The down Cornish Riviera passing through Lostwithiel station headed by Castle class 4-6-0 No 5058 Earl of Clancarty.

In Cornwall, on the main line between Plymouth and Penzance, is Lostwithiel. This small town was of considerable importance even as far back as the Middle Ages and since then its fortunes have fluctuated with the rise and fall of several different trades and industries, including a period when it was designated a Stannary town with the right to assay locally mined tin.

In the last century the mining of tin and all its associated trades more or less finished in this area, and it was fortunate for the town when the new main railway line from Plymouth to Penzance was routed through the Fowey valley with a major station built in Lostwithiel. Alongside the station was a large goods shed with extensive sidings to accommodate the original broad gauge rolling stock, and extensive workshops were developed to service this new industry. At the beginning of this century more than a hundred men were employed by the GWR and the prosperity of the town was guaranteed for the foreseeable future. The station changed very little for most of this time, until factors affecting the rest of the country's rural railways ineluctably led to its decline.

In 1976 the station buildings on the down platform at Lostwithiel were demolished. For such a small town they were grand examples of GWR station design, with cantilevered awnings on either side of the waiting-room, in which a fire was often lit for the additional comfort of the passengers. A group of local residents turned up at 7am on the morning of demolition day, silently watching the bulldozers move in to carry out the inevitable.

A pressure group in town had worked hard to save the buildings over the previous months, even travelling to Parliament with a petition asking for their preservation. If only they had survived for ten more years new British Rail policy might have recognised the fact that here was a classic example of a Victorian country station which should be cherished, and that aesthetically the station should have been maintained as it was originally. As things were, no maintenance or painting had been carried out for years, and rot and decay had been allowed to create havoc in the wooden structure. It was said in town that, just like the footbridge a few years earlier, for something reported to be unsafe it took a 'hell of a hammering' to get it down. Three years later the Brunel-designed booking hall on the up platform went the same way, to be replaced by a design of 1980s vintage of which the best that can be said is that it is cleaner than the old one.

The flowers and gardens of the station are still cared for lovingly and, where there are not enough flower beds, tubs and window boxes are filled for summer showing. The palm trees on the platform are still there. Unusually severe frosts culled them all back to ground level a few winters ago but miraculously they have all survived. It's a pity that station buildings cannot imitate nature and grow again from their demolished foundations.

Fortunately there are still older people around who can remember life in the earlier part of this century, when the station was still the main centre of communication and an extremely important asset to the town. On the main line goods were delivered regularly, met by the local carrier with his horse and wagon or his hand cart. The bakers used some locally milled flour but the rest was sent down from Plymouth with sugar from Bristol and barrels of treacle at Christmas time.

There was a special siding on the up line where lamb carcasses, freshly slaughtered in the nearby 'killing house', were loaded onto trains to be taken up-country. At this time the area now occupied by the milk factory, as locals call it, and the playing fields was known as Hicks Moor with Hicks slaughterhouse situated close to the railway line. The trade in lamb carcasses continued from May to September. Live cattle and pigs were brought in to the local market, and transported out again, by train. The narrow river bridge between the station and the town must have been jammed with conflicting flows of livestock just as it is now with cars. The site of the market is now a car park, but there are still rings and chains in the enclosing walls where once cattle were tethered.

In its heyday this station was a busy place. Several porters as well as a booking clerk and station master were needed to deal with the passengers. There were three signalmen and two men in the goods yard, and the adjacent railway workshops employed up to a hundred men. The railway was the largest employer in the town, and with the trade it attracted the community must have thrived in this period. Stories of eccentric characters still survive. There was the porter called Albert, otherwise known as Hop-along because he used to hop along to the nearby Globe Inn between trains. In contrast to Albert was the ticket collector who was so polite he became a legend. As he took the tickets he would raise his cap with a 'Than-kew' which became well imitated by all the regulars. There was another local man who, early in every spring, would wait on the footbridge until the platform was full of up-country folk waiting for their connections. At the right moment he would

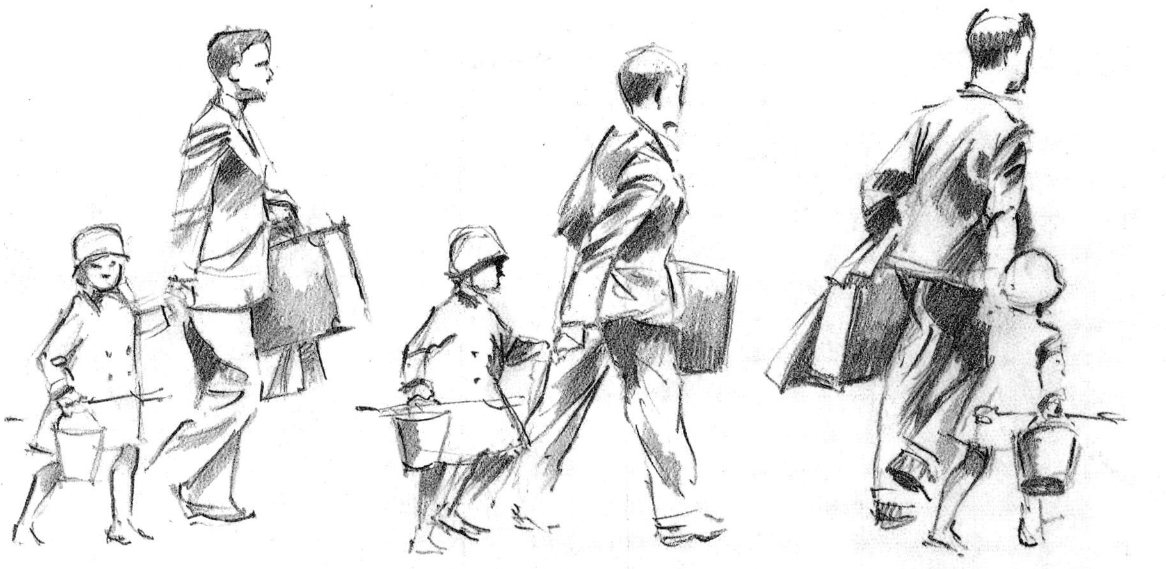

From video of Schools TV prog - sequence of 'walking figures' - station location

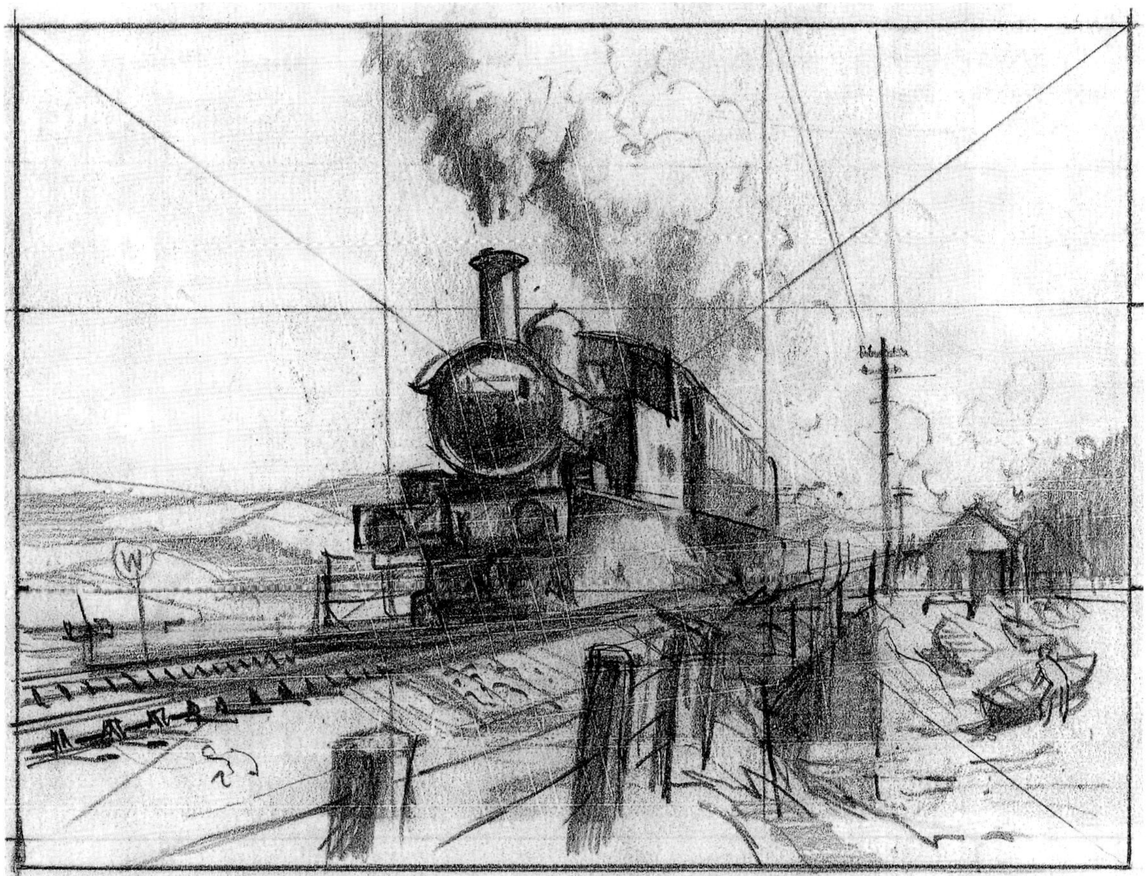

Sketch for 'Leaving Golant' 1400 class engine.

call 'Cuckoo', as real as the bird sound could be. This would cause great excitement on the platform and perhaps resulted in many letters to *The Times*! This performance went on for years in every spring and was a source of great delight to the locals.

During the Second World War large numbers of American servicemen were billeted round the town and there was much rail activity leading up to the D-Day embarkation from the Fowey estuary. Although the number of goods sidings had steadily increased over the years to deal with the variety of traffic, new sidings were built on the down side of the station funded, it was said, by the Americans to accommodate the anticipated activity. There was never again to be a time when all these goods sidings were needed. The bypass road in Lostwithiel had been opened in 1939 and after the war, with road connections improved, the decline of the railway system began.

At Lostwithiel a line branches off to Fowey. It follows a perfect riverside route down towards the estuary where for decades ships have collected their cargoes of china clay. The clay was once transported mainly by rail from the quarries around the St Austell area. The clay trains are now the only rolling stock permitted on this beautiful branch line, except for the odd special when ornithologists can delight in the close proximity to the river as the line runs down towards the sea.

An auto-train used to run regularly on this line. A timetable for 1909 shows five trains a day running in each direction and by 1932 this service had increased to ten on weekdays and twelve on Saturdays. The train was known locally as the Rattler and amongst the regular passengers were those local children who had been 'lucky' enough to pass the 11 Plus to Fowey Grammar School. It is difficult to imagine a better start or finish to a school day than a trip on a steam-hauled train down a picturesque riverside line to the delightful town of Fowey. No doubt these pleasures became commonplace with familiarity and perhaps it was only when the line was closed to passengers that people appreciated what had been.

Apart from locals who used the line it was the route for holidaymakers staying at the Fowey Hotel, who would change at Lostwithiel from their mainline trains from Paddington. Prior to the Fowey branch closure there was a public enquiry.

To justify the closure decision passenger figures were produced by the enquiry inspector, and apparently it was only later that local people realised the figures comprised only the mainline passengers who changed at Lostwithiel for Fowey. The number of local travellers for whom the branch was the only connection with Fowey had not been included. But objection came too late to save the line.

Even after the Fowey branch was closed mainline trains continued to stop at Lostwithiel until the 1970s, but gradually the service decreased. By this time locals were preferring to use cars to travel up to Plymouth or down to Truro and there were seldom many people waiting on the platform. The engineering works had long gone, moving down to the larger sheds at St Blazey, and there was not much activity compared with the old days.

So the prestigious 125s rush through Lostwithiel now, to be picked up at Bodmin Road for Paddington or Penzance, and the bus-like Sprinters are the only stopping trains. But at least this station has survived, and enough of its past can still be detected from the remaining bare bones to remind us of the important role it once played in the life of this town.

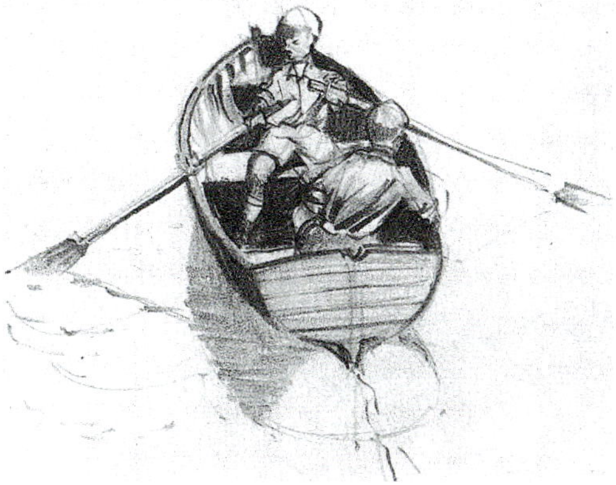

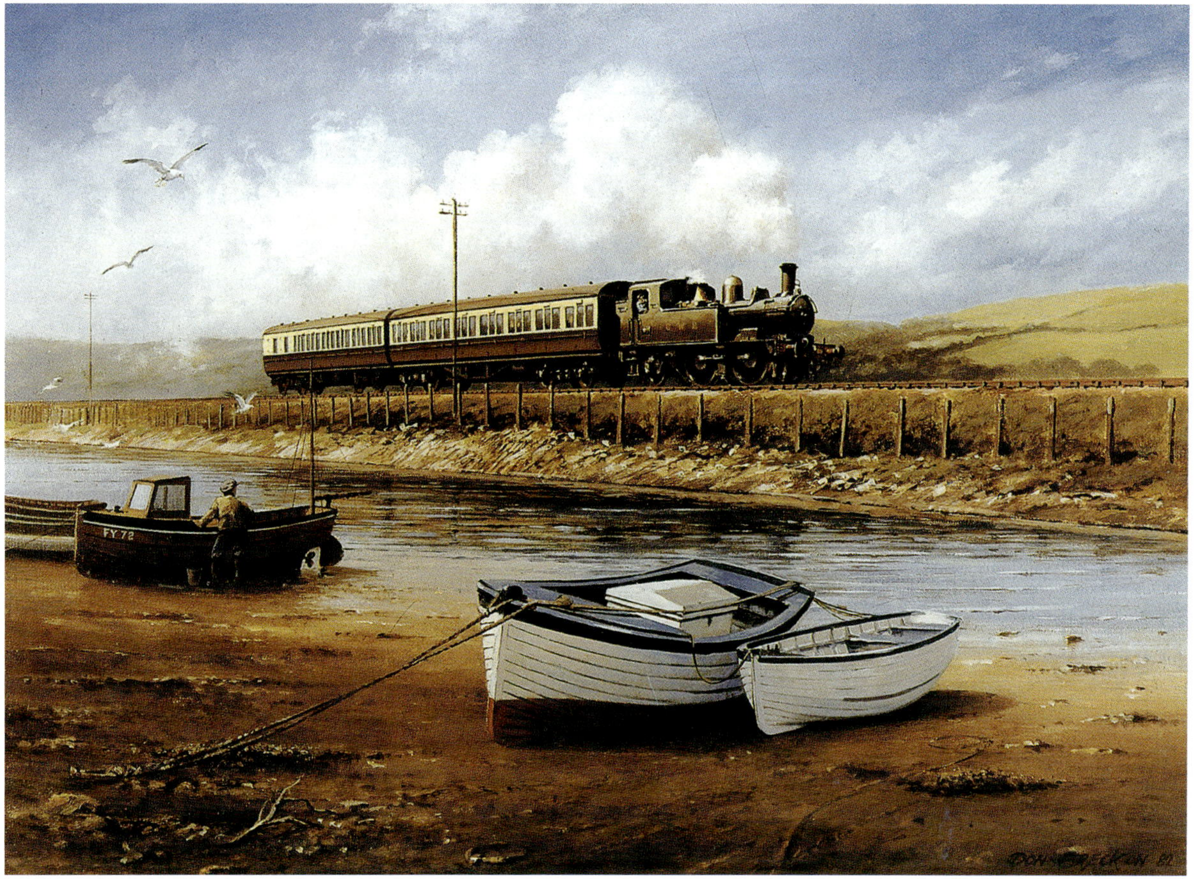

Train to Fowey (1982)
The train from Lostwithiel to Fowey approaches Golant beside the tidal estuary of the River Fowey.

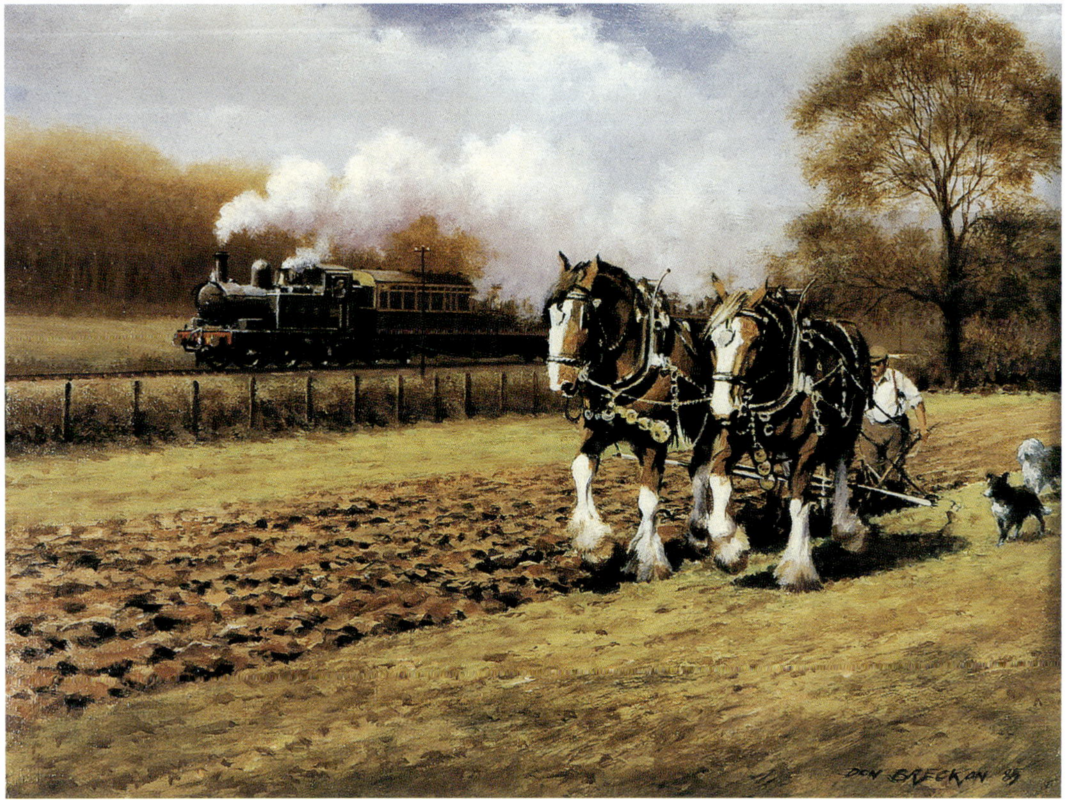

Ploughing (1985)
GWR 0-4-2T of the 1400 class and auto-trailer passing horses at work with the plough.

Lostwithiel Station in the 1950s (opposite)
Castle class 4-6-0 No 5041 Tiverton Castle *rolls into Lostwithiel at the head of a Plymouth train as the connecting branchline train to Fowey takes water at the end of the down platform. The building in the left foreground was demolished in 1976 and the main building to the right was dismantled in 1981.*

Before British Rail demolished the building to the left on the down platform of the station I wandered in through the door of the waiting-room. Inside was an atmosphere which carried me back many years to the railway journeys of my youth. The horsehair sofas, the old posters, and a fire crackling in the grate were all straight from the age of steam.

Stepping out again into the 1970s and looking up at the splendid awning cantilevered out over the mainline platform and the Fowey branch line on the other side, I took a photograph standing where the old footbridge had crossed the line. The photograph duly went into my reference files and from time to time I looked at it as the basis for a painting. It was incomplete, however, as it did not include the main station building on the up side and by then both buildings had been dismantled. Then along came a book by John Vaughan entitled *Diesels in the Duchy* – the only book of diesels I have – and there was a photograph of the up building at approximately the angle I wanted.

Choosing a wide 40in × 20in canvas I proceeded to weld the two views together, a rather complicated task as it turned out, but finally the picture was sketched out. The branch line train to Fowey was going to be out of sight except for a sliver on the extreme left and I felt that this was a pity. Then I discovered that it took water at the end of the platform so I placed the train there, leaving me a space to include the china clay wagons in the siding beyond. Now I had to think about the mainline train. Too close and it would obscure the main building; too far back and it would be only a head-on view. After much shunting about I finally decided on the best position.

The figures were chosen carefully to help the composition. If the porter to the right was moving forward it would suggest that the train was about to stop and was not just passing through. The man at the ticket window is the only figure in shadow on the right and echoes the figures on the left in the shadow of the awning. On the other hand there is the contrast of the dark family group silhouetted against the light under the awning with the sunlit couple to the right against the dark of the palm trees. I couldn't resist the train spotters – two younger excitable ones and the lad, head in hands, who does not seem impressed by the sight of a Castle class locomotive. Or perhaps he is dreaming of being an engine driver himself.

One figure featured prominently for most of the working time on the painting but, sadly, had to be painted out. A young lady in a white dress was sitting on the platform seat in the foreground, but she was 'throwing' the composition so she had to leave!

Lostwithiel Station 1950s was included in an exhibition in the town when Lostwithiel celebrated the 800th anniversary of the granting of its charter, and I like to think it brought back a few memories to those who remember the station in its heyday. It is also pleasing that the painting is now owned by a local man who was a wartime evacuee to the town and who first stepped off the train from Paddington to start his new life just a few yards into this scene.

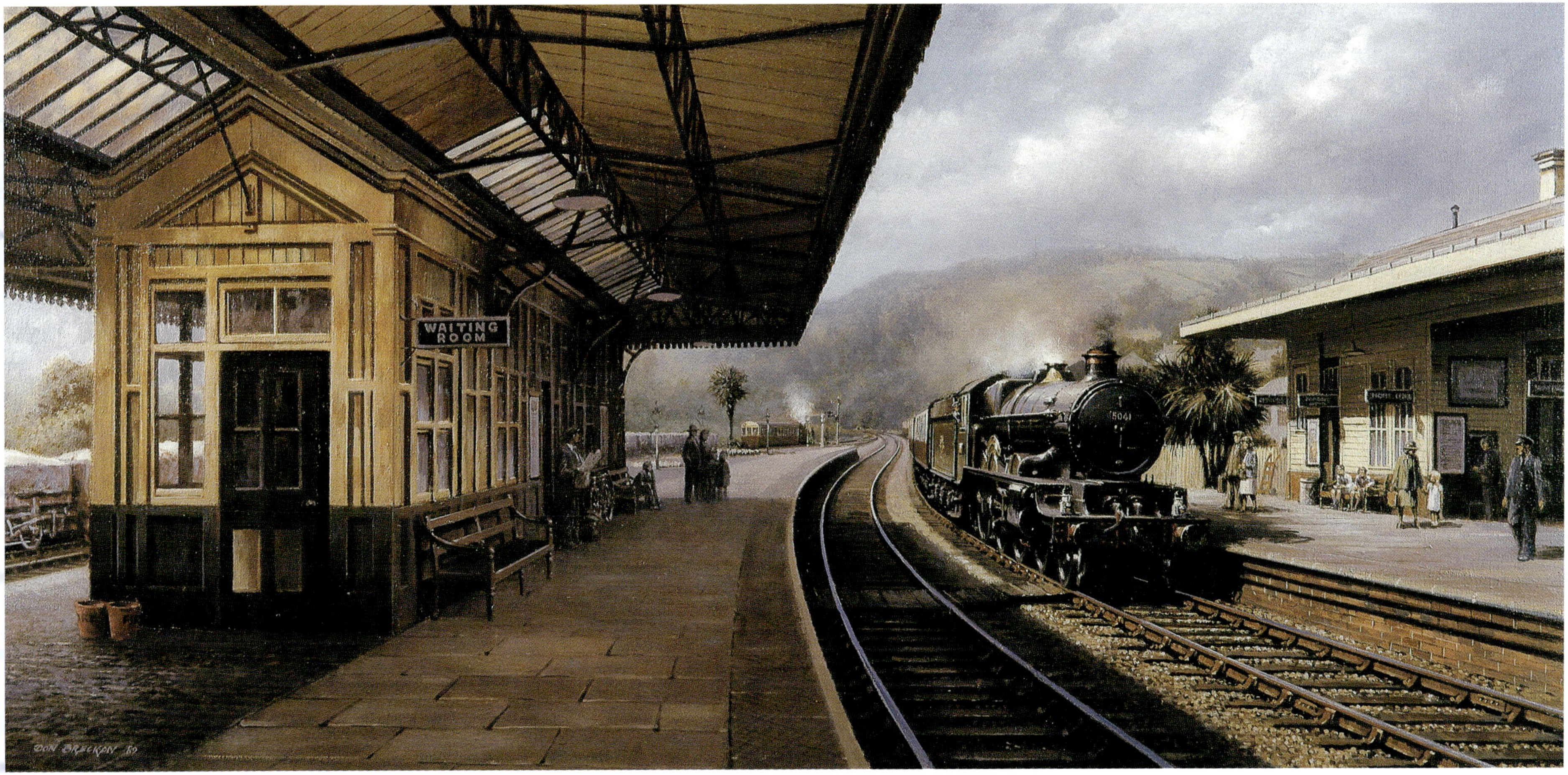
WAITING ROOM

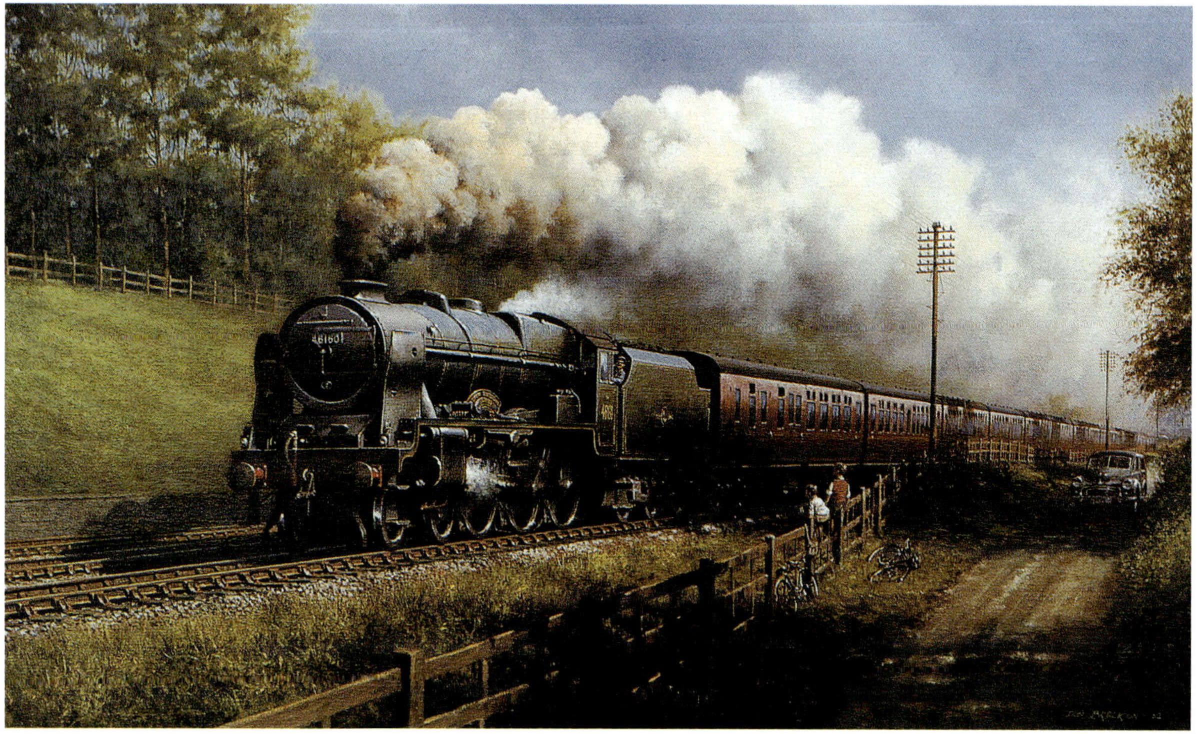

Queen Victoria's Rifleman (1982)
Midland Region's rebuilt Royal Scot class No 46160 Queen Victoria's Rifleman *is shown with two trainspotters and an approaching Morris Minor Traveller.*

Winter Express
GWR King class locomotive No 6023 King Edward II *rushes through a snow-covered landscape at the head of an express. On the line beside the track a local man pauses in his chat with the postman, who is driving a Morris GPO van, to look at the passing train. No 6023 was built in 1930 and withdrawn in 1962, having been fitted with a double chimney five years earlier. After twenty-two years in Barry scrapyard the locomotive was bought for eventual restoration to full working order.*

I was commissioned to paint a King class locomotive heading an express through a snow-covered landscape with a postal van as a secondary point of interest. Though to me they lack the elegance of the Castles there is no denying the powerful appearance of the Kings, so I decided to pull the locomotive forward in the painting to emphasise this quality. To offset the rushing train I halted the van in the lane and introduced a conversation with a local man – perhaps about weather conditions! The cottage on the right followed logically, providing a link with either the man or the postal delivery.

The postal service has been associated with the railways since 1830 and until quite recently postal workers were very much part of the railway scene. Day and night the mail would arrive and depart from stations in the little red Post Office vans, and platform trolleys loaded with sacks of letters and parcels would be waiting on the platform. In my National Service days I frequently waited on station platforms in the middle of the night, along with others, for a train back to camp. It was often chilly and our spirits were at a low ebb but we were cheered a little by groups of postal workers gathered around their trolleys laughing and joking. How could anyone be so cheerful at 2am?

The Post Office trains had something special about them. Halted at a level crossing one night I was surprised to see one rushing through, the lights of the signalbox flicking across the blank coaches with the letters 'Royal Mail' on each one. John Grierson's classic documentary film *Night Mail* (1936) about the down West Coast Postal was a record of the working of these trains. In the film the lineside exchange of mail at speed was shown in full detail. Apparatus on the coach and beside the track enabled bags of mail to be collected and dropped off as the train rushed past. This came to an end in 1971 but the Great Western Railway Centre at Didcot has assembled a set of equipment for public demonstration of this once-routine link between the railway and the Royal Mail.

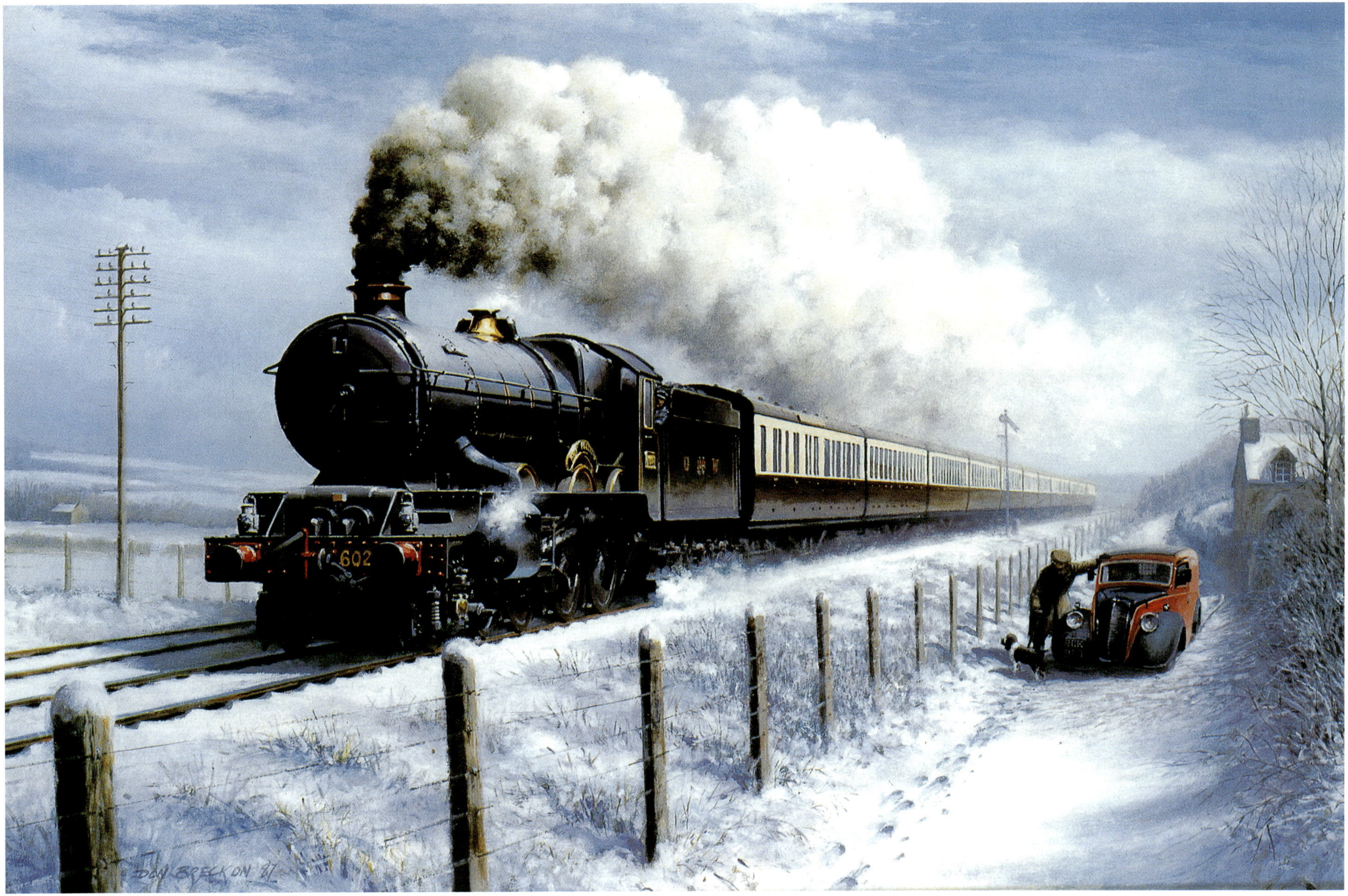
602
DON BRECKON

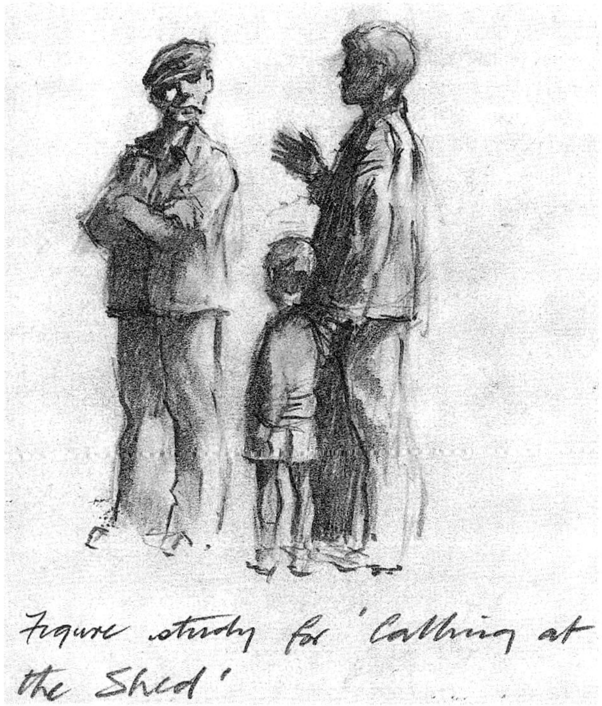

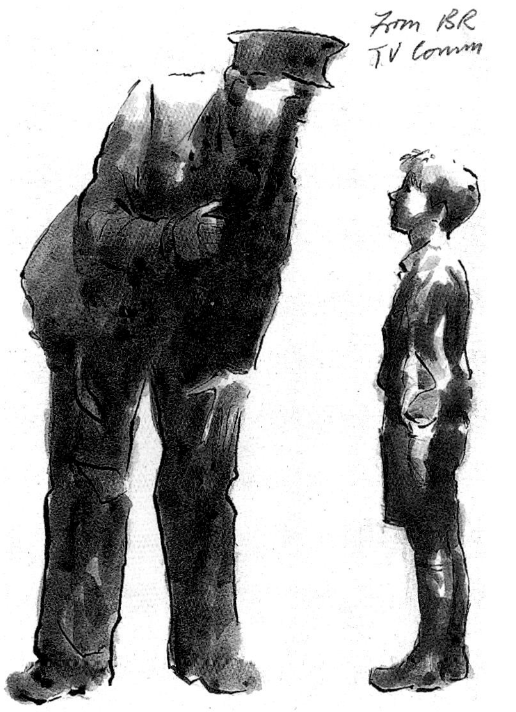

Visitors to the Shed

A father asks permission for his son to look over the engine at the small country engine shed at Tetbury in Gloucestershire. Down the track a single coach is waiting at the branch terminus for the 1400 class 0-4-2T No 1404 to collect it for the seven mile run to Kemble on the main line. Tetbury station and the branch closed in 1964.

Branch line engines were usually based at the terminus for operating convenience and the small country shed seemed to fit the meaning of the word much more than the large sheds found near mainline stations. In fact the appeal lay in its size, the little shed not overwhelming the surroundings but in time being embraced by the countryside in which it was built.

I chose Tetbury as a subject because the station building could be included in the scene and the sloping field behind the shed gave a good backdrop. An added bonus was that the 1400 class engines worked on the line so I could have one standing in the sunshine ready for duty. These engines had real character, being rather like the locomotive equivalent of an Austin Seven or a Morris Minor! With their tall chimneys they seemed old-fashioned, though they were only built in 1935 as a development of an earlier design.

The engine and shed were sketched in with the station in the distance. Figures would bring the scene to life and the driver and fireman were the obvious choices. I decided, however, that a visitor to the group would add a new aspect, perhaps linking the foreground to the distant station. Out of this came the idea of the father and son, who as outsiders bring a new dimension to the scene in their relationship to the crew of the engine.

'All right if the lad looks around?' might be the opening gambit, or 'Can the boy have a look?', with the man trying to sound as casual as possible, hiding his own curiosity and excitement which may well have been greater than the boy's. Many will remember their fathers saying this at some time in their childhood as they strolled into an exciting place previously 'out of bounds' to the public. Of course there was always the risk of refusal and of the son realising that Dad was not all-powerful after all, but it was usually worth the chance.

In this scene the situation hangs, I think, in the balance. Father and son have already strayed across the tracks and if the old driver is a stickler for the rules he may give them an abrupt answer. The fireman looks on with interest to see how his mate will react.

The Tetbury branch line had an interestingly named halt a little to the north of Tetbury. Driving near the town I saw a sign pointing across the fields to Trouble House Halt. It sounded just the place where a group of passengers in a 1940s British film would be stranded on a wild night. Michael Flanders and Donald Swann wrote a song in the sixties called 'Slow Train' which was about the closing of branchline stations and they included that intriguing name – Trouble House Halt.

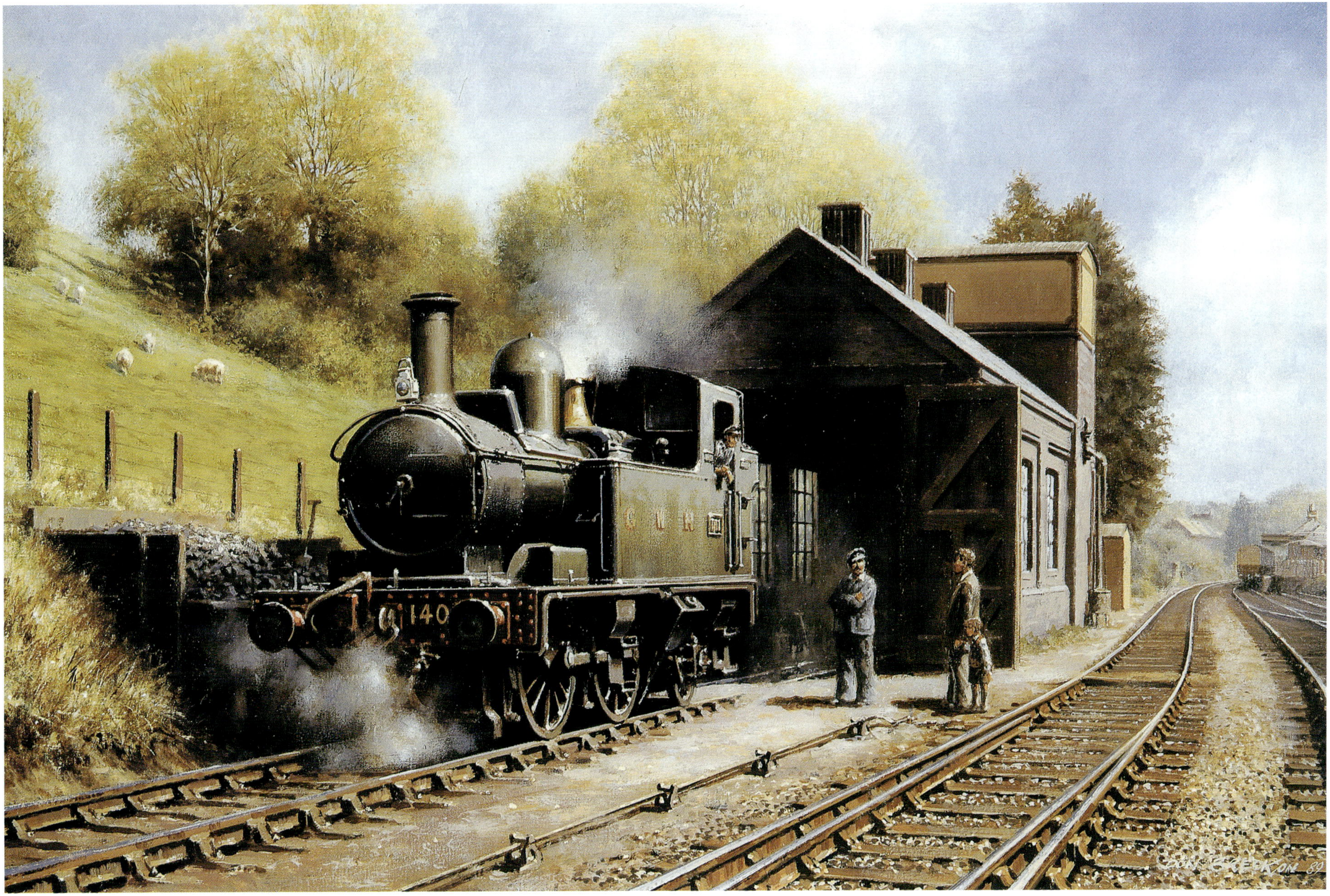
G W R
140

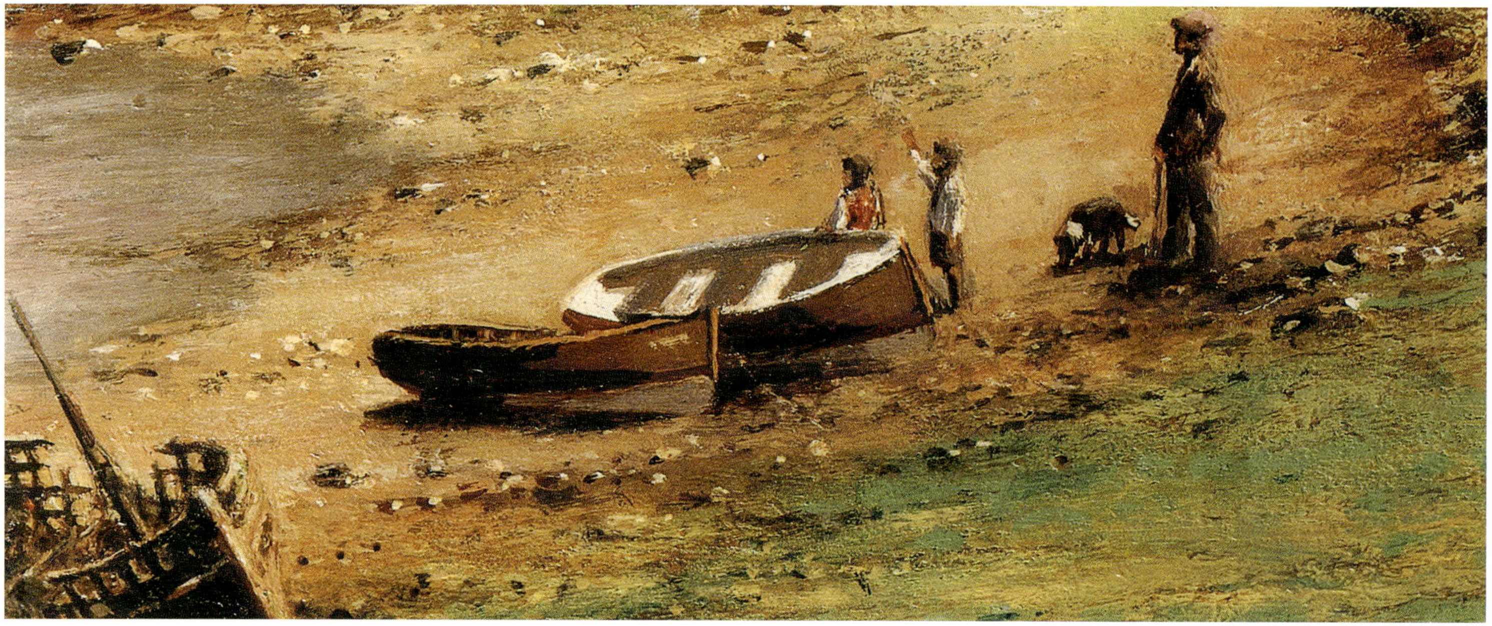

Skye Boat Train

An LMS Black Five 4-6-0 heads the boat train to Kyle of Lochalsh along the shore of Loch Carron near Strome Ferry. After the 82-mile rail journey from Inverness the train would connect with the boat at Kyle of Lochalsh for the crossing to the Isle of Skye. The Black Fives worked both freight and passenger trains on the line from the 1930s to the end of steam in the 1960s.

The scenery of the west Highlands of Scotland is magnificent. Lochs and mountains create views of a grandeur which stirs the emotions. My mother was born in Portree on the Isle of Skye so I have a special affection for this part of the world.

The Victorian railway builders must have viewed the landscape with considerable apprehension, however, as they struggled to build their line towards the Western Isles. In fact the Dingwall and Skye Railway made a temporary stop when it reached Strome Ferry on the shore of Loch Carron. It was ten miles short of its destination at Kyle of Lochalsh but the money ran out, due largely to an enforced detour into the hills north of Strathpeffer to Raven Rock. The landowners of Strathpeffer barred the railway from intruding into their privacy!

Nevertheless, determined to connect with the isles, the railwaymen built a pier at Strome from which a steamer service was operated to the Hebrides by the Highland Railway, of which the Dingwall and Skye was a part. This situation was to last for twenty-three years, until competition from a rival company forced the completion of the line. In 1893 the North British Railway, bitter rival of the Highland, started to build a line from Fort William to Mallaig, thus creating a more direct route of access to Skye. The Highland Railway had to complete those last ten miles to counter this threat to its service. It was to prove the most expensive piece of railway engineering of its day. After four years, 31 rock cuttings, and 29 bridges, and at a cost of £20,000 per mile, the first train ran through to Kyle of Lochalsh.

With the grouping of Britain's railways in 1923 the Kyle line became part of the LMS and the Mallaig line part of the LNER, so the rivalry continued, though less intensely. With nationalisation both lines became part of British Rail and began to decline as road improvements attracted traffic away from the rail routes. The shadow of closure hung over them. It is perhaps ironic that this new emphasis on roads and the resulting increase in tourism may have opened a new future for the railways of north-west Scotland. Steam trains have returned to the Mallaig line and rail tour specials are organised regularly from Inverness to Kyle of Lochalsh.

I have wanted to paint the Scottish railway scene for a long time and after a holiday in this area I came back inspired! A photograph by John Goss gave the exact location but having started the painting, it had to wait until I returned to the scene the following year before it could make progress. The favourite viewpoint for this part of the line is from land belonging to a farmer of rare breeds. When I asked permission to cross the land for a better view I was directed towards the llama! 'All the photographers find that a good location.' I got the references I needed and managed to avoid the llama. Even then the painting was not straightforward because the landscape dominated the train more than in any other railway painting I had previously tackled. I began to understand how those Highland Railway engineers had felt!

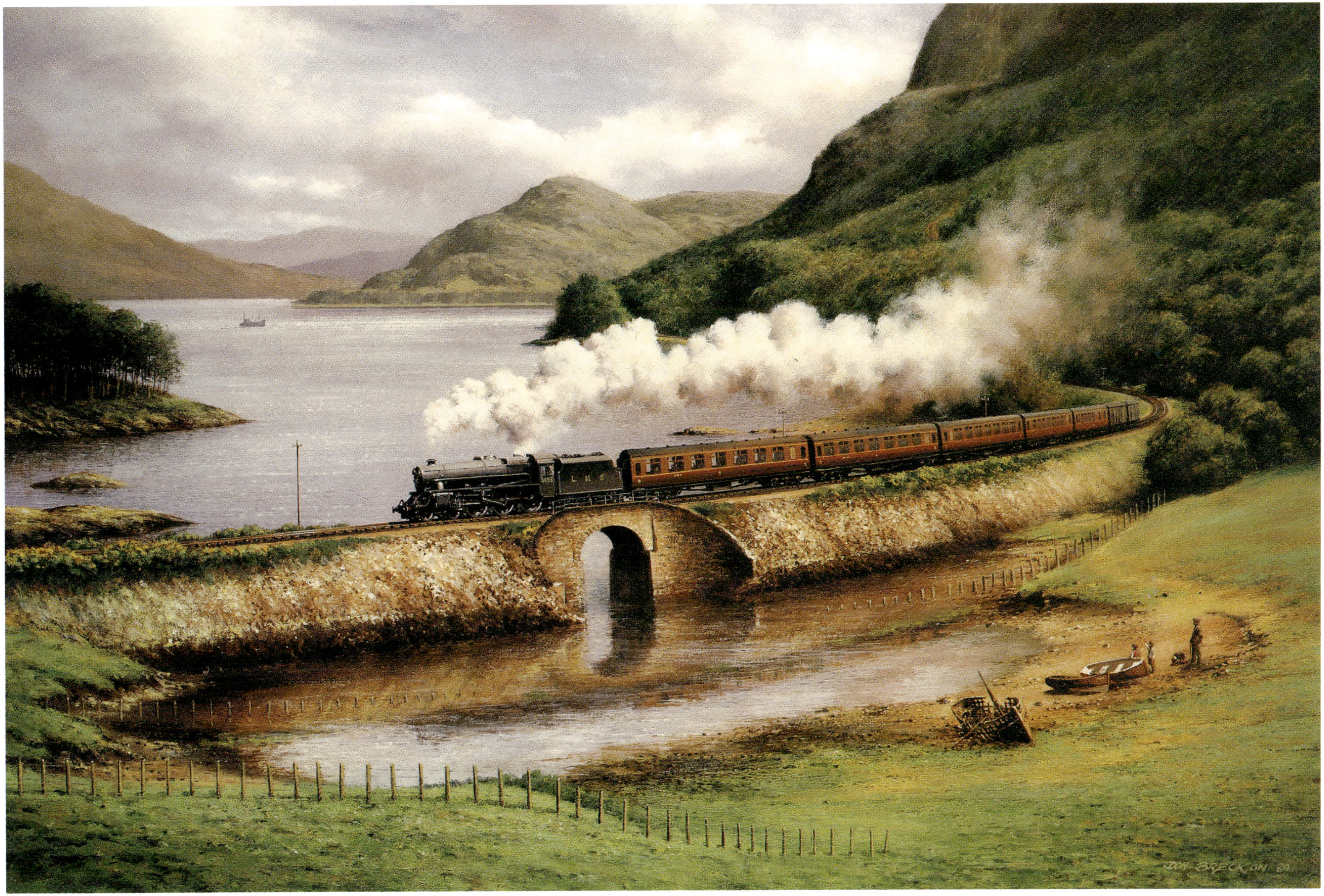
DON BRECKON 89

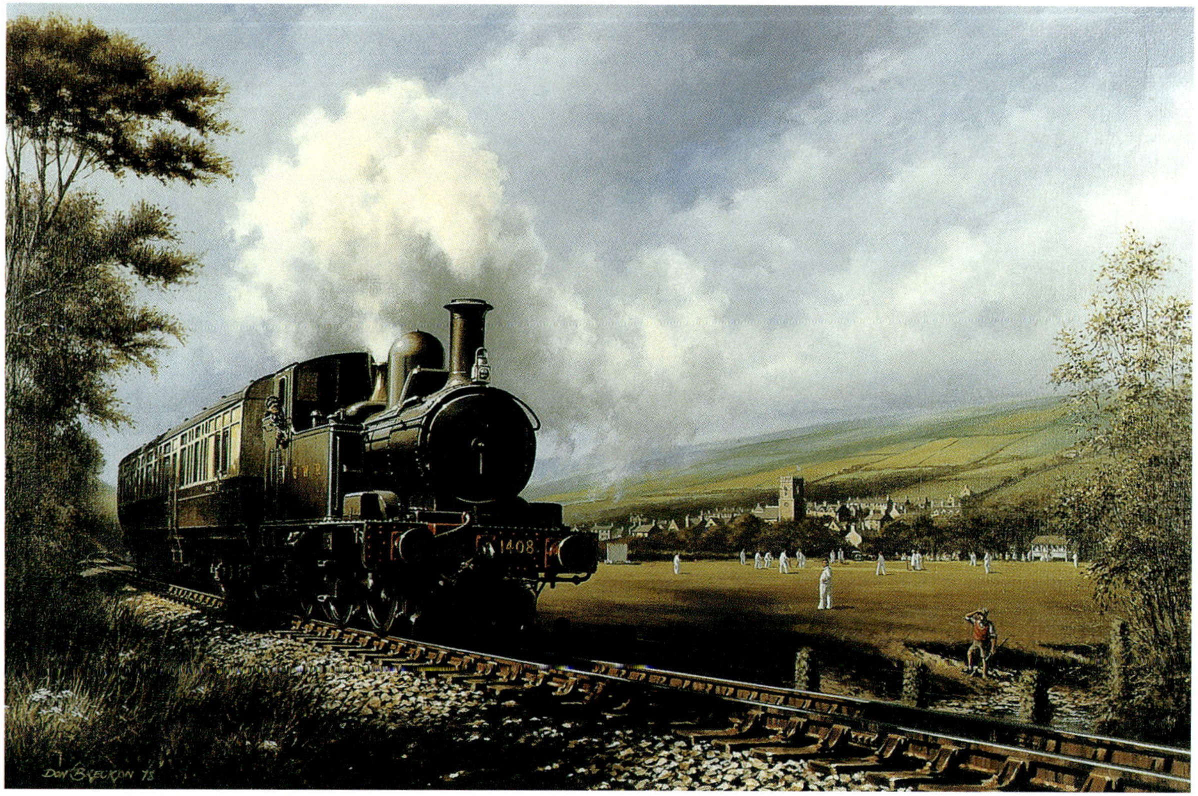

The Cricket Match (1978)
A branch line train headed by 0-4-2T No 1408 of the GWR passes as the village cricket match is in progress.

My father was a Yorkshireman and a keen cricketer. My own involvement with the game was limited by an inability to bowl, catch or hit the ball, but despite this handicap I enjoyed playing 'cricket' on the waste ground near our home, and frequently watched him play the 'proper' game. So the images of white-clad figures on a green field with blue sky beyond has a special significance for me.

Even today the village cricket match still retains the special atmosphere which seems to belong to a more leisurely age. Nothing very dramatic seems to happen but it is a heart-warming sight which epitomises English village life in summer. Imagine the old branch-line railway passing close enough to glimpse the action. For a few moments the train would become a travelling grandstand as the passengers watched the bowler pace up for the next delivery. His arm would swing over, and – the scene would disappear behind the trees!

This is the atmosphere I wanted to capture in this composition. The train would be in the foreground with the field beyond but well to the far left so the detail of the cricketers and the distant village could be seen. By losing part of the train in shadow and lightening the field in contrast, the problem of the relationship between train and setting was solved. The boy in the corner of the field shades his eyes to look at the train, having been drawn away from spectating by the delights of a little stream and the railway. One player is having such a quiet time near the boundary that he is easily distracted by the passing train which is about to cross our view of the scene and obscure the match and the village. This was just the situation as I remembered it – that the cricket field was just glimpsed from the train, and soon lost to view.

When this painting was completed in 1978 it was entitled *Sunday Afternoon* and included in an exhibition in Bournemouth where it was apparently sold. I never knew where it went from there, as is so often the case, but always have referred to it as 'the cricket match painting'. I was delighted when it turned up on the market again recently, in a gallery near the south coast. I was able to see it again, and photograph it properly before it was sold. Glimpsed – but soon lost to view once more!

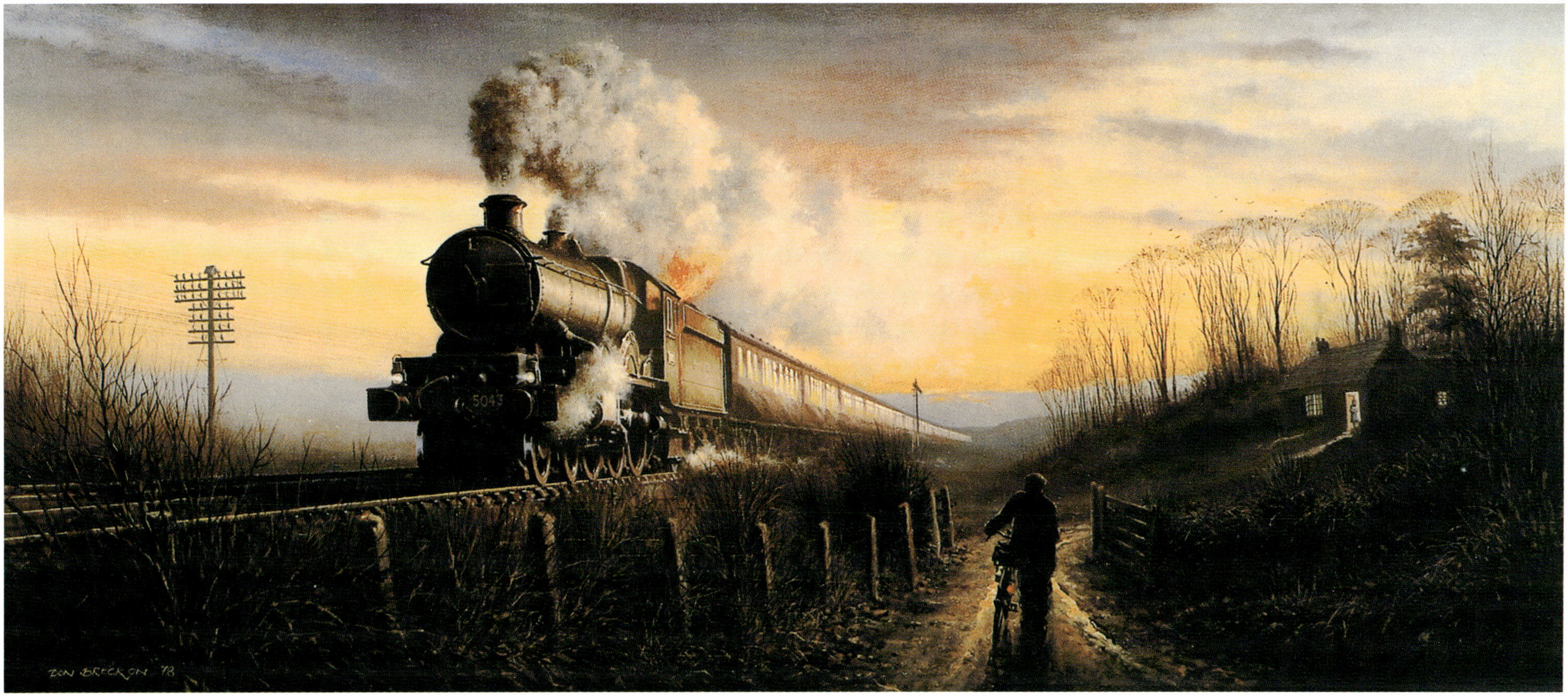

Earl of Mount Edgecumbe (1978)
Castle class 4-6-0 No 5043 Earl of Mount Edgecumbe *heads an up express at sunset.*

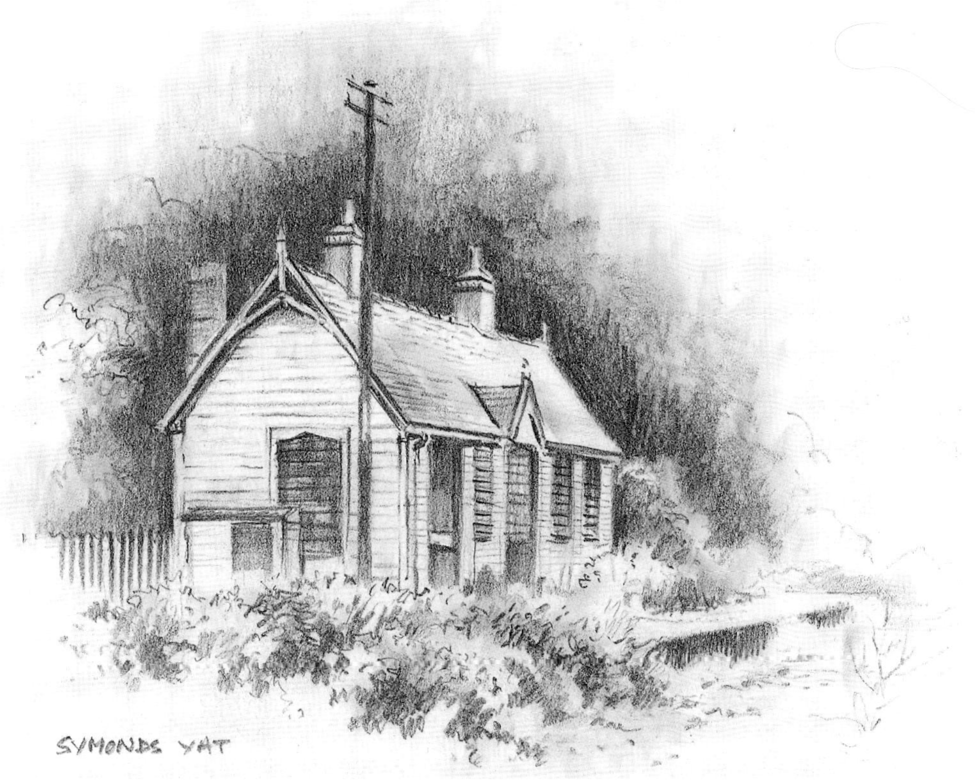

Incident at Symonds Yat

As passengers alight from the train at Symonds Yat, they are startled by the roar of aircraft engines. Three Hawker Typhoon fighter bombers sweep past over the river, making a simulated attack on the station. They carry the black and white 'invasion stripes' in preparation for service in Europe after D-Day. The train from Monmouth is headed by a 5700 class 0-6-0 pannier tank locomotive No 7771 which was built in 1931 and withdrawn in 1961.

The brief for this commission from Mr Williams was so descriptive that I can do no better than to quote it word for word.

In those days I would cycle to Symonds Yat for a good spell of spotting and to enjoy the scenery. The line was served by push-pull sets, and sometimes a railcar, with pannier-hauled goods trains. The river at this point was, and still is, very attractive with the surface broken by rocky outcrops producing small white water rapids.

The scene in the 1940s therefore was for the most part total tranquillity, the only noises being the babbling water, rustling leaves and the occasional station bell. Every now and again a burst of activity heralded the arrival of a train from Ross or Monmouth. All this in itself would qualify for a delightful study. However on this particular occasion that I recall, and which I would like you to capture, the station was occupied by a standing pannier and push-pull coach and the platform was alive with the activity of various types of passengers and staff. There were a few locals returning from shopping and, because it was market day in Ross-on-Wye, one old rustic struggling with a nanny goat whose leg was tethered to a piece of twine. There were a couple of aristocratic gentlemen with fishing gear and a serviceman on leave. Then there was myself, as usual ears and eyes agog, lapping up the scene. During the next few moments the atmosphere and character of the whole scene was transformed.

Up until that moment the only concession to the fact that a World War was in progress was the presence of the servicemen on the platform. Suddenly a different sound echoed back and forth off the walls of the valley. Around the far bend in the river, coming from the Monmouth direction, three RAF Typhoons came swooping and banking, following each other in line astern in a mock attack on the station. The planes were decorated with the distinctive black and white stripes on the underside of the wings which had been adopted as an aid to identification by the Allied forces on the ground prior to the launching of the invasion for D-Day.

By the time they drew level with the train they were only feet above the river. In a flash and with a wave from the pilots they were gone, climbing back up into the sky up the valley and out of sight. All the people in and around the train were caught in various poses of unpreparedness and their postures of reaction can be imagined. The scene settled back to normality – the hissing engine, the shuffling passengers, the doors slamming, the guard's whistle, and off the train went, down the line to Monmouth.

Preparation sketches for the painting were a confused mass of alterations as the problems of the train, the people on the platform and the planes were brought together. 'It's three pictures in one,' someone said, and they were not far wrong. The answer was to rise above the scene and look down on the train. This brought the river and the planes into view and enabled the people at the far end of the platform to play a part in the scene. Having sorted out the composition a new problem cropped up. The passengers would not be able to see the aircraft because the coach would block their view! Even the sound would have been muffled to those standing close to the train. In the end I worked on a line-of-sight policy and those standing away from the train are looking at the aircraft whilst others are busying themselves with other things – especially the man with the goat!

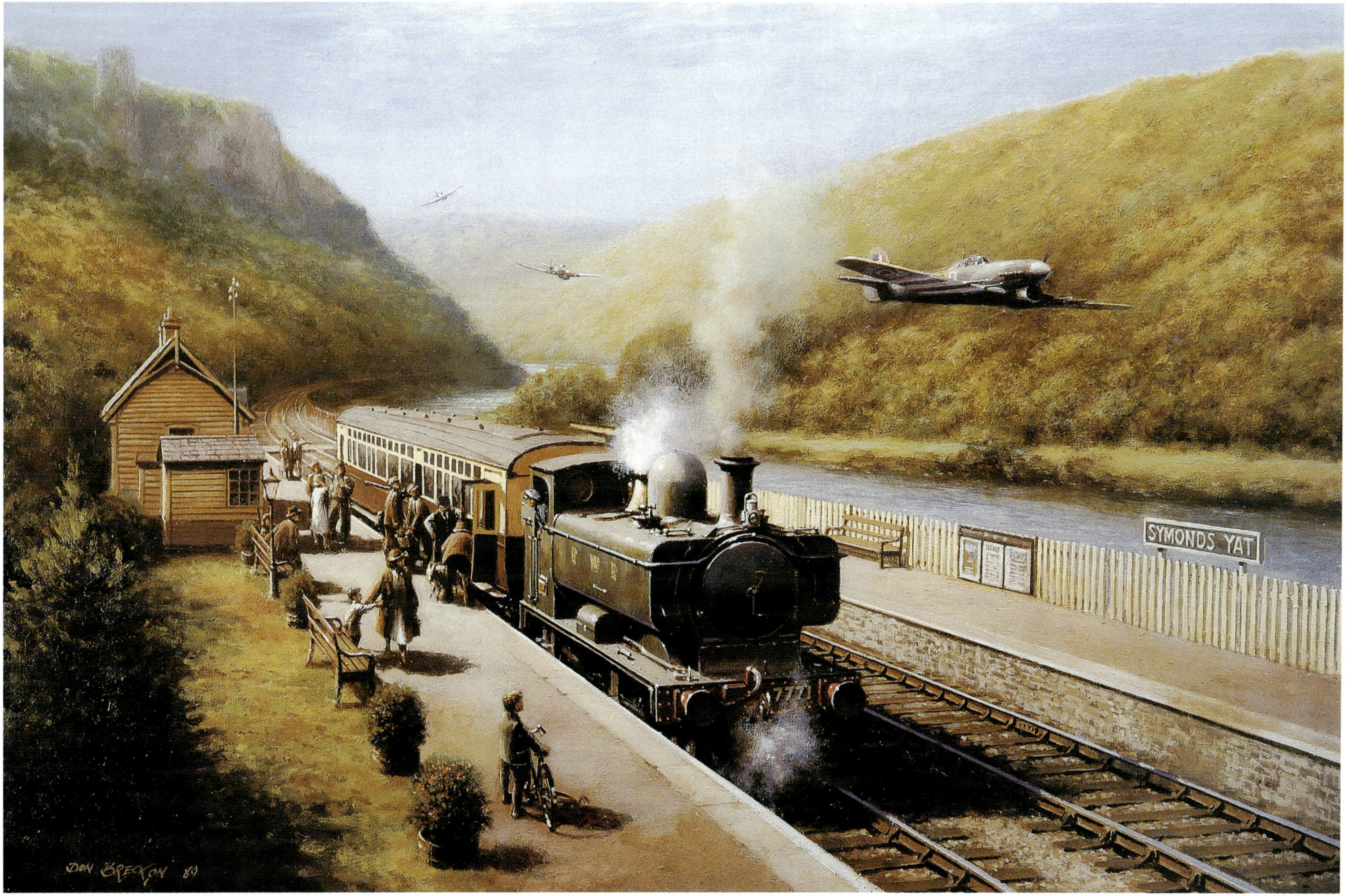
SYMONDS YAT
DON BRECKON '89

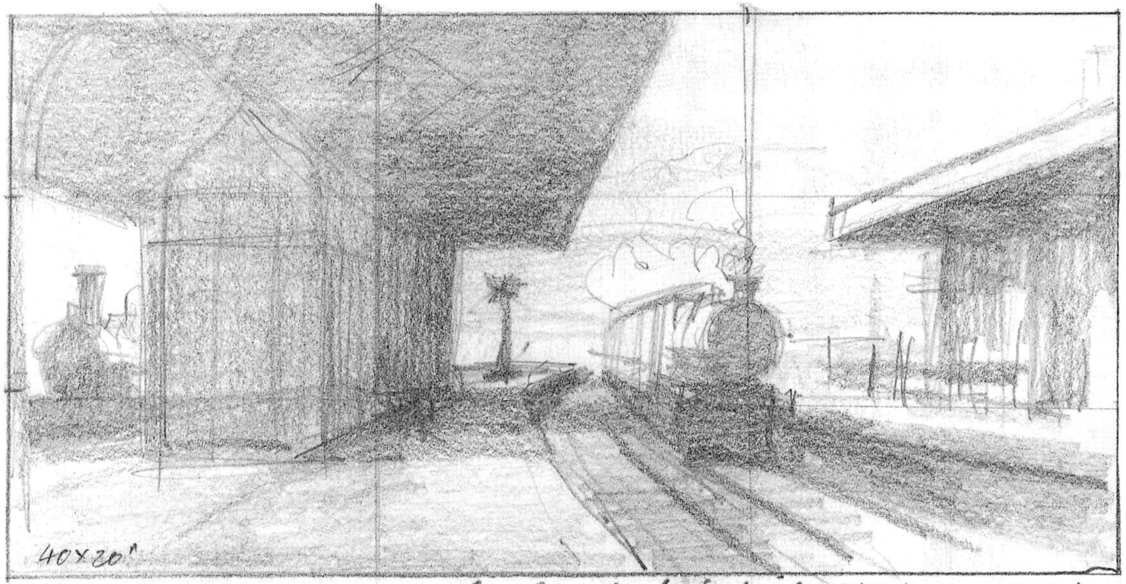

Tonal sketch layout for Lostwithiel Station 1950's

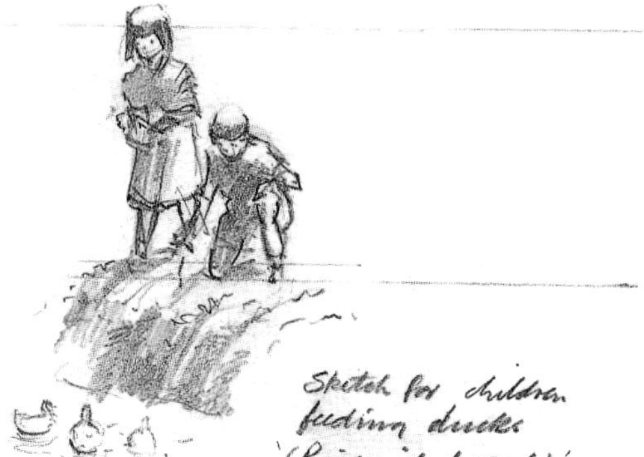

Sketch for children feeding ducks ('Riverside Local)'

WORKING DRAWINGS

Pages from my sketch books, showing some of the preparatory work for the paintings in this book.

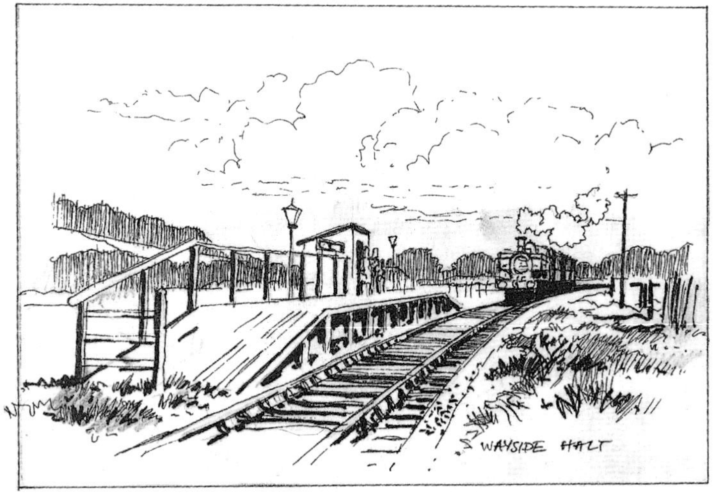

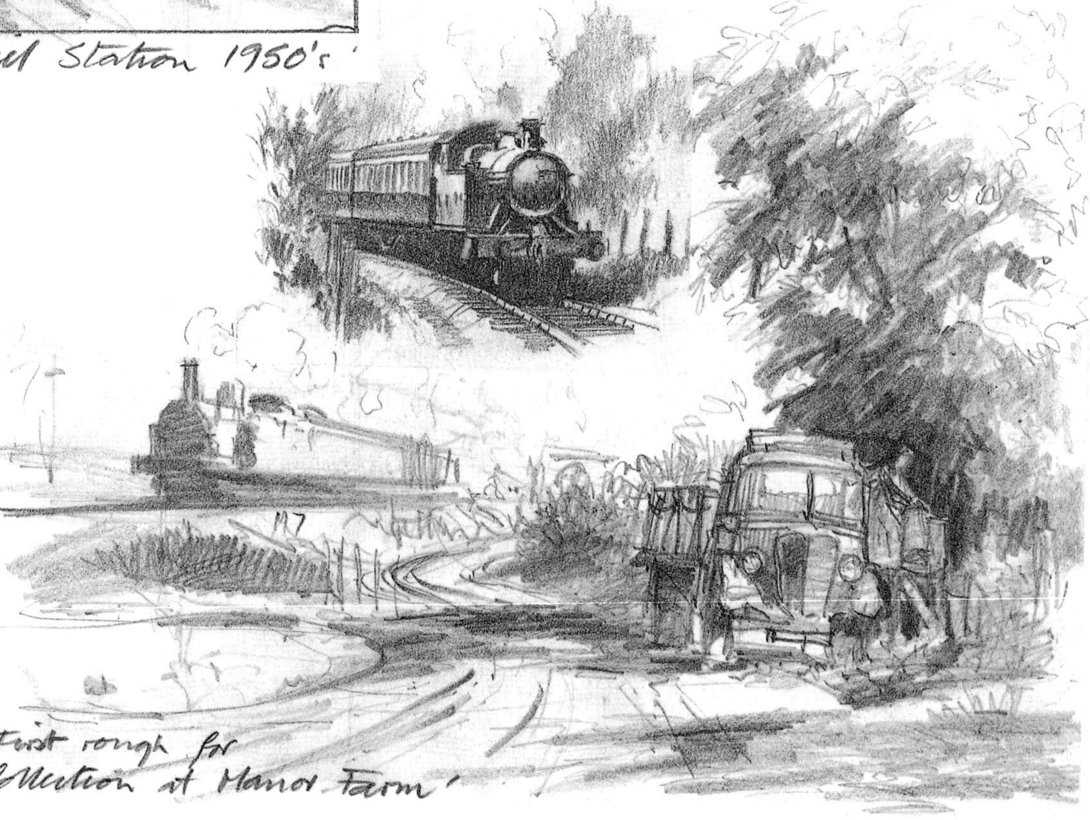

First rough for 'Collection at Manor Farm'

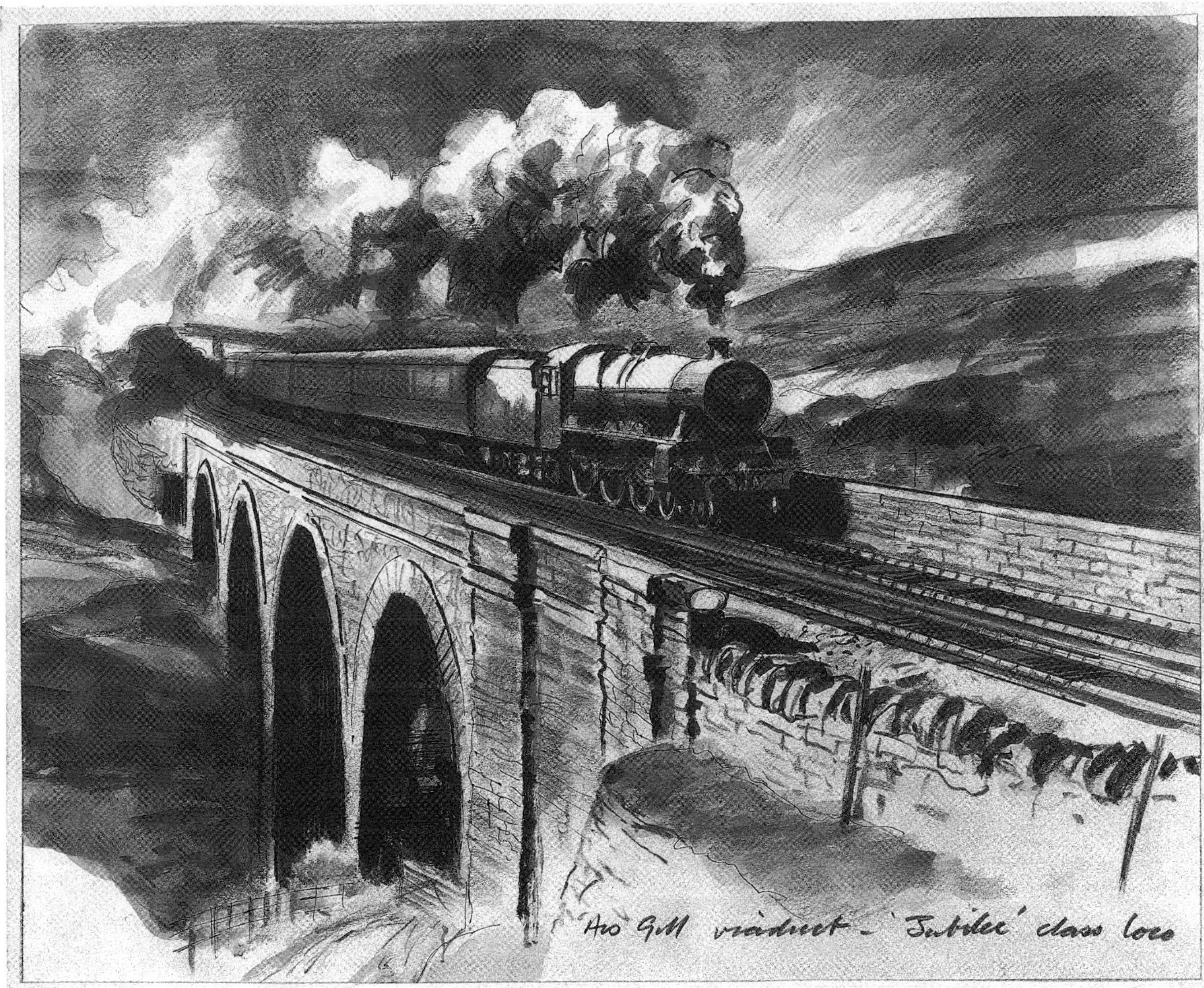
'Ais Gill viaduct – 'Jubilee' class loco

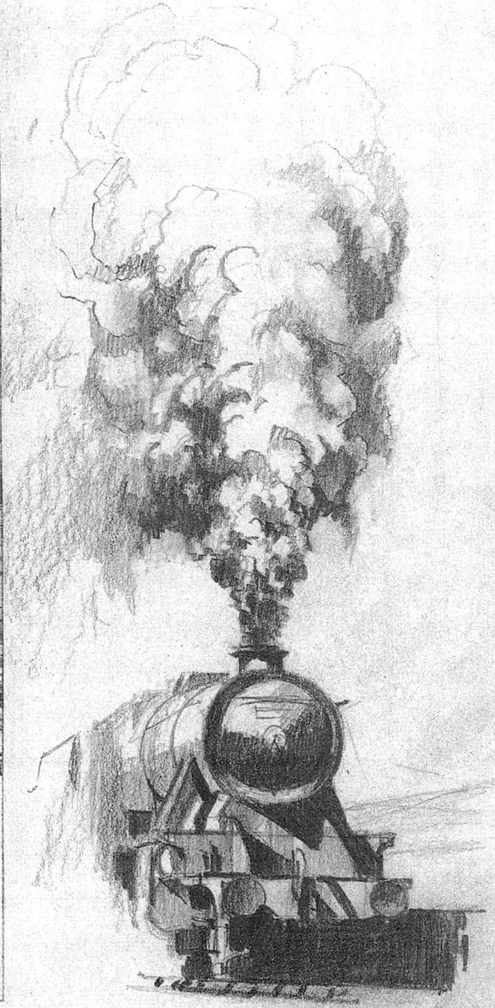

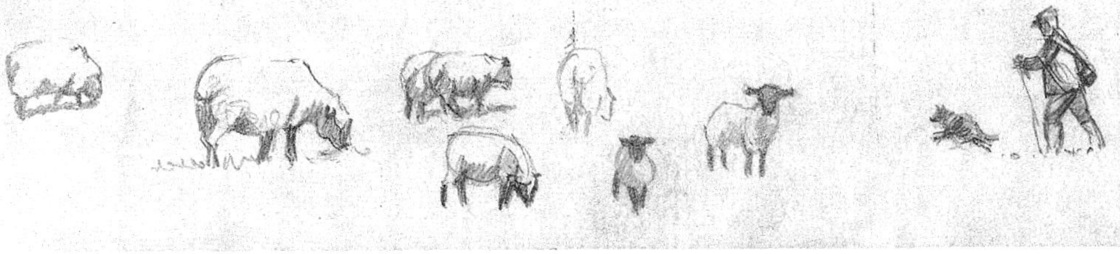

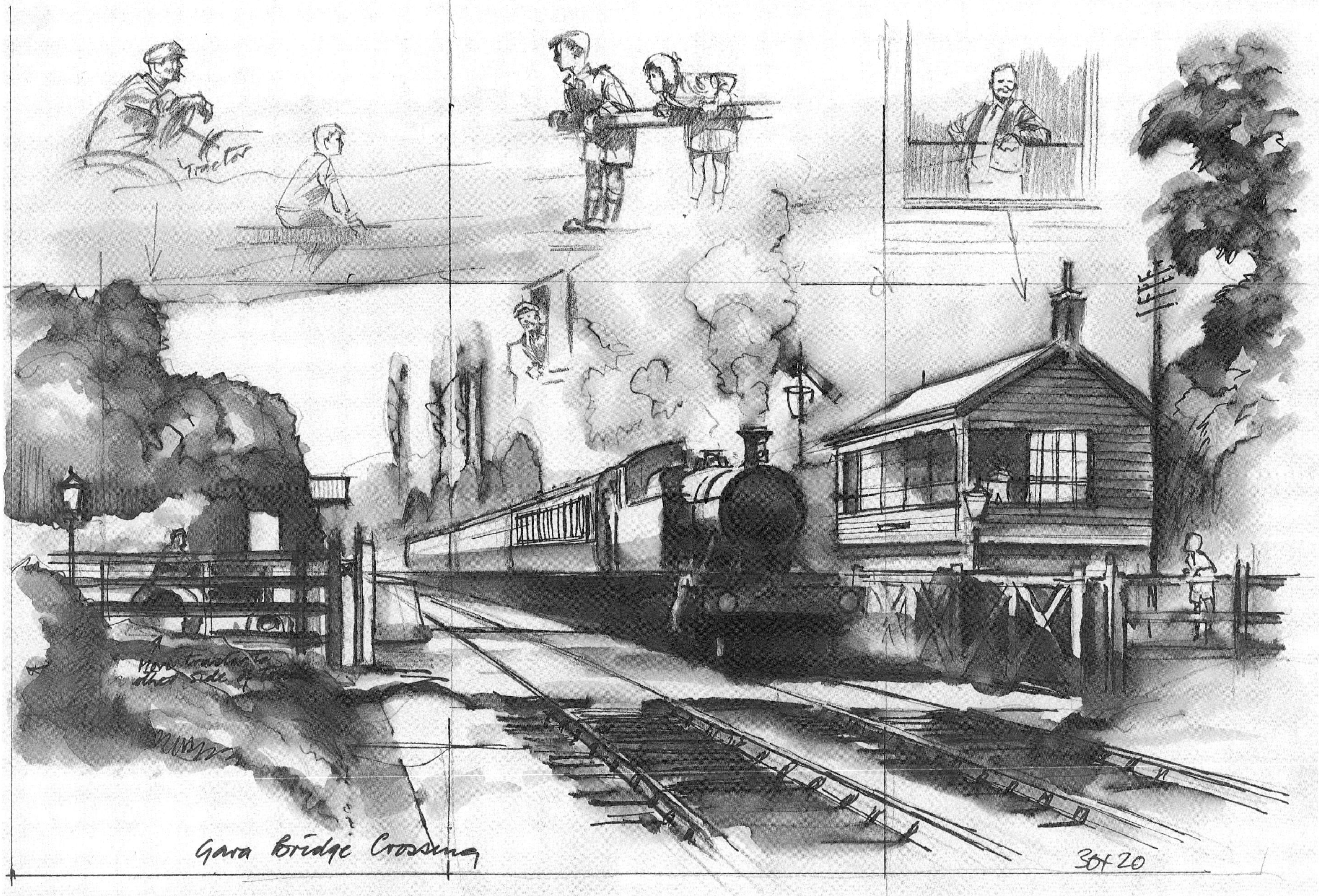
Tractor
Move tractor to
other side of
Gara Bridge Crossing

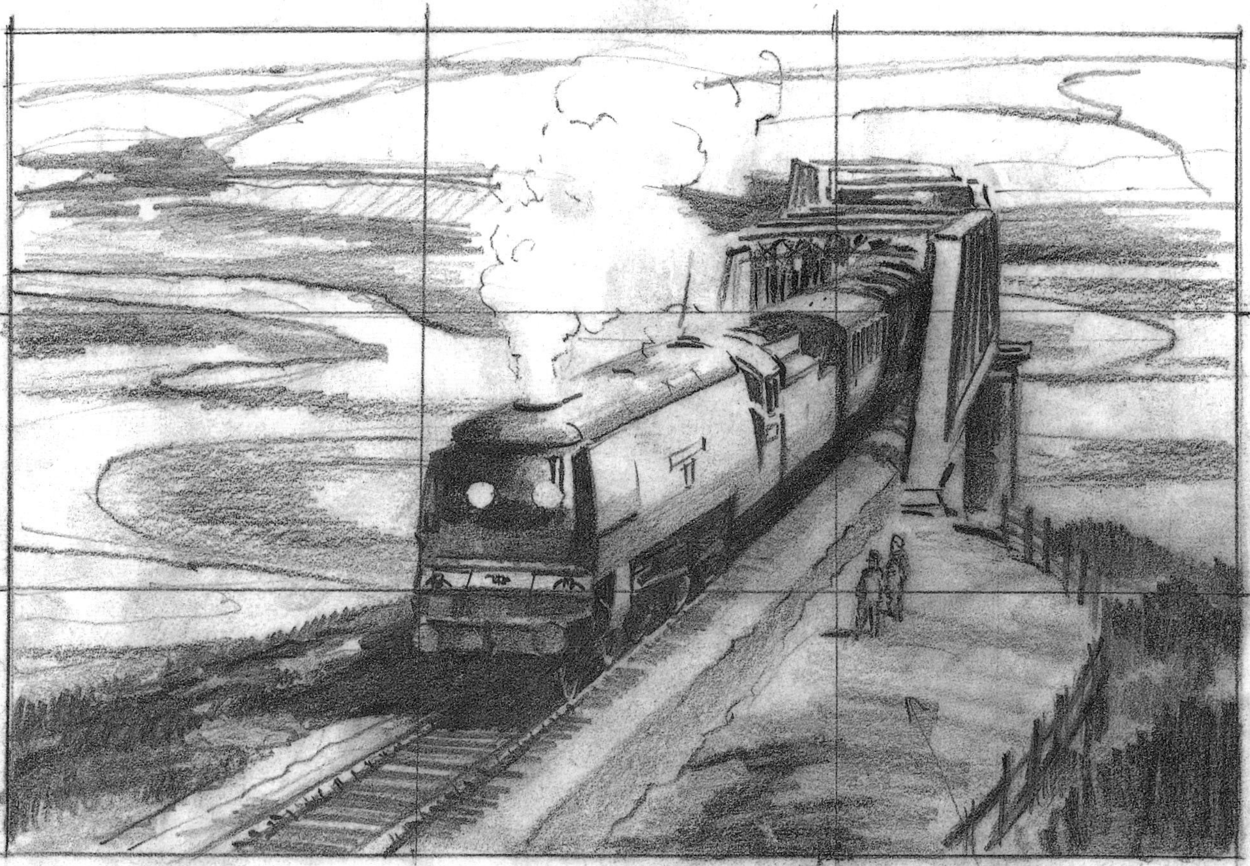

"APPROACHING PADSTOW" West Country class crossing Little Petherick Creek Bridge with train from Waterloo (Early 50's) 30 × 20"

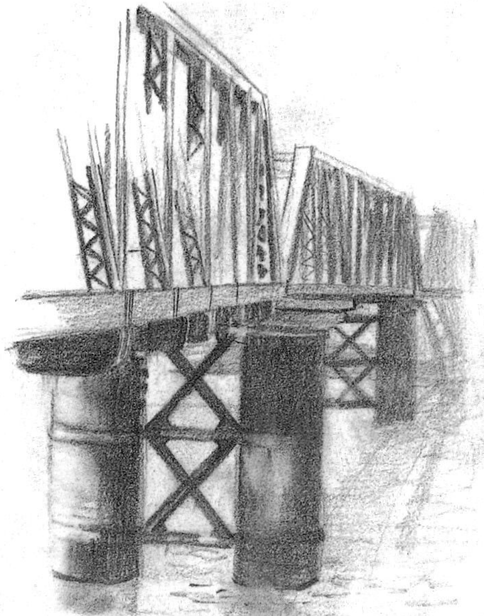

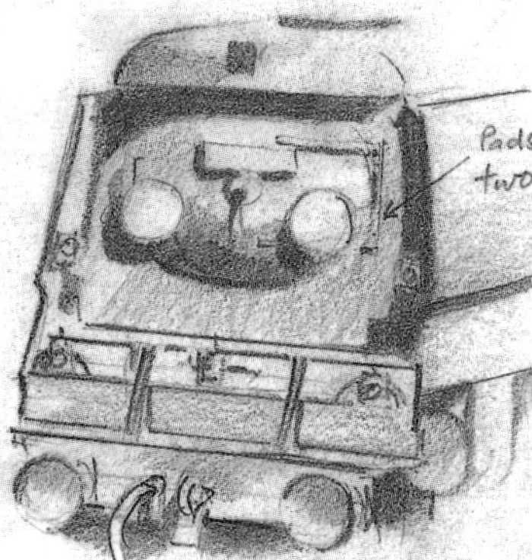

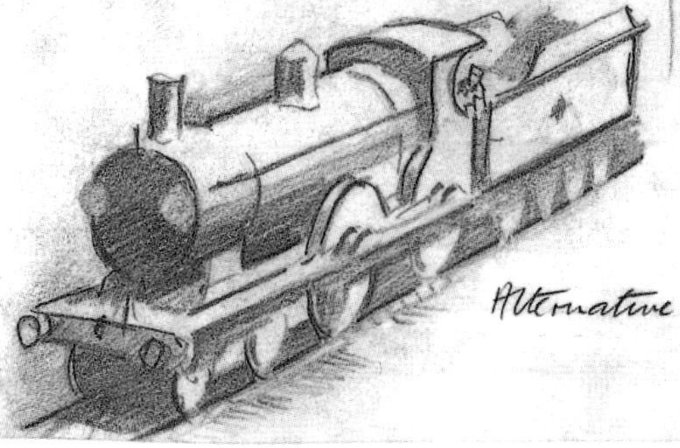

Alternative engine - T9

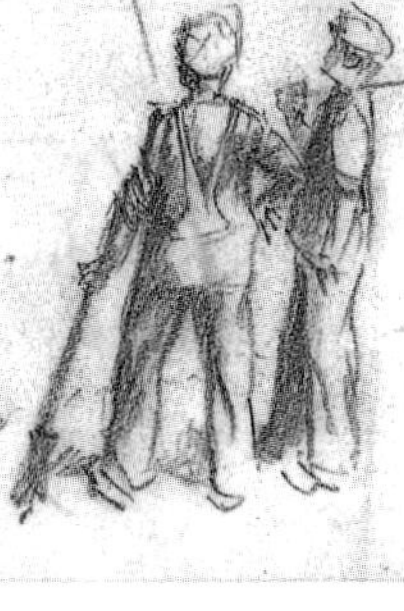

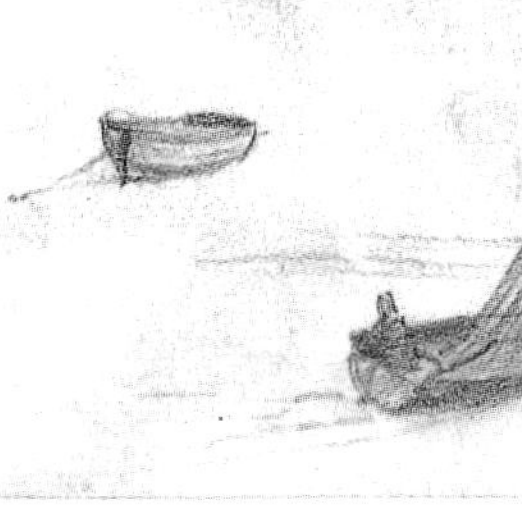

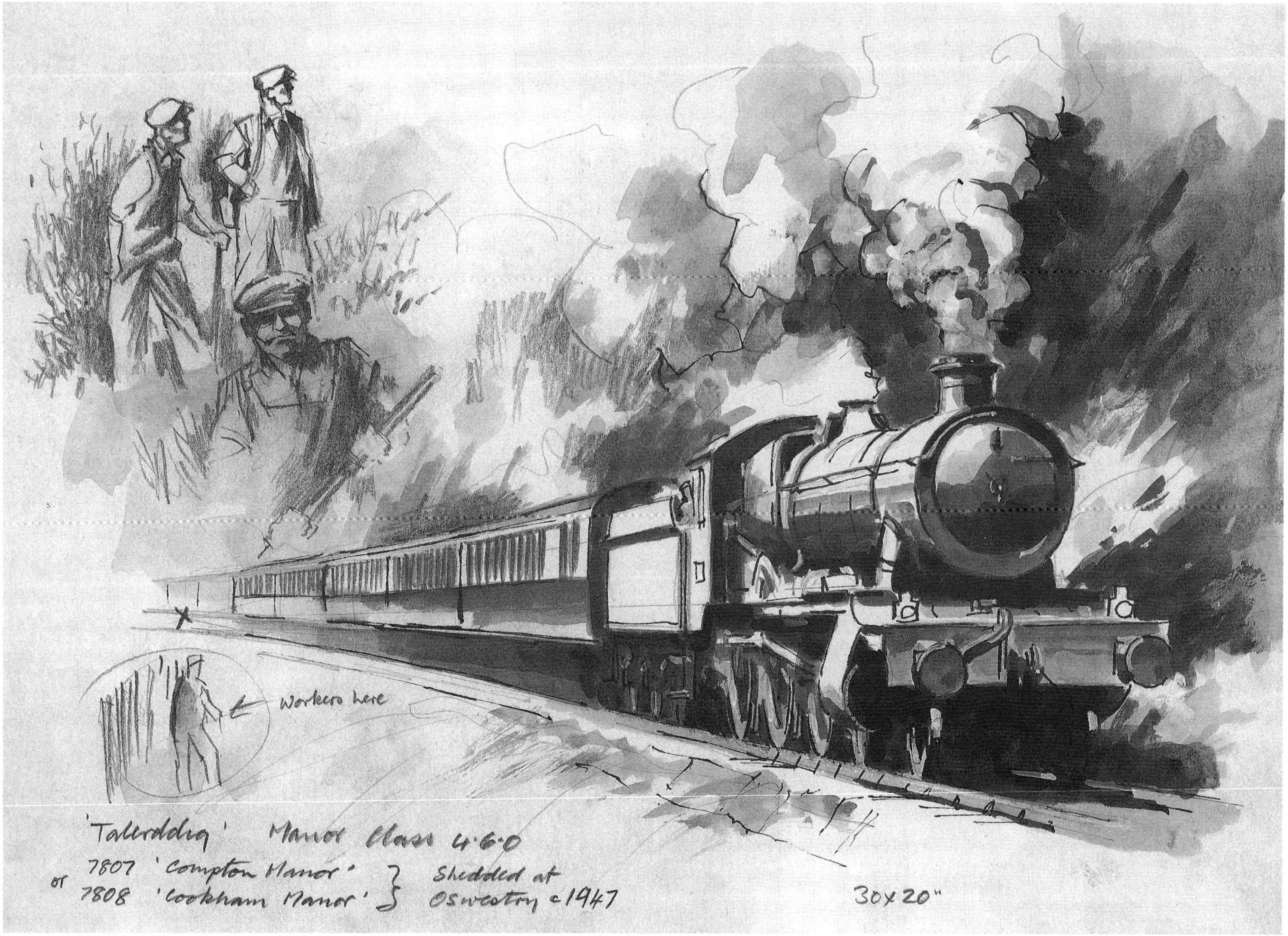
Workers here
'Talerddig' Manor class 4-6-0
7807 'Compton Manor'
or
7808 'Cookham Manor'
Shedded at Oswestry c1947
30x20"

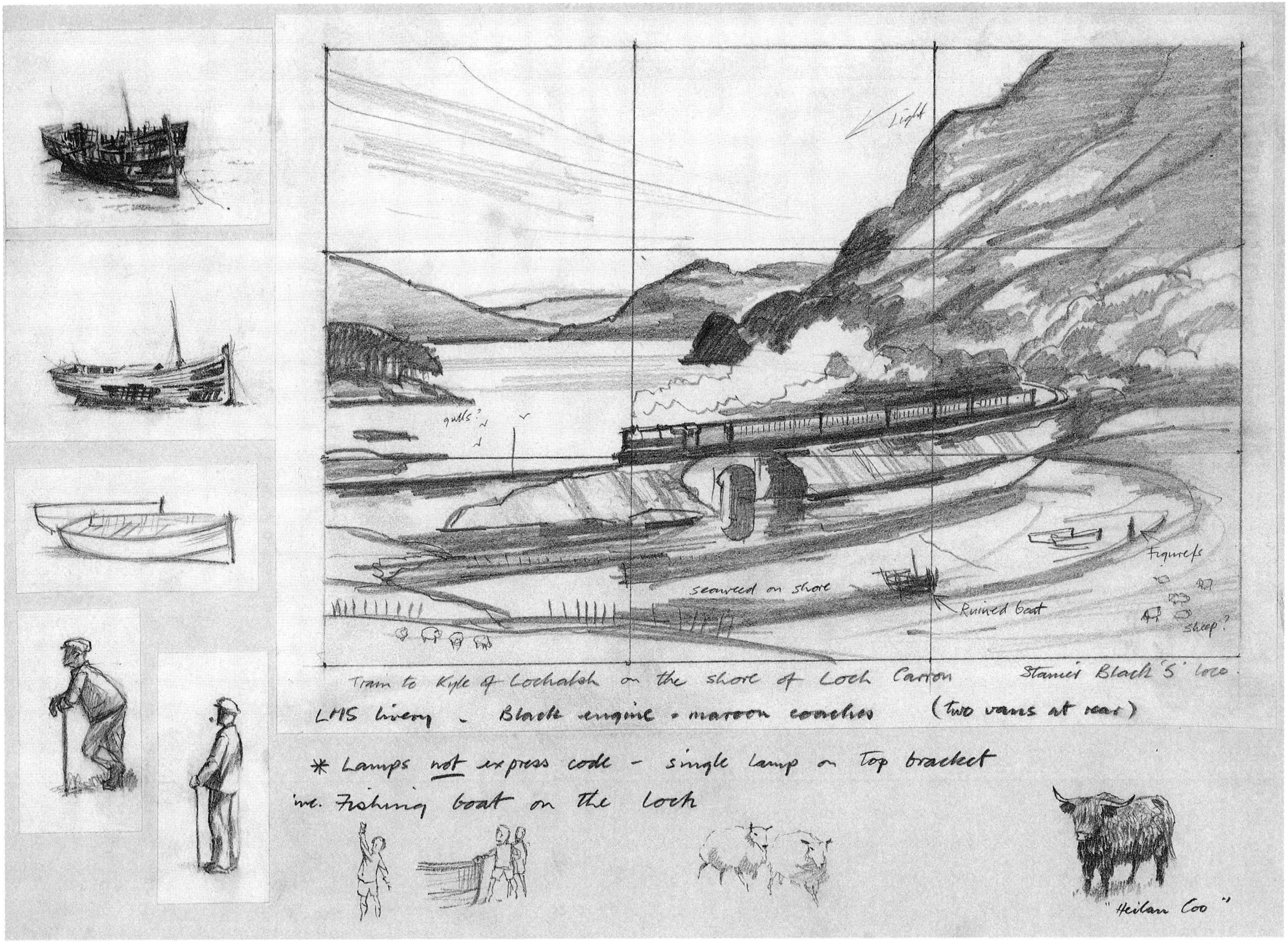
Light
gulls?
seaweed on shore
Ruined boat
Figures
sheep?
Train to Kyle of Lochalsh on the shore of Loch Carron
Stanier Black '5' loco
LMS livery - Black engine - maroon coaches (two vans at rear)
* Lamps not express code - single lamp on Top bracket
inc. Fishing boat on the Loch
"Heilan Coo"

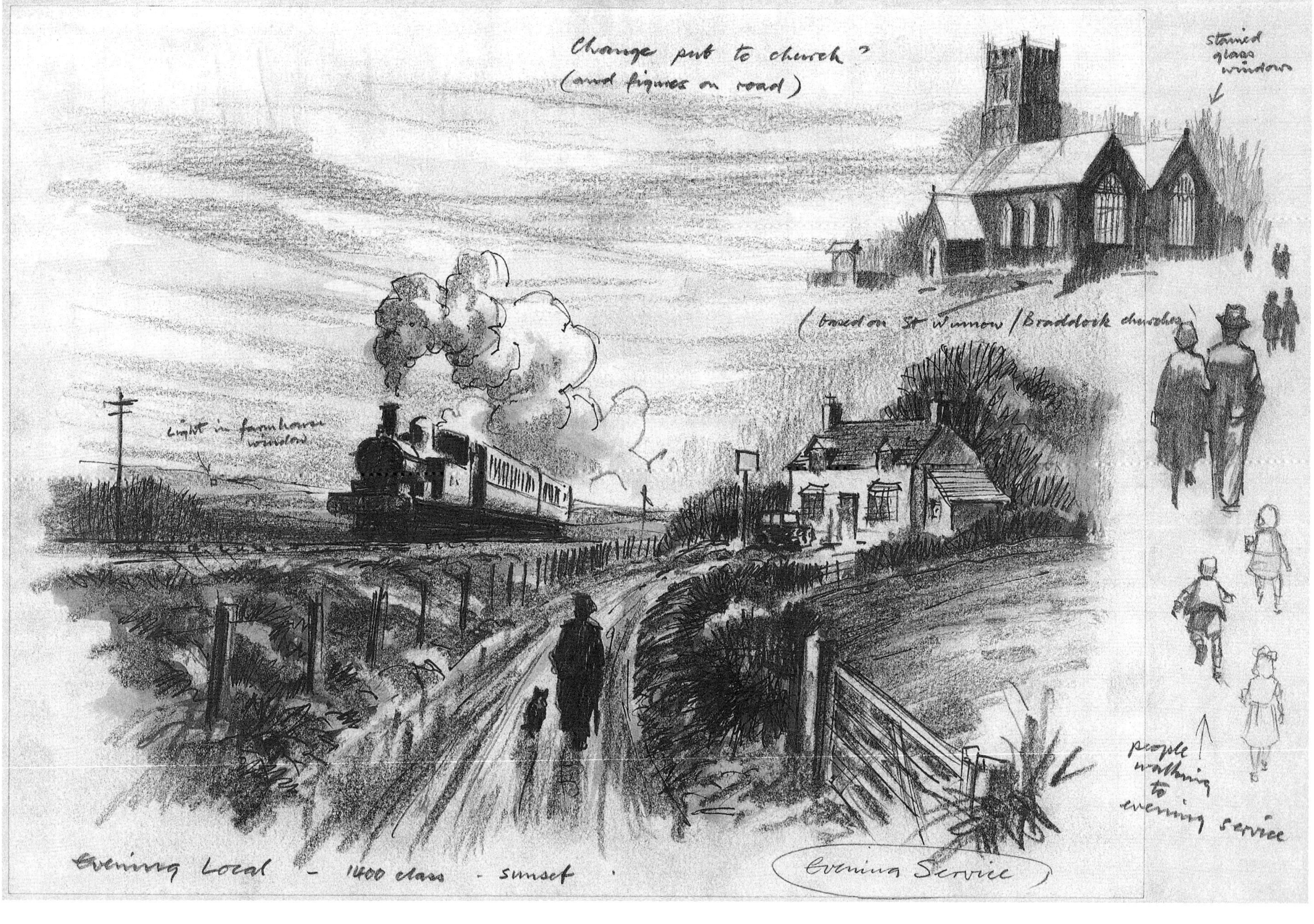

Change put to church ?
(and figures on road)
stained glass window
(based on St Winnow / Braddock churches)
light in farmhouse window
people walking to evening service
Evening Local - 1400 class - sunset .
Evening Service

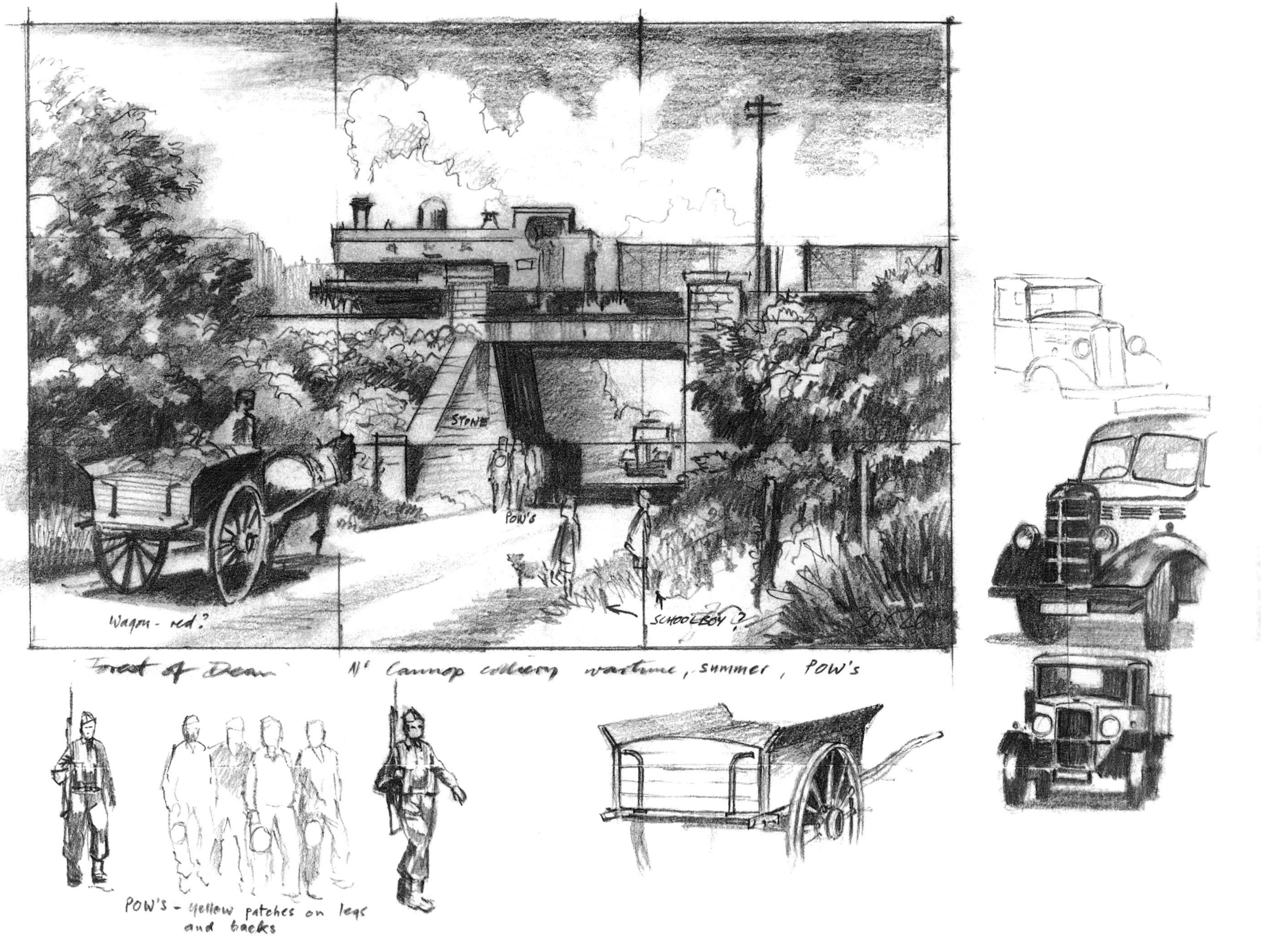
STONE
POW's
Wagon - red?
SCHOOLBOY ?
Forest of Dean
Nr Cannop colliery wartime, summer, POW's
POW's - yellow patches on legs
and backs

From a Railway Carriage

Robert Louis Stevenson

Faster than fairies, faster than witches,
Bridges and houses, hedges and ditches;
And charging along like troops in a battle,
All through the meadows the horses and cattle:
All of the sights of the hill and the plain
Fly as thick as driving rain;
And ever again, in the wink of an eye,
Painted stations whistle by.

Here is a child who clambers and scrambles,
All by himself and gathering brambles;
Here is a tramp who stands and gazes;
And there is the green for stringing the daisies!
Here is a cart run away in the road
Lumping along with man and load;
And here is a mill and there is a river:
Each a glimpse and gone forever!

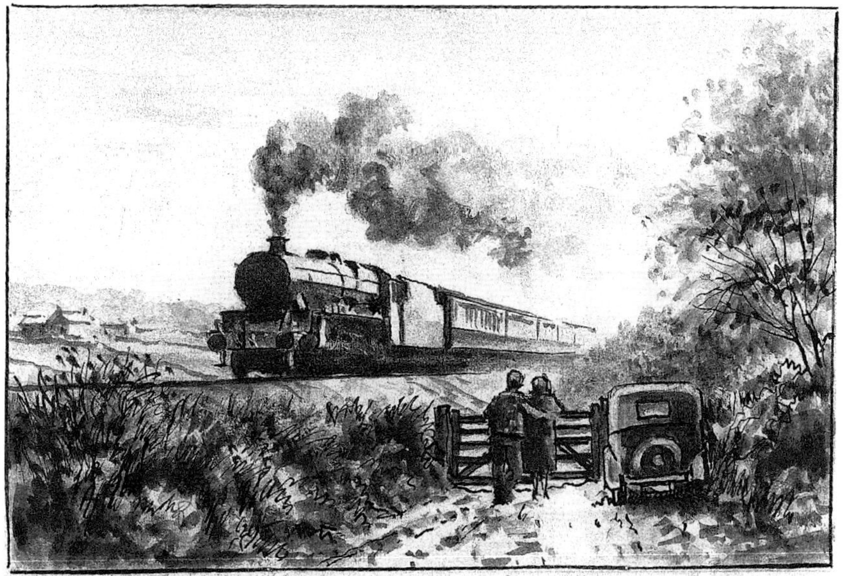

'Jubilee' courting couple and Austin Seven